T0146951

THE INDIVISIBLE REMAINDER

THE INDIVISIBLE REMAINDER

Slavoj Žižek

VERSO

London • New York

First published by Verso 1996
© Slavoj Žižek 1996
This edition published by Verso 2007
All rights reserved

The moral rights of the author have been asserted

1 3 5 7 9 10 8 6 4 2

Verso
UK: 6 Meard Street, London W1F 0EG
USA: 388 Atlantic Ave, Brooklyn, NY 11217
www.versobooks.com

Verso is the imprint of New Left Books

ISBN-13: 978-1-84467-581-4
ISBN-10: 1-84467-581-5

British Library Cataloguing in Publication Data
A catalogue record for this book is available from the British Library

Library of Congress Cataloging-in-Publication Data
A catalog record for this book is available from the Library of Congress

Printed in the USA

Contents

Before the Beginning • The unconscious act • The
contraction of Being • Drives and their rotary motion •
From freedom to a free subject • The divine madness •
Schellingian politics • The primordial dissonance •
'Symbolic castration' • The paradox of reflection • The
virtual reality of Ideas • The ascent from Eternity to Time •
The 'enchainment' • 'Selfhood as such is spirit' •
Existence and its Ground • Evil as the perverted unity of
Existence and Ground • The three levels of freedom •
The materialist notion of subject • The Absolute 'out
of mind' • The 'formula of the world'

From subjectivization to subjective destitution • Desire
versus drive • 'The voice is a voice' • 'And' as a category •
The ambiguous status of *lalangue* • What is idealism? • The
'repressed' genesis of modernity • *Die Versagung*: from
Paul Claudel . . . • . . . to France Prešeren • The dialectical
transubstantiation • How does the Spirit return to
itself? • There is no subject without an empty signifier •
The precipitate identification • The semblance of the
'objective Spirit' • The symbolic sleight of hand • 'A is *a*' •
Voice as a supplement • The shofar • How not to read
Lacan's 'formulas of sexuation' • Femininity as masquerade •

In praise of hysteria • 'Desire is the desire of the Other'

The 'wired' desire • The Cartesian cyberpunk •
Cynicism as reflected ideology • Cynicism versus irony •
Quantum physics' 'thesis eleven' • 'Complementarity' •
Against historicism • How does one make a rat
human? • Five lessons of the 'double-slit' • *Creatio
ex nihilo*

Introduction

As a Slovene, I have always been attentive to those few places in his writings and letters in which Freud mentions a Slovene or Slovenia; since Slovenia was part of the Austrian Empire in his time, it is surprising that these mentions are so rare. Apart from the dismissive but none the less enigmatic reference to an '*unanalysierbares*' ('unanalysable') Slovene patient in a letter to the Italian analyst Edoardo Weiss[1], there is another, perhaps even more significant case.

During one of his summer vacations, Freud visited Škocjan caves, a magnificent subterranean cave system in southern Slovenia – the extent to which descending into subterranean caves served him as a metaphor for entering the netherworld of the unconscious is well known. So, in the midst of his walk in this fascinating dark universe, Freud suddenly turned pale, faced with an unpleasant surprise: there, standing in front of him in these twilight depths, was another visitor to the caves, Dr Karl Lueger, Mayor of Vienna, a right-wing Christian demagogic populist and notorious anti-Semite. . . . What we must be careful not to miss here is the wordplay with *Lueger* which, of course, in German immediately associates with *Lüge*, a lie. It was as if this contingent encounter staged for Freud the fundamental truth of his teaching, the truth concealed by the obscurantist New Age approach according to which, upon penetrating the ultimate depth of our personality, we discover there our true Self, to whom we must then open ourselves – that is, allow him or her free expression: quite to the contrary, however, what we discover in the deepest kernel of our personality is a fundamental, constitutive, primordial *lie*, the *proton pseudos*, the phantasmic construction by means of which we endeavour to conceal the inconsistency of the symbolic order in which we dwell.

One can see here how Lacan (and, indeed, Freud) belies Foucault's insertion of psychoanalysis in the line of development that begins with the Christian practice of confession – his assumption that in the course of the psychoanalytic cure the subject-analysand discloses, probes into, brings to light, the truth about himself hidden deep in his unconscious: what the subject encounters in the unfathomed 'depths' of him- or herself is, on the contrary, a *primordial lie*. Psychoanalysis therefore emphasizes the obverse of Václav Havel's famous dissident motto 'life in truth': the 'natural state' of the human animal is to live in a lie. Freud's uncanny encounter condenses, as it were, two closely connected Lacanian theses: the Master is unconscious, hidden in the infernal world, *and* he is an obscene impostor – the 'version of the father' is always a *père-version*. In short, the lesson for the *Ideologiekritik* is that there is no *Herrschaft* which is not supported by some phantasmic enjoyment.

A personal experience revealed this inherent obscenity of Power to me in a most distastefully-enjoyable way. In the 1970s I did my (obligatory) military service in the old Yugoslav People's Army, in a small barracks with no proper medical facilities. In a room which also served as sleeping quarters for a private trained as a medical assistant, a doctor from the nearby military hospital held his clinic once a week. On the frame of the large mirror above the washbasin in this room, the soldier had stuck a couple of postcards of half-naked girls – a standard resource for masturbation in those pre-pornography times, to be sure. When the doctor paid us his weekly visit, all of us who had reported for medical examination sat on a long bench alongside the wall opposite the washbasin, and were examined in turn.

One day, while I was waiting to be examined, it was the turn of a young, half-illiterate soldier who complained of pains in his penis (which, of course, was in itself sufficient to trigger obscene giggles from all of us, the doctor included): the skin on its head was too tight, so he was unable to draw it back normally. The doctor ordered him to pull down his trousers and demonstrate his trouble; the soldier did so and the skin slid down the head smoothly, though the soldier was quick to add that his trouble occurred only during erection. The doctor then said: 'OK, then, masturbate, get an erection, so that we can check it!' Deeply embarrassed and red in the face, the soldier began to masturbate in front of all of us but, of course, failed to produce an erection; the doctor then took one of the postcards of half-naked girls from the mirror, held it close to the soldier's head and started to shout at him: 'Look! What breasts, what a cunt! Masturbate! How is it that you don't get an erection? What kind of a man are you! Go on, masturbate!' All of us in the room, *including the doctor himself*, accompanied this spectacle with obscene laughter; the unfortunate soldier himself soon joined us with an embarrassed giggle, exchanging looks of solidarity with us while he continued to masturbate. . . . This scene brought about in me an experience of quasi-epiphany: *in nuce*, there was everything in it, the entire panoply of Power – the uncanny mixture of imposed enjoyment and the humiliating exercise of Power, the agency of Power which shouts severe orders but simultaneously shares with us, his subordinates, obscene laughter bearing witness to a deep solidarity. . . .

One could also say that this scene exemplifies the *symptom* of Power: the grotesque excess by means of which, in a unique short circuit, attitudes which are officially opposed and mutually exclusive reveal their uncanny complicity, where the solemn agent of Power suddenly starts to wink at us across the table in a gesture of obscene solidarity, letting us know that the thing (i.e. his orders) is not to be taken too seriously, *and thereby consolidating his power*.[2] The aim of the 'critique of ideology', the analysis of an ideological edifice, is to extract this symptomal kernel which the official, public ideological text simultaneously disavows and needs for its undisturbed functioning. One is tempted to say that each of the three main politico-ideological positions ('Right', 'Centre', 'Left') relies on such an unacknowledged yet unavoidable supplement: the 'Right' finds it difficult to conceal its fascination with the myth of a 'primordial' act of violence supposed to ground the legal order; the 'Centre' counts on innate human egotism (between the lines, liberalism as a rule addresses the individual's egotistic indifference to other people's plight); the 'Left', as has long been discerned by perspicacious conservative critics from Nietzsche onwards, manipulates with *ressentiment* and the promise of revenge ('Now it's our turn to . . .').

The conclusion to be drawn from this, however, is not that there is no escape, that every subversion of the existing power structure is false, illusory, caught in advance in the network of what it endeavours to undermine, but the exact opposite: every power structure is necessarily split, inconsistent; there is a crack in the very foundation of its edifice – and this crack can be used as a lever for the effective subversion of the power structure. . . . In short, the foundations of Power can be shaken because the very stability of its mighty edifice hinges on an inconsistent, fragile balance. The other conclusion to be drawn is deeply solidary with the preceding one, although it may give rise to the false impression of contradicting it: perhaps the moment has come to leave behind the old Leftist obsession with ways and means to 'subvert' or 'undermine' the Order, and to focus on the opposite question – on what, following Ernesto Laclau, we can call the 'ordering of the Order': not how can we undermine the existing order, but *how does an Order emerge out of disorder in the first place*? Which inconsistencies and splittings allow the edifice of Order to maintain itself?

The philosopher who came closest to this obscene shadowy double of public Power was F.W.J. Schelling: there is no *Geist* without *Geisterwelt*, no pure spirituality of *Logos* without the obscene spectral 'spiritual corporeality' of the living dead, and so on. This perversion of spirituality and ideality is not something that accidentally befalls them: its possibility is contained in the very notion of spirituality. This Schellingian notion of 'spiritual corporeality' enables us to establish an unexpected link with Marx. Today, it is clearly established that Schelling prefigures a series of key Marxian motifs, up to Marx's 'revolutionary' reproach to Hegel's dialectics according to which the speculative-dialectical resolution of the contradiction leaves the actual social antagonism intact (Hegel's 'speculative positivism').[3] The roots of the Marxian problematic of 'commodity fetishism' in Schelling provide another link to this series. That is to say: why, precisely, did Marx choose the term *fetishism* in order to designate the 'theological whimsy' of the universe of commodities? What one should bear in mind here is that 'fetishism' is a *religious* term for (previous) 'false' idolatry as opposed to (present) true belief: for the Jews, the fetish is the Golden Calf; for a partisan of pure spirituality, fetishism designates 'primitive' superstition, the fear of ghosts and other spectral apparitions, and so forth. And the point of Marx is that the commodity universe provides the necessary fetishistic supplement to 'official' spirituality: it may well be that the 'official' ideology of our society is Christian spirituality, but its actual foundation is none the less the idolatry of the Golden Calf: money.

In short, Marx's point here is deeply Schellingian: there is no spirit without spirits-ghosts, no 'pure' spirituality without the obscene spectre of 'spiritualized matter'. The first to accomplish this step 'from spirit to spirits' in the guise of the critique of pure spiritual idealism, of its lifeless 'negative' nihilism, was precisely Schelling who, in the dialogue *Clara* (1810), drove a wedge into the simple complementary mirror-relationship of Inside and Outside – between Spirit and Body, between the ideal element and the real element which together form the living totality of the Organism – by drawing our attention to the double surplus that 'sticks out' . On the one hand, there is the *spiritual element of corporeality*: the presence, in matter itself, of a non-material but physical element, of a subtle corpse, relatively independent of time and space, which provides the material base of our free will (animal magnetism, etc.); on the other hand, there is the *corporeal element of spirituality*: the materializations of the spirit in a kind of pseudo-stuff, in substanceless apparitions (ghosts, living dead). It is clear how these two surpluses comprise *in nuce* the logic of the opposition of commodity fetishism and of the Althusserian Ideological State Apparatuses (ISAs): commodity fetishism involves the uncanny 'spiritualization' of the commodity-body, whereas ISAs materialize the spiritual, substanceless big Other of ideology.[4]

However, are not Schelling's obscure ruminations about the Absolute prior to the creation of the world simply *out of touch* with our post-Enlightened pragmatic universe? Among the numerous platitudes proposed by Karl Popper, one idea stands out as more inane than the rest: that of an inherent link between philosophical 'totalism' ('strong' philosophy striving to grasp the Absolute) and political totalitarianism – the idea that a thought which aims at the Absolute thereby lays the foundation for totalitarian domination. It is easy to mock this idea as an exemplary case of the inherent imbecility of analytical philosophy, of its inferiority to the dialectical (and/or hermeneutical) tradition – however, do not Adorno and Horkheimer, the two great opponents of the Popperian orientation, put forward what ultimately amounts to the same claim in their *Dialectics of Enlightenment*?

To begin with, one is tempted to venture an 'empirical' refutation of this notion of an inherent link between philosophical 'totalism' and political totalitarianism: on the one hand, the philosophy that legitimizes a totalitarian political regime is generally some kind of evolutionary or vitalist relativism; on the other hand, the very claim to a 'contact with the Absolute' can legitimize an individual's resistance to a terrestrial political power – the link is thus far from necessary and self-evident; rather, the opposite. Is not the ultimate argument against this link provided by Schelling, who advocates the strongest version of the philosophy of the Absolute (in Part I of *Weltalter* he attempts to present the Past as the 'age' of God Himself prior to creation), yet who, *in the name of this very reference to the Absolute, relativizes the State* – that is, conceives it as something contingent, unachieved-incomplete in its very notion?

How, then, do we stand with regard to Schelling today? The co-ordinates of the contemporary philosophico-ideological scene are provided by two orientations: 'postmodern' relativist New Sophists (from neo-pragmatists to deconstructionists) and New Age obscurantists. For both these orientations the reference to Schelling, to his critique of Hegel and of modern idealism in general, is of crucial importance. The New Sophists emphasize how Schelling was the first to introduce a crack into Hegel's panlogicist edifice by asserting the motifs of contingency and finitude; the New Age obscurantists perceive Schelling as the philosopher who accomplished the 'Jungian' turn by asserting the notions of *Weltseele*, primordial Wisdom, sexualized cosmology, and so on.

Again, the relationship between Schelling and Hegel is the knot, the junction at which 'everything is decided'. According to the predominant *doxa*, in Hegel's absolute idealism and panlogicism the self-movement of the Idea generates its own content and retroactively grounds its own presuppositions, whereas Schelling introduced a gap which opens a way for the post-Hegelian problematic of finitude: the Hegelian Idea can comprehend only the ideal necessity of a thing, *what* a thing is, the thing in its conceptual determination, in its notional possibility; what is out of its reach is the contingent fact *that* something exists at all, a fact which depends on a free act of creation.

This surplus which eludes notional self-mediation can be discerned exemplarily apropos of the problematic of Evil: Hegel reduces Evil to the subordinated moment in the self-mediation of Idea *qua* supreme Good, whereas in Schelling Evil remains a permanent possibility which can never be fully 'sublated [*aufgehoben*]' in and by the Good. A *doxa* – a cliché, even – on Schelling is that in his philosophy the subject can assert its self-presence only against the background of an obscure, dense, impenetrable *Grund* which withdraws-into-self the moment it is illuminated by the light of Reason: *logos* can never fully mediate/ internalize this Otherness of the Ground – in its elementary dimension, *Grund* is nothing but the impediment of an Otherness which maintains forever its externality. . . .

Is this comprehension of the Hegelian dialectical process as the self-mediation of the Notion which externalizes itself, posits its content in its independence and actuality, and then internalizes it, recognizes itself in it, adequate? Our premiss, of course, is that it is not. Our aim, however, is not simply to defend Hegel against Schelling's critique by demonstrating how Schelling misses his target and ultimately fights a straw man – this would be a rather boring, purely academic exercise. Our thesis is more complex: in the case of Schelling, as well as that of Hegel, what we may call a *formal envelope of error* (the standard misleading image of Schelling as the philosopher of irrational Ground, of *Weltseele*, etc.; the standard misleading image of Hegel as the philosopher of absolute idealism, of the accomplished self-mediation of the Notion, etc.) conceals, and simultaneously contains, an unheard-of subversive gesture which – herein resides our ultimate premiss – *is the same in both cases*. What is effectively at stake in our endeavour, therefore, is not to pit Hegel's wits against Schelling but to discern the contours of this gesture with regard to which the standard readings of Schelling and Hegel, these two 'formal envelopes of error', are simply two modalities to avoid it, to render it invisible. Our second premiss, of course, is that it is Lacan's psychoanalytic theory which enables us to approach this gesture, the only true *Sache des Denkens*.

So why, exactly, do we focus on the *Weltalter* drafts? Jean-Claude Milner[5] recently attempted to enumerate the features which distinguish great works of *materialist* thought, from Lucretius' *De rerum natura* through Marx's *Capital* to the work of Lacan. The main feature is their *unfinished* character: these works seem to tackle the same nodal problem again and again (the genesis of the commodity fetishism in Marx; the 'knot' that links the Real, the Symbolic, and the Imaginary in Lacan); although they ultimately fail, although their work remains a fragment, their very failure is theoretically extremely productive. Our point, of course, is that Schelling's *Weltalter* drafts belong to this same series, with their repeated failure to provide the definitive formulation of the 'beginning of the world', of the passage from the pre-symbolic chaos of the Real to the universe of *logos*. What is of special interest here is that Schelling has no problem with penetrating the obscure netherworld of pre-symbolic drives ('God prior to the creation of the world') – where he fails again and again is in his *return* from this 'dark continent' to our common universe of language.

This book was written in the hope that it will contribute to our perception of Schelling's *Weltalter* drafts as one of the seminal works of materialism. This claim cannot but provoke an immediate response: Schelling a materialist? Isn't he, rather, the last great representative of anthropomorphic, pre-scientific theosophy? In his Introduction to the first French translation of Schelling's 'Philosophical Investigations into the Essence of Human Freedom', Henri Lefebvre wrote that this treatise 'is certainly not true, but is none the less very important for the truth'.[6] This statement can also serve as our guideline – on condition that we do not miss its paradox: the point is not to reject what is not true in Schelling, the false ('obscurantist', 'theosophico-mythological') shell of his system, in order to attain its kernel of truth; its truth, rather, is inextricably linked to what, from our contemporary perspective, cannot but appear as blatantly 'not true', so that every attempt to discard the part or aspect considered 'not true' inevitably entails the loss of the truth itself – there is no way of throwing out the dirty bath water without losing the baby.

That is to say: how does one usually interpret this intermingling of the untrue with truth in Schelling? One of the commonplaces about Schelling is that he is a philosopher of transition, located in the break between two epochs – one foot still within the universe of speculative Idealism whose theme is the immanent self-deployment of the eternal Absolute; his other foot already encroaching into the post-Hegelian universe of finitude–contingency–temporality. Although Schelling's *Weltalter* drafts (1811 to 1815) contain all the ingredients for an 'analytics of finitude' founded on the structure of temporality,[7] he maintains that the three temporal dimensions of Past, Present and Future are not simply the horizon of human finite temporality but designate the three 'ages' of the Absolute itself. . . . The implicit presupposition of such a reading, of course, is that one has to reject the Absolute, the System, and so on, and to assert all that prefigures the subsequent development (Marx's critique of Hegel, Heidegger's analysis of temporality, etc.).

Heidegger himself provided the most concise formula of such a reading with his claim that Schelling's philosophy – the 'system of freedom' – is characterized by an implacable and unsolvable tension between its two constitutive terms, freedom and system: according to Heidegger, of course, the fatal limitation of Schelling resides in his adherence to system: that is to say, it is the framework of system which condemns Schelling's endeavour to comprehend adequately the essence of freedom to failure. . . . In short – as Marc Richir, a commentator otherwise favourable to Heidegger, ironically summarizes Heidegger's position – the frame of the system prevents Schelling from already becoming Heidegger, and developing the analytics of finitude.[8]

Our reading is radically opposed to such a reduction of Schelling to an 'intermediate' phenomenon whereby, in order to obtain the analytics of finitude, one has only to cast off the form of the Absolute: we are as far as possible from dismissing Schelling's narrative of the Absolute as an incoherent short circuit between the post-metaphysical problematic of contingency–temporality–finitude and the metaphysical problematic of the Absolute. Schelling's place is indeed 'intermediate', yet it is precisely as such, as a kind of 'vanishing mediator' between the Idealism of the Absolute and the post-Hegelian universe of finitude–temporality–contingency, that his thought – for a brief moment, as it were in a flash – renders visible something that was invisible beforehand and withdrew into invisibility thereafter. Therein consists the unique intermediate position of Schelling, his double non-contemporaneity to his own time: he belongs to three discursive domains – he simultaneously, as it were, speaks three languages: the language of speculative idealism; the language of anthropomorphic–mystical theosophy; the post-idealist language of contingency and finitude. The paradox, of course, is that *it was his very 'regression' from pure philosophical idealism to pre-modern theosophical problematic which enabled him to overtake modernity itself.* That is to say: on the one hand Schelling is the last great representative of the pre-modern 'anthropomorphic' sexualized vision of the universe (some of his pupils carried this notion to extremes – J.J. Goerres, for example, in his voluminous *Sexual System of Ontology*); on the other hand, only a thin invisible line separates him from openly asserting, in a thoroughly postmodern vein, the *impossibility* of the sexual relationship – that is, a fundamental 'out-of-joint', a disturbed balance – as the positive ontological constituent of the universe.

In dealing with Schelling's *Weltalter*, one should always bear in mind the precise discursive context of his endeavour: his ultimate aim was to realize the so-called 'oldest systematic programme of German Idealism' from his youth, and to deliver the system of 'rational mythology' which would present the highest insights into the nature of the Absolute in a popular-mythological form, thereby setting in motion a total spiritual-political renovation of the German nation via the surmounting of the deadlocks of modernity. How are we to account for this step from logical presentation to mythical narrative *today*, in our discursive context? Does not this step involve 'regression' to a version of New Age mythology? When, at the key points of their theoretical edifice, Freud and Lacan also resorted to a mythical narrative (Freud's myth of the primordial father in *Totem and Taboo*, his reference to Plato's myth of androgynous primordial man in *Beyond the Pleasure Principle*; Lacan's myth of 'lamella' in his *Four Fundamental Concepts of Psycho-Analysis*), they were driven by the same necessity as Schelling: the need for the form of mythical narrative arises when one endeavours to break the circle of the symbolic order and to give an account of its genesis ('origins') from the Real and its pre-symbolic antagonism. In short, Schelling's *Weltalter* is to be read as a *metapsychological* work in the strict Freudian sense of the term.

Notes

1. For a detailed analysis of this reference, see Chapter 1 of Slavoj Žižek, *For They Know Not What They Do*, London: Verso 1991.

2. In what, then, would the subversive antipode to this obscenity of power consist? Let me again evoke a personal experience from the last years of Communist rule in Slovenia, when the Communists, well aware that their days were numbered, tried desperately to please everyone. Ljubljana student radio interviewed an old Communist cadre – a real one, in a grey suit, with clumsy manners, etc. – bombarding him with provocative questions about his sexual life; desperate to please, the cadre delivered the right answers, but in wooden bureaucratese – sexuality as an important component of his socialist personality; observing naked women and touching their intimate parts gave an important incentive to his creative efforts. . . . What was truly subversive in this show was the grotesque discrepancy between the position of enunciation (stiff bureaucratese) and the sexualized, intimate content.

3. For this indebtedness of Marx to Schelling, see Manfred Frank, *Der Unendliche Mangel an Sein*, Frankfurt: Suhrkamp 1975.

4. For a more detailed elaboration of this point, see Slavoj Žižek, 'Introduction: The Spectre of Ideology', in *Mapping Ideology*, London: Verso 1994.

5. See Jean-Claude Milner, *L'œuvre claire*, Paris: Seuil 1995.

6. F.W.J. Schelling, *La liberté humaine*, Introduction de Henri Lefebvre, Paris: Rieder 1926, p. 7.

7. See Alan White, *Schelling: An Introduction to the System of Freedom*, New Haven, CT and London: Yale University Press 1983, p. 142.

8. See Marc Richir, 'Schelling et l'utopie métaphysique', in F.W.J. Schelling, *Recherches sur la liberté humaine*, Paris: Payot 1977, p. 176.

PART I

F.W.J. Schelling, or, At the Origins of Dialectical Materialism

Schelling-in-itself:
The 'Orgasm of Forces'

Before the Beginning

How, then, should one begin an essay on Schelling? Perhaps the most appropriate way is by focusing on the *problem of Beginning itself*, the crucial problem of German Idealism – suffice it to recall Hegel's detailed elaboration of this problem and all its implications in his *Science of Logic*. Schelling's 'materialist' contribution is best epitomized by his fundamental thesis according to which, to put it bluntly, *the true Beginning is not at the beginning*: there is something that precedes the Beginning itself – a rotary motion whose vicious cycle is broken, in a gesture analogous to the cutting of the Gordian knot, by the Beginning proper, that is, the primordial act of decision. The beginning of all beginnings, the beginning *kat' exohen* – 'the mother of all beginnings', as one would say today – is, of course, the '*In the beginning was the Word*' from the Gospel according to St John: prior to it, there was nothing, that is, the void of divine eternity. According to Schelling, however, 'eternity' is not a nondescript mass – a lot of things take place in it. Prior to the Word there is the chaotic-psychotic universe of blind drives, their rotary motion, their undifferentiated pulsating; and the Beginning occurs when the Word is pronounced which 'represses', rejects into the eternal Past, this self-enclosed circuit of drives. In short, *at the Beginning proper stands a resolution, an act of decision which, by differentiating between past and present, resolves the preceding unbearable tension of the rotary motion of drives*: the true Beginning is the passage from the 'closed' rotary motion to 'open' progress, from drive to desire – or, in Lacanian terms, from the Real to the Symbolic.

One is tempted to evoke here 'The Sole Solution', a thoroughly Schellingian science-fiction story by Eric Frank Russell which describes the inner feelings of someone filled with doubt, someone who turns around in a futile circle and cannot reach a decision, who makes all kind of plans which are then immediately aborted. Finally, he makes up his mind and says: 'Let there be light!' In short, what we took, all through the story, for the groaning of some confused idiot turns out to be the hesitation of God immediately before the act of creation. The beginning thus occurs when one 'finds the word' which breaks the deadlock, the vicious cycle, of empty and confused ruminations.

In this precise sense, the problem of the Beginning is the problem of 'phenomenalization': how does it happen that God pronounces the Word and thereby discloses Himself, appears to Himself? We must be careful not to miss this crucial point: as with Hegel, the problem is not how to attain the noumenal In-itself beyond phenomena; the true problem is how and why does this In-itself split itself from itself at all, how does it acquire a distance towards itself and thus clear the space in which it can appear (to itself)? How, then, can this phenomenalization of God, this pronunciation of the Word in Him which magically, in an unfathomable way, dispels the impenetrable darkness of drives, occur? *It can occur only on condition that the rotary motion of drives which precedes the Beginning is itself not the primordial, unsurpassable fact.* That is to say, the notion of the vortex of drives as the ultimate foundation, the 'origin of all things', renders inconceivable the fact of freedom: how can a Word emerge out of this vortex and dominate it, confer on it its shape, 'discipline' it? Consequently, this ultimate Ground [*Grund*] of reality, the primordial vortex of drives, this Wheel of Fate which sooner or later engulfs and destroys every determinate object, must be preceded by an unfathomable X which thereupon, in a way yet to be explained, 'contracts' drives.

Is not the primordial vortex of drives, however, the ultimate ground which nothing can precede? Schelling would be in entire agreement with this, adding only that the point in question is precisely the exact status of this 'nothing': prior to *Grund*, there can be only an abyss [*Ungrund*] – that is to say, far from being a mere *nihil privativum*, this 'nothing' which precedes Ground stands for the 'absolute indifference' *qua* the abyss of pure Freedom which is not yet the predicate-property of some Subject but, rather, designates a pure impersonal Willing [*Wollen*], which wills nothing. How can we, finite, mortal humans, find access to this abyss of freedom which is the primordial origin of all things? Schelling's fundamental premiss here is radically 'anthropocentric': man is not merely an epiphenomenon in the universe, a negligible grain of dust – among all created things, he is the only one to possess the 'power of the centre', and stands as such in direct contact with the abyss of primordial freedom:

> One must allow to man a principle which is outside and above the world; for how could he alone of all creatures follow back the long path of

developments from the present into the deepest night of the past, he alone ascend to the beginning of times, if there were not in him a principle before the beginning of times? Poured from the source of things and the same as the source, the human soul has a conscience/co-knowledge [*Mitwissenschaft*] of creation.[1]

Here, however, we have proceeded too hastily. What one should do is reconstruct all the steps which led Schelling to assert the identity between human freedom and the primordial abyss which is 'the source of things'. Schelling was first and foremost a philosopher of freedom, a philosopher who tackled the 'impossible' task of *thinking freedom within the framework of a philosophical system* – of elaborating a philosophical system that would not preclude freedom. What, precisely, is a system?

Let us tackle this problem via a perhaps unexpected detour, taking as our starting point Robert Zemeckis's *Flintstones*. Apart from providing an exemplary lesson on the notion of the 'primitive' (the anachronistic 'projection' of today's features into the 'primitive' Stone Age past renders visible the elementary structure of today's society in its distilled form, reduced to its bare essentials), the main interest of the film lies in its 'premiss' of establishing a perfect correlation between the two series (our contemporary late-capitalist consumer life; the Stone Age), so that anxiety constantly gnaws at the spectator: will the film succeed in finding a Stone Age counterpart to all the phenomena of our society – that is to say, will it succeed in transposing modern high-tech inventions into Stone Age conditions without cheating (cars run by feet; planes flown by birds attached to their wings; a parrot serving as a dictaphone; etc.)? A professor of modern philosophy at Ljubljana University recently had an analogous experience: at an oral exam, a student invented for every question an excuse for not answering it – Spinoza's God? Sorry, I'm member of a religious sect which prohibits me from pronouncing God's name in public, so I can't answer the question. Leibniz's monads? Leibniz says monads are self-enclosed and have neither doors nor windows; I'm claustrophobic and cannot speak about them, it causes me too much anxiety. . . . Again, we obtain a 'system' when we accept the premiss of completing the list and including the entire history of philosophy: Thales? Sorry, he claimed that the origin of all is water, and I can't swim, I'm afraid of drowning. Plato? According to Plato, ideas dwell in the air, far above earth, but I have a fear of heights; the mere thought of Plato's ideas makes me giddy . . . etc., etc.

Schelling's point is a somewhat similar radical uncertainty: will a philosopher succeed in containing everything within his system? Or will he, sooner or later, stumble upon an element which will unmask his vain pretence and reveal his impotence? Significantly, it is Hegel's system which most often gives rise to such an anxiety in the reader: according to the *doxa*, Hegel is the philosopher who claims to account for everything, so at every dialectical turn one waits anxiously – will he again succeed in 'performing his trick' and providing a convincing semblance of rational explanation, or will he finally be caught red-handed and forced to admit his imposture? The 'system' always involves such a highly reckless premiss that the two series (of experiential reality and of the conceptual network) will be fully correlated, and this permanent anxiety over the outcome of this enterprise is what Schelling relies on – the fact that the universe is rationally ordered, caught in a causal nexus; is not self-evident, but precisely something to be explained: 'The whole world is thoroughly caught in reason, but the question is: how did it get caught in the network of reason in the first place?'[2] Here Schelling inverts the standard perspective: the problem is not how, in an universe regulated by inexorable natural laws, freedom is possible – that is, where, in the determinist universe, there is a place for freedom which would not be a mere illusion based on our ignorance of the true causes – but, rather, how the world as a rational totality of causal interconnections made its appearance in the first place. (As we shall see later, Schelling accomplishes a similar turn apropos of the ontological proof of God: the problem, for him, does not reside in the leap from the notion of God to God's reality – reality is always-already given, it pertains to the original ex-stasis of our mind, so the true problem is, rather, how do we pass from the raw fact of God's (Absolute's) meaningless existence to His notion – that is, how does God give birth to *logos*, how does He pronounce the Word and posit Himself as Reason?) For Schelling, then, the primordial, radically contingent fact, a fact which can in no way be accounted for, is freedom itself, a freedom bound by nothing, a freedom which, in a sense, *is* Nothing; and the problem is, rather, how this Nothing of the abyss of primordial freedom becomes entangled in the causal chains of Reason.

The unconscious act

It may seem that this notion of freedom has nothing whatsoever to do with what we usually, in our everyday life, understand by this word. What Schelling wants to accomplish, however, is precisely to undermine the abstract philosophical notion of freedom via a reference to our most concrete existential experience: for him, freedom is not, in the usual idealist vein, the full autonomy of the Absolute, its power to deploy its content 'freely', to determine itself independently of any external limitations, to posit its limitations as its self-determinations; rather, it concerns the most concrete experience of the tension within a living, acting and suffering person between Good and Evil – there is no actual freedom without an unbearable anxiety. So how does Schelling establish a link between freedom *qua* primordial Void and the concrete experience of freedom?

Let us tackle this problem *in medias res*, at the pathetic climax of Schelling's *Philosophical Investigations into the Essence of Human Freedom*, where he endeavours to articulate the most radical dimension of human freedom. Schelling refers here to Kant who, in his *Religion Within the Limits of Reason Alone*, had already drawn attention to the mysterious paradox of our ethical reasoning: when one encounters a truly evil person, one cannot avoid the impression that in accomplishing his horrifying acts he is merely following the necessity inscribed in his nature; that it is not in his power to act differently – he is simply 'made like that'; the mystery resides in the fact that – notwithstanding this impression, and in apparent contradiction to it – *we hold him fully responsible for his acts*, as if his evil nature itself is contingent on his free choice:

> ... despite the undeniable necessity of all actions, and although every man must admit, if he is mindful of himself, that he is by no means accidentally or voluntarily evil or good, yet the evil man, for instance, seems to himself anything but compelled (since compulsion can be felt only in becoming, not in being), but acts willfully, not against his will. That Judas became a traitor to Christ, neither he nor any creature could alter; and yet he betrayed Christ not under compulsion, but willingly and with full freedom. ... How often it happens that from childhood on, from a time when, from an empirical point of view, we can scarcely credit someone with freedom and deliberation, a person shows a tendency towards evil from which can be foreseen that he will never yield to discipline and teaching, and who subsequently actually brings forth the bad fruit we foresaw in the bud. And yet no one doubts his responsibility; everyone is as convinced of this person's guilt as would be possible only if each individual action had been in his control.[3]

Schelling bears witness here to his extraordinary ability to account for a very tangible ethical experience in the terms of a most audacious philosophical speculation: like Kant, he is closest to our concrete life-experience in his wildest speculations. Following in Kant's footsteps, he explains the paradox of freedom by invoking a *noumenal, extra-temporal act of self-positing by means of which a man creates himself, chooses his eternal character*. The first thing to note here is the anti-Fichtean sting in the tail: this act of primordial decision by means of which I choose myself cannot be attributed to I *qua* subject of self-consciousness – the act which creates me as a subject conscious of itself, of its specific character (i.e. by means of which I create–posit myself as such) can only be unconscious:

> This general judgment of a tendency towards evil which in its origin is entirely unconscious and even irresistible as being an act of freedom, points to a deed and thus to a life prior to this life – except that it is not thought of as preceding in time, since the intelligible is outside of time altogether. There is greatest harmony in creation, and nothing is as separate and successive as we must portray it to be, but in the prior the subsequent, too, is already coacting, and everything happens at once in one magical stroke. Thus man, who now appears determined and definite, apprehended himself in the first creation in a determined form, and is born as the one he is from eternity, since by this deed even the nature and constitution of his corporealization are determined.[4]

Anti-Fichtean here is Schelling's assertion of *a radical split – an ontological incompatibility, even – between consciousness and freedom*, in clear contrast not only to Fichte but also to the commonplace association of freedom with consciousness ('I decide freely when I make a conscious choice, whereas an unconscious decision is by definition no decision at all, but something blindly imposed'). In a sense Schelling is 'more Fichtean than Fichte himself': while he fully endorses Fichte's thesis according to which the very essence of man is his own act, he does not confine this act to self-consciousness but situates it in terms of the real kernel of man's being which precedes consciousness – man contracts his very being, his eternal character (in the double meaning of the verb which is crucial for Schelling: to harden-condense-concentrate into a consistent form of being *and* to get infected with being) by means of an unconscious primordial act of decision.[5] Schelling reinterprets along these lines the theological problematic of *predestination*: predestination no longer refers to God's arbitrary decision concerning my damnation or salvation; rather, the subject *predestines himself* – produces the 'cipher of his destiny', as Lacan would have put it – when, in an extra-temporal, eternally past, always-already-accomplished unconscious free act, he chooses the eternal character of his temporal existence. Within his temporal self-experience, of course, this free decision appears to him in the guise of its opposite: as an inexorable necessity.[6]

Here Schelling activates the opposition of *being* and *becoming*: from the standpoint of temporal *becoming*, man is caught in, conditioned by, the necessary chain of causes and effects; his emergence is conditional upon – results from – a complex causal network; from the standpoint of eternal *being*, he is free: he is an entity which posits itself, starts out of itself in the abyss of freedom – in the temporal process of becoming, he merely becomes what he always-already was. The common-sense 'evolutionary' view subordinates being to becoming: becoming is the truth of being, the genesis of a thing provides the key to what this thing is – one knows what a thing is when one is able to explain how it arose, where it proceeded from. Schelling, however, in accordance not only with Hegel but also with Marx (for whom, as he put it in the Introduction to *Grundrisse*, the anatomy of man is the key to the anatomy of ape), inverts the relationship between the terms: 'becoming' designates a mere temporal realization of what a thing, in its eternal essence, always-already is. In the order of finite-unfree entities, becoming effectively has the advantage over being: finite entities are not self-centred, they do not possess what Schelling calls the 'power of the centre'; their essence lies elsewhere, outside themselves, which is why one can explain a finite entity by rendering visible the causal network upon which its existence is conditional. Man *qua* free being, on the contrary, has the 'power of the centre', which is why one can understand man's temporal becoming, his life story, only by means of a reference to his eternal being (timeless character).

In the psychoanalytic perspective, of course, this primordial act of free self-positing cannot but appear as the real of a fantasy-construction: the status of the primordial act is analogous to that of the Freudian parricide – although it never effectively took place within temporal reality, one has to presuppose it hypothetically in order to account for the consistency of the temporal process. The paradox of this primordial act is the same as that of Baron Münchhausen pulling himself out of the swamp by lifting himself by the hair – in both cases, the subject is somehow already here prior to his existence and then, by way of a free act, creates–posits himself, his own being. What we encounter here is the temporal loop which defines the structure of a fantasy: prior to his very being, the subject is miraculously present as a pure gaze observing his own nonexistence. Apropos of this primordial noumenal act of self-predestination in which freedom and necessity coincide, Schelling ventures a crucial step further than Kant: he relates it to the Absolute itself – a step which is strictly prohibited within the Kantian perspective. That is to say, according to Schelling, in this act of free self-positing by means of which man tears the chain of causal necessity asunder, he touches the Absolute itself as the primordial abyss-origin of all things:

> ... this differentiation cannot occur in time; it occurs outside all time and hence is concurrent with the first creation (though as an act distinct from it). Although man is born in time, he is created in the beginning of creation (the center). The act by which his life in time is determined does

not itself belong to time, but to eternity, nor does it precede time, but moves through time (untouched by it) as an act by its nature eternal. Through this act man's life extends to the beginning of creation; thus through it he is beyond creation as well, free and himself eternal beginning.[7]

Consequently, when Schelling conceives freedom as the suspension of the Ground, the term 'Ground' is to be comprehended here in both its principal senses: Ground as the 'firm ground', the only foundation out of which the spiritual edifice can grow, and Ground as reason-cause (in the sense of the 'principle of sufficient ground'). The emergence of Freedom means that Spirit has posited itself as such in opposition to its impenetrable-inert Ground, that it has acquired a distance towards its Ground and can now 'make free with it', *and* that the 'chain of being' is broken – that is to say, Spirit is no longer determined by the network of causality. Freedom is thus *stricto sensu* the moment of eternity – it stands for the suspension of the temporal chain of (sufficient) reasons-causes, for the leap from the enchainment [*Verkettung*] of finite, determinate entities into the abyss of their primordial origin, of the 'source of things'.

In the experience of freedom, in the vortex we perceive for a brief moment when we confront a groundless act of freedom, we 'rejoin the Absolute' – that is, we re-establish contact – our identity, even – with the primordial origin outside temporal reality, with the abyss of eternity prior to the fall into the world of creatures. Man is directly linked to the Absolute in so far as he occupies a unique place among created things: what re-emerges in him (and in him only) is a 'possibility-potentiality of being [*Seinkönnen*]' which does not immediately collapse into actuality. Other actually existing entities do not relate to possibility as such; in them, a possibility is simply realized; man only relates to possibility as such – for him, a possibility is in a sense 'more' than actuality, as if the actualization-realization of a possibility somehow already 'betrays' or 'devalues' it. This opposition, of course, coincides with the opposition between necessity and freedom: an unfree entity simply is, it coincides with its positive actuality, whereas (as Schelling asserts, announcing thereby the existentialist problematic) a free being can never be reduced to what it is, to its actual, positive presence – its 'project', the undecidable opening of what it might do or become, its 'want-to-be', is the kernel of its very existence.

Here Schelling goes even a step further: the primordial act of free decision is not only man's direct contact with the primordial freedom as the abyss out of which all things originate – that is, a kind of short circuit, of direct overlapping, between man and the Absolute; this act of contracting being, of choosing one's eternal nature, *has to be a repetition of the same act of the Absolute itself.* In opposition to Kant, who conceives the primordial act of decision as the founding gesture of a free (human) subject, and with the speculative audacity which characterizes his thought, Schelling thus ventures to *ascribe this act to the Absolute itself* – why?

With the emergence of man, the first cycle of creation is concluded, since in man, as we have just seen, freedom is posited as such – we are thereby again at the origins, in the absolute indifference: that is, the deepest essence of man is the abyss of freedom as pure indifference, as a willing which wants nothing. This means that – in so far as the universe *qua* multitude of entities effectively exists – the Absolute (God) Himself had to accomplish an analogous act on Himself: He had to disengage Himself from the primordial indifference and to posit the universe, reality. Man's act of decision, his step from the pure potentiality-essentiality of a will which wants nothing to an actual will, is therefore a *repetition* of God's act: in a primordial act, God Himself had to 'choose Himself', His eternal character – to contract existence, to *reveal* Himself. In the same sense in which history is man's ordeal – the terrain in which humanity has to prove its creativity, to actualize its potential – nature itself is God's ordeal, the terrain in which *He* has to disclose Himself, to put His creativity to the test. Schelling delineates the contours of this unheard-of primordial act of God Himself in the last pages of the second draft of *Weltalter*:

> The deed, once accomplished, sinks immediately into the unfathomable depth, thereby acquiring its lasting character. It is the same with the will which, once posited at the beginning and led into the outside, immediately has to sink into the unconscious. This is the only way the beginning, the beginning that does not cease to be one, the truly eternal beginning, is possible. For here also it holds that the beginning should not know itself. Once done, the deed is eternally done. The decision that is in any way the true beginning should not appear before consciousness, it should not be recalled to mind, since this, precisely, would amount to its recall. He who, apropos of a decision, reserves for himself the right to drag it again to light, will never accomplish the beginning.[8]

The key to this enigma of the primordial deed is that 'it is done eternally [for all time], i.e. it is eternally [at any time] already done, therefore past'.[9] What is thereby resolved is the tension between eternity and the singularity of the act: how can an act, unique by definition, a happenstance, be *eternal*? What is done eternally (in the sense of remaining, in its very withdrawal, the eternal foundation of the present, not just something disappearing in the recess of the past) must be eternally (at any time always-already) done, and is therefore inherently past – that is, it has to belong to a past which was never present. This is what the predicate 'unconscious' designates: a past which, although it never existed, persists as a durable foundation of the present. The paradox of such an 'eternal past' is constitutive of *time*: there is no time without reference to a past which was never present – that is to say, temporality, in its original dimension, is not a single line of events that runs from the past through the present to the future, but involves the tension of a relationship to an act which, precisely in so far as it was never present, in its very withdrawal, is always here as the (past) foundation of the present.

The contraction of Being

As we have already indicated, however, this eternal act of decision – which, by separating past from present, opens up temporality – is not what comes first, at the outset of the 'ages of the world'. First, at the outset of His 'pre-history', prior to the Beginning itself, God unavoidably, of the blind necessity which characterizes the workings of Fate (according to the first draft of *Weltalter*), 'contracts' Being – that is, a firm, impenetrable Ground. (Schelling, of course, plays upon the double meaning of the term 'contraction': to tighten-compress-condense *and* to catch, to be afflicted with, to go down with ... [an illness] – the primordial Freedom 'contracts' Being as a painful burden which ties it down ...).[10] Prior to this primordial contraction, to this act of engendering–ejecting one's Ground, God is – as Schelling inimitably puts it in the second draft of *Weltalter* – a pure Nothingness which 'enjoys its own non-being'.[11]

Significantly, Schelling resorts to the same formulation when, in his *Letters on Dogmatism and Criticism*, he describes the falsehood of a person entertaining the notion of his own death: when one indulges in fantasies about one's own death, one always imagines oneself as miraculously surviving it and being present at one's own funeral in the guise of a pure gaze which observes the universe from which one is already absent, relishing the imagined pathetic reactions of relatives, and so on. We are thereby again at the fundamental time-loop of the fantasy: to be present as a pure gaze prior to one's own conception. Is not the God prior to the primordial contraction, this pure gaze which finds enjoyment in contemplating its own non-being, also therefore a fantasy-formation at its purest? Schelling emphasizes again and again that the passage of the pure *Seinkönnen* of the primordial Abyss into the contracted Ground cannot be accounted for or 'deduced': it can be described (narrated) only *post festum*, after it has already taken place, since we are dealing not with a necessary act but with a free act which could also not have happened – however, does this not amount to an implicit admission of the fact that its status is that of a retroactive fantasy?

God *qua* pure Freedom which has not yet contracted being thus, *stricto sensu*, does not exist: the spontaneous, self-generated 'breach of symmetry' – we are tempted to say: the primordial 'vacuum fluctuation' which sets in motion the development of the Absolute – is the primordial contraction by means of which God acquires being.[12] This contraction of/into being is necessarily followed by a counter-stroke of expansion – why? Let us step back for a moment and reformulate the primordial contraction in terms of the passage from a self-contented Will which wants nothing to an actual Will which effectively wants something: the pure potentiality of the primordial Freedom – this blissful tranquillity, this pure enjoyment, of an unassertive, neutral *Will which wants nothing* – actualizes itself in the guise of a *Will which actively, effectively, wants this 'nothing'* – that is, the annihilation of every positive, determinate content. By means of this purely formal conversion of potentiality into actuality, the blissful peace of primordial Freedom thus changes into pure contraction, into the vortex of 'divine madness' which threatens to swallow everything, into the highest affirmation of God's egotism which tolerates nothing outside itself. In other words, the blissful peace of primordial Freedom and the all-destructive divine fury which sweeps away every determinate content are one and the same thing, only in a different modality – first in the mode of potentiality, then in the mode of actuality: 'the same principle carries and holds us in its ineffectiveness which would consume and destroy us in its effectiveness'.[13]

Upon experiencing itself as negative and destructive, the Will opposes itself to itself in the guise of its own inherent counter-pole, the Will which *wants something*, that is, the positive Will to expansion. However, this positive Will's effort to break through the bars of its self-imposed contraction is doomed to fail, since the antagonism of the two Wills, the contractive one and the expansive one, is here *under the dominant, in the power, of contraction* – one can say that prior to the pronunciation of the Word, God Himself is 'in the power of B'. He, as it were, repeatedly dashes against His own wall: unable to stay within, He follows His urge to break out, yet the more He strives to escape, the more He is caught in His own trap. Perhaps the best metaphor for this rotary motion is a trapped animal which desperately strives to disengage itself from a snare: although every spring only tightens the snare, a blind compulsion leads it to make a dash for it again and again, so that it is condemned to an endless repetition of the same gesture. . . .

What we have here is Schelling's grandiose 'Wagnerian' vision of God in the state of an endless 'pleasure in pain', agonizing and struggling with Himself, affected by an unbearable anxiety, the vision of a 'psychotic', mad God who is absolutely alone, a One who is 'all' since He tolerates nothing outside Himself – a 'wild madness, tearing itself apart'.[14] The horror of this rotary motion resides in the fact that it is no longer impersonal: God already exists as One, as the Subject who suffers and endures the antagonism of drives. Here Schelling provides a precise definition of anxiety: anxiety arises when a subject experiences simultaneously the impossibility of closing itself up, of withdrawing fully into itself, and the impossibility of opening itself up, admitting an Otherness, so that it is caught in a vicious cycle of pulsation – every attempt at creation-expansion-externalization repeatedly 'aborts', collapses back into itself. This God is not yet the Creator, since a proper act of creation posits the being (the contracted reality) of an Otherness which possesses a minimal self-consistency and exists *outside* its Creator – this, however, is what God, in the fury of His egotism, is not inclined to tolerate.

And, as Schelling emphasizes again and again, even today this all-destructive divine vortex remains the innermost base of all reality: 'if we were able to penetrate the exterior of things, we would see that the true stuff of all life and existence is the horrible'.[15] In this sense, all reality involves a fundamental antagonism and is therefore, sooner or later, destined to fall prey to Divine fury, to disappear in the 'orgasm of forces'.[16] 'Reality' is inherently fragile, the result of a temporary balance between contraction and expansion which can, at any moment, 'run amok' and explode into one of the extremes.[17] Hogrebe resorts here to an analogy from cinema: if the projection of a film is to give rise to an 'impression of reality' in the spectator, the reel has to run at the proper speed – if it runs too quickly, the movement on the screen is blurred and we can no longer discern different objects; if it is too slow, we perceive individual pictures and the effect of continuity which accounts for the impression that we are watching 'real life' is lost.[18] Therein resides Schelling's fundamental motif: what we experience as 'reality' is constituted and maintains itself through a proper balance in the tension between the two antagonist forces, with the ever-present danger that one of the two sides will 'be cracked', run out of control and thus destroy the 'impression of reality'.

Is not this speculation confirmed by the basic premiss of contemporary cosmology according to which the 'reality' of our universe hangs in the balance – hinges on the fragile balance between expansion and gravitation? If the expansion were just a little stronger, the universe would 'explode', dissipate, no firm, stable object would form; if, on the contrary, it were just a little weaker (or gravitation a little stronger), it would long ago have 'collapsed', fallen in. . . . In the domain of intersubjectivity, one often encounters a child who, in order to impress his peers, is ready to 'go to extremes' and to accomplish a 'crazy' suicidal act regardless of its self-destructive consequences (say, to finish a bottle of whisky in one minute). This 'fanatical' disposition, this propensity to 'go to extremes', has to be contained, 'normalized', by activating the counter-tendency, as in quantum physics, where one arrives at a stable finite situation through the 'renormalization' of two opposed infinities.

Let us refer again to Hogrebe, who evokes another nice analogy from athletics:[19] just before the start, the runner has to 'contract'-concentrate himself, to 'immobilize' himself, to turn himself into a statue, so that he can then, at the sound of the pistol, spring up and run as fast as possible – or, as Lenin would have put it, 'one step backwards, two steps forward'. In this precise sense the Beginning is the opposite of the Process itself: the preparatory-contractive 'step back', the setting up of a foundation which then serves as the springboard for taking off and rushing forward – in short, the denial [*Verneinung*] of what follows, of what is the beginning: 'only in the denial is there a beginning'.[20]

On a somewhat higher, more 'spiritual' level, one usually fails to take note of how a free play of our theoretical imagination is possible only against the background of a firmly established set of 'dogmatic' conceptual constraints: our intellectual creativity can be 'set free' only within the confines of some imposed notional framework in which, precisely, we are able to 'move freely' – the lack of this imposed framework is necessarily experienced as an unbearable burden, since it compels us to focus constantly on how to respond to every particular empirical situation in which we find ourselves. Suffice it to recall the paradoxical lesson of so-called 'closed' societies: when an ideological edifice is imposed as the obligatory frame of reference (as it was with Marxism in 'actually existing Socialism'), the subject is relieved of the pressure to ponder all the time upon the basic conceptual schema – the rules of the game are clearly defined, so one can devote one's intellectual energy to the game itself. . . . On a rather different plane, the same experience is regularly reported by Japanese scientists: questioned by their Western colleagues on how they can stand the stiff hierarchy and the rules of ritualized courtesy which regulate inter-subjective relations even in scientific communities (openly to contradict a higher authority is considered extremely coarse behaviour, etc.), they claim that these imposed rules of proper conduct enable them to dismiss from their mind any concern about intersubjective tensions, and to concentrate wholly on scientific work and inventions.

The most acute philosophical formulation of this motif of 'discipline as the condition of freedom' is found in Hegel who, in 'Anthropology' (Subsection A of Part I of his *Philosophy of Mind*[21]), emphasized the liberating aspect of habit: it enables us to dispense with continuous, time-consuming worries about how to react to the multitude of ever-new empirical situations surrounding us. Habit provides ready-made answers which can be applied blindly, without reflection; when a habit becomes our second nature which we follow spontaneously, this very unawareness of the rules which regulate our activity sets our mind free for higher spiritual matters. In short, what effectively sets us free is the 'mechanical' contraction of our dealing with immediate surroundings in the network of habits which forms our 'second nature'. The supreme example, of course, is *language* itself as the paradigm of all institutions: one is effectively able to think freely only when one is fully accustomed to the language in which one thinks – when one loses awareness of its rules and learns to follow them 'blindly'. The moment one has to pay attention to the rules of grammar, and so on, one's thought no longer moves freely, but begins to drag – the free expansion of thinking has its Ground in the 'contraction' of grammatical and other rules. The example of custom clearly demonstrates that contraction is not the external opposite to free expansion: the free activity of thinking does not assert itself *against* custom; rather, it takes place *in the very medium of (linguistic) custom* – we 'think freely' only when we follow the rules of language without being aware of them.[22]

Finally, when all is said and done, this is what *self-identity* is about: a self-identity is never fully transparent – the more it is 'self-', the more it implies a minimum of opaque contraction which holds it together and thus prevents it from dispersing. When Derrida says that the identity of Kafka's text is achieved not

> within an assured specular reflection of some self-referential transparency – and I must stress this point – but in the unreadability of the text, if one understands by this the impossibility of acceding to its proper significance and its possibly inconsistent content, which it jealously keeps back[23]

he is yet again closer to Schelling and Hegel than may appear: the kernel of unreadability that resists and belies every interpretative appropriation – that is, the very feature which makes a text forever 'non-identical to itself', the unappropriable foreign ingredient-body on account of which a text always eludes and defers its being-comprehended – is the ultimate guarantee of its identity; without this unassimilable kernel, the text would lack any proper consistency, it would be a transparent medium, a mere appearance of *another* essential identity.

This co-dependence of expansion and contraction is best expressed by means of Lacan's formula of fantasy $ ◊ a: there can be no $, no void of expansion, of self-overtaking and giving away, without a minimal contraction into an element in which the subject's positive support is condensed; without the 'glue' of this object, the subject would simply 'give itself away' and lose the minimum of consistency on account of which one can speak of a subject.

Perhaps the supreme ideologico-political example of contraction is provided by today's religious and ethnic fundamentalisms which are emerging as a reaction to the withering-away of the Nation-State. The key fact of today's world is the unheard-of expansion of capitalism, which is less and less bound by the form of the Nation-State, capitalism's hitherto fundamental unit of contraction, and asserts itself more and more in direct 'transnational' form; the reaction to this boundless expansion which threatens to sweep away every particular self-identity are 'postmodern' fundamentalisms as the violent 'contraction' of social life into its religious-ethnic roots. Is not this contraction a kind of mocking imitation of the Schellingian primordial act of choosing one's own eternal character? In rediscovering one's ethnic roots or religious tradition (all of which, of course, are faked retroactive projections), a social group as it were chooses its eternal nature – that is, freely decides what it always-already was. . . .

Drives and their rotary motion

It is easy to demonstrate how Jan de Bont's *Speed* varies the well-known Hollywood formula of the production of a couple: one needs the extremely stressful situation of a bus full of hostages in order to engage Keanu Reeves (whose gay proclivities are well known) in a 'normal' heterosexual relationship – the film ends in accordance with the most traditional Oedipal scenario (the killing of the obscene paternal figure – Dennis Hopper – consolidates the love couple of Reeves and Sandra Bullock). The fact that one needs such extreme stress to produce a couple is definitely an index of today's perturbations in the relationships between the sexes. There is, however, another, deeper way (or rather, closer to the surface, and for that very reason more pertinent): at first the wild driving of the bus (its speed has to remain above 50 miles per hour: the moment it falls lower, the bomb will explode. . .) is experienced as a permanent state of suspense, a stressful endless nightmare – our only wish is for this state to end as soon as possible; sooner or later, however, the spectator becomes aware that the wild driving of the bus is a metaphor for *life itself*. In so far as life is also a permanent state of tension, a run whose 'speed' (the heartbeat) must not fall beneath a certain pace if we are to remain alive, the longed-for end of the wild run is simply *death* itself. In short, what is at first experienced as a *threat to life* reveals itself as the ultimate metaphor of *life itself*. . . .[24]

This mad driving of the bus in *Speed* – its agitated, nervous, jumpy, unbalanced character – provides an accurate metaphor of what Schelling has in mind with the rotary motion of drives: the attitude towards the universe implied in the notion of rotary motion is the very opposite of what one usually perceives as 'wisdom': the rotary motion of drives does not offer a pacifying view of totality which calmly rotates around itself and follows its own course, blessedly indifferent towards (and elevated beyond) our petty worries and anxieties, but, rather, a kind of crazy merry-go-round whose run has to be discontinued. . . .

This logic of pre-symbolic antagonism, of the rotary motion of drives, should not be confused with the *Lebensphilosophie* problematic of the pre-logical life-substance of 'irrational' drives: the status of rotary motion prior to the Beginning is thoroughly logical, since we are dealing with a *failed* logic, with an endlessly repeated effort to begin – that is, to posit the identity-and-difference between the (logical) Subject and Predicate. Prior to the Beginning, there is in a sense only the failed Beginning, failed attempts at the Beginning – a sterile repetition caught in its own vicious cycle, a faltering effort which repeatedly collapses back into itself, unable to 'take off' properly. As Hogrebe conclusively demonstrated, the endless oscillation between contraction and expansion is propelled by the impossibility of formulating the 'stable' relationship between S and P that forms the structure of a propositional judgement: the subject (also and above all in the logical sense of the term) 'contracts' itself, withdraws into itself and annihilates its predicative content; whereas in the ensuing gesture of expansion, it passes over into the predicate and thereby loses the firm ground of its self-consistency.

Another confusion to be avoided here is with the common-sense notion (to which, from time to time, all great theoreticians of antagonism succumb – not only Schelling, but also Freud in *Civilization and its Discontents*, for example) of Eros and Thanatos or expansion and contraction as the two opposed forces engaged in an unending and unrelenting battle for domination. The co-dependence of the two antagonistic forces does not reside in the fact that one force needs the other as the only ground against which it can assert itself (no light without darkness, no love without hate. . .); the logic at work here is much closer to what Marx had in mind apropos of his crucial concept of a 'tendency' which can lead to counter-effects: the long-term 'tendency' of the profit rate to fall, for example, can set in motion the 'defence mechanisms' of Capital which – in the short term, at least – *raise* the profit rate.[25]

As Jacqueline Rose has demonstrated, Melanie Klein's depiction of the pre-symbolic antagonisms of psychic life involves an analogous mechanism: one and the same cause can bring about opposite effects – that is, it sets in motion a process whose outcome is radically undecidable: excessive aggression can be counteracted by a suppression of aggression, *or trigger an upward spiral of more and more aggression.* Homosexuality can arise out of the very anxieties generated by too-strong heterosexual fantasies; at times anxiety and guilt check libidinal development, at other times they enhance it (since the subject, as a reaction to anxiety and guilt, is pushed towards the integrative work of restitution). . . . One should not miss the crucial point here: homosexuality emerges not as the revolt of the suppressed 'polymorphous perversity', or whatever, against the heterosexual phallic economy, but *as a reaction to the very excessive strength of heterosexual fantasies.* It was Freud who, in *The Ego and the Id,* indicated this paradoxical logic when he emphasized how the 'progress' of culture is founded upon a libidinal 'regression' or regressive fixation. One cannot escape this paradox by recourse to the infamous distinction between the two 'aspects' or 'levels': the point is not that what, at the level of culture, stands for a form of 'progress' is, at the level of biological maturation, a regressive fixation; the problem is that libidinal 'progress' itself can take place only as a reaction to an excessively 'regressive' libidinal fixation, just as a highly developed moral sensitivity can emerge only as a reaction to an excessive propensity to Evil. Or – to take a further example from Klein – the very precocious formation of an overdeveloped ego can start to function as an obstacle to its further development, and vice versa.[26]

Two characteristics of this paradoxical causality should be retained: a cause is inherently undecidable, it can enhance either the feature it stands for or its opposite; and, above all, there is no 'proper measure' in the relationship between a cause and its effect – the effect is always in excess with regard to its cause, either in the guise of the excessive upward spiral (aggression leads to more and more aggression) or in the guise of the excessive counteraction (awareness of aggression brings forth a fear of 'overreacting' which deprives the subject of the 'normal' measure of aggressive self-assertion).[27] This undecidability in the cause should not, therefore, be confused with symbolic retroactivity in which the intervention of a 'quilting point [*point de capiton*]' retroactively stabilizes-totalizes the field and specifies the efficiency of the causes – that is, the way the causes will act.[28]

The common-sense logic of complementary couples of opposites to which Schelling often succumbs, and which forms the very core of the 'formal envelope of error' in his thought (one needs Evil, since Good can assert itself only in the guise of the unrelenting effort to overcome Evil; Light can emerge only by overcoming the resistance of Darkness, by 'penetrating the darkness' and illuminating it, etc.), obfuscates the properly *perverse* economy in which Evil is not merely the background of Good, the opposite principle which the Good needs in order to assert itself, but maintains and supports the Good in a much more direct and uncanny way. Let us recall the proverbial Catholic attitude towards adultery: in principle the Church is opposed to pornography, adultery, perversities, and so on; if, however, a moderate dose of it (an occasional visit to a brothel; talk peppered with perverse fantasies or a recourse to pornography destined to enliven the stale sexuality of the consorts) can save a marriage, it is not only tolerated but even actively recommended – an exemplary case of Lacan's thesis according to which perversion, far from being subversive, is a socially constructive posture. During the shooting of *Fitzcarraldo* in the Amazon jungle, a Catholic priest implored Werner Herzog to engage prostitutes from a nearby town as the only way to prevent the white members of his crew raping the Indian women . . . . One should not be surprised by the current regular outbursts of sexual scandals, usually of a perverse nature, in precisely those political parties or movements which advocate rigid conservative morality – from the British Conservative Party (where a series of scandals rendered ridiculous the motto of its moral majority campaign, 'Back to basics!': the MP who thundered threats against single mothers fathered two illegitimate children; another fighting 'unnatural' sexual practices on behalf of Christian values was revealed to be gay; a third died of self-suffocation during masturbation. . .) to American TV preachers (Jim Bakker's encounter with a prostitute and his financial manipulations; Jimmy Swaggart's weird sexual practices with prostitutes. . .). There is no 'contradiction' here: the pervert's transgression is inherent to the moral Order, it serves as its main support.

When Jimmy Swaggart claimed that although he is a sinner his permanent fight against the temptations of Sin (i.e. against his perverse inclinations) gives him the right to preach, he thoroughly obfuscated the true state of things: his perversions were not merely the obstacle he had to fight and to surmount again and again in order to assert his Faith, they were a direct support of his Faith – the occasional 'detour' through Sin enabled him to sustain the burden of Faith. Therein resides the Hegelian 'reversal of the reversal' by means of which we surpass the external co-dependence of opposites: Sin is not simply the obverse of Faith but its inherent constituent – that is to say, one can maintain one's

Faith against the threat of the complete predominance of Sin only by resorting to (a regulated, contained, yet unavoidable minimal amount of) Sin itself. Sometimes, a marriage in deep crisis can be saved from the threat of divorce and a fall into common debauchery only by applying the necessary minimum of pornography, adultery, and so on. In other words, the 'contraction' of Sin provides the minimum of firm ground on which Faith can arise, so that if we subtract Sin, Faith dissipates in boundless expansion. So the point is not that the ethical domain is the field of the eternal struggle between Virtue and Sin; the point is, rather, that *Virtue itself can get the upper hand over Sin only by resorting to (a moderate, controlled, measure of) Sin.*[29]

One more thing should be noted about the blind rotary motion of God prior to the pronouncement of the Word: this motion is not yet temporal, it does not occur 'in time', since time already presupposes that God has broken free from the closed psychotic circle. The common expression 'from the beginning of time. . .' is to be taken literally: it is the Beginning, the primordial act of decision/resolution, which constitutes time – the 'repression' of the rotary motion into the eternal Past establishes the minimal distance between Past and Present which allows for the linear succession of time.

Here we encounter the first of Schelling's many anti-Platonic 'stings': eternity prior to the Word is the timeless rotary motion, the divine madness, which is *beneath* time, 'less than time'. However, in contrast to those who emphasize Schelling's affinity with Heidegger's assertion of temporality as the ultimate, unsurpassable horizon of Being, it should be said that nowhere is Schelling farther from Heidegger, from his analytics of finitude, than in his conception of the relationship between time and eternity. For Schelling, eternity is not a modality of time; rather, it is time itself which is a specific mode (or rather, modification) of eternity: Schelling's supreme effort is to '*deduce' time itself from the deadlock of eternity.* The Absolute 'opens up time', it 'represses' the rotary motion into the past, in order to get rid of the antagonism in its heart which threatens to drag it into the abyss of madness. On the other hand – and, again, in clear contrast to Heidegger – freedom for Schelling is the moment of 'eternity in time', the point of groundless decision by means of which a free creature (man) breaks up, suspends, the temporal chain of reasons and, as it were, directly connects with the *Ungrund* of the Absolute. This Schellingian notion of eternity and time – or, to put it in more contemporary terms, of synchrony and diachrony – is therefore to be opposed to the standard notion of time as the finite/distorted reflection of the eternal Order, as well as the modern notion of eternity as a specific mode of temporality: *eternity itself begets time in order to resolve the deadlock it became entangled in.* For that reason, it is deeply misleading and inadequate to speak about eternity's 'fall into time': the 'beginning of time' is, on the contrary, a triumphant ascent, the act of decision/differentiation by means of which the Absolute resolves the agonizing rotary motion of drives, and breaks out of its vicious cycle into temporal succession.

Schelling's achievement here is a theory of time whose unique feature is that it is not formal but qualitative: in contrast to the standard notion of time that conceives the three temporal dimensions as purely formal determinations (the same 'content' 'travels', as it were, from the past through the present to the future), Schelling provides a minimal qualitative determination of each temporal dimension. The rotary motion of drives *is in itself past*: it was not once present and is now past, but *is past from the beginning of time*. The split as such is present – that is, the present stands for the moment of division, of the transformation of drive's undifferentiated pulsation into symbolic difference, whereas the future designates the reconciliation to come. The target of Schelling's critique here is not only the formalism of the standard notion of time but also, perhaps even primarily, the unavowed, hidden prerogative of the present involved in it – for Schelling, this prerogative equals the primacy of mechanical necessity over freedom, of actuality over possibility.

From freedom to a free subject

Schelling's 'dialectical materialism' is therefore encapsulated in his persistent claim that one should presuppose an eternally past moment when God Himself was 'in the power (exponent) of B', at the mercy of the antagonism of matter, without any guarantee that A – the spiritual principle of Light – would eventually prevail over B – the obscure principle of Ground. Since there is nothing outside God, this 'crazy God' – the antagonistic rotary motion of contracted matter – has to beget out of Himself a Son, that is, the Word which will resolve the unbearable tension.[30] The undifferentiated pulsation of drives is thus supplanted by the stable network of differences which sustains the self-identity of the differentiated entities: in its most elementary dimension, the Word is the medium of differentiation.

Here we encounter what is perhaps the fundamental conceptual opposition of Schelling's entire philosophical edifice: the opposition between the atemporal 'closed' rotary motion of drives and the 'open' linear progression of time. The act of 'primordial repression' by means of which God ejects the rotary motion of drives into the eternal past, and thereby 'creates time' – opens up the difference between past and present – is *His first deed as a free Subject*: in accomplishing it, He suspends the crippling alternative of the subjectless abyss of Freedom and the Subject who is unfree, caught in the vicious cycle of rotary motion.[31] *Here God is in exactly the same position as man on the verge of his timeless act of choosing his eternal character*: it is only via this act of primordial decision that God's freedom becomes the actual 'freedom to do Good or Evil' – that is to say, He has to choose between self-withdrawal and opening up, between psychotic madness and the Word. The difference between God and man, of course, is that God inevitably chooses the Good (pronounces the Word, creates Order out of chaos), whereas man no less inevitably incurs the Fall – in both cases, the choice is simultaneously free and 'forced'. This notion of God's primordial act of decision also enables Schelling to answer the standard reproach to theodicy: why did God create the universe with so much evil and suffering in it? Does this not confront a believer with the embarrassing alternative: either God is evil, or He is not omnipotent? Schelling in no way contests the amount of Evil in the world; he never resorts to the old excuse from the theological bag according to which what we (mis)perceive as Evil is merely a tiny part of a larger divine plan above the reach of the human mind. Quite to the contrary, Schelling's great 'conservative' motif is that our universe, the earth, is the domain of unspeakable horrors which sprang up as God's excrement – left to its own resources, without God's intervention, humanity is lost. His point, however, is that *Creation – the pronunciation of the Word in God – was, as such, a victory of Good over Evil*: in opting for Creation, God shifted from the contractive power B to the expansive power A.

This primordial act of 'repression' which opens up the dimension of temporality *is itself 'eternal', atemporal*, in strict analogy with the primordial act of decision by means of which man chooses his eternal character. That is to say: apropos of Schelling's claim that man's consciousness arises from the primordial act which separates present-actual consciousness from the spectral, shadowy realm of the unconscious, one has to ask a seemingly naive but crucial question: what, precisely, is the unconscious here? Schelling's answer is unambiguous: the 'unconscious' is not primarily the rotary motion of drives ejected into the eternal past; rather, the 'unconscious' is the very act of *Ent-Scheidung* by means of which drives were ejected into the past. Or – to put it in slightly different terms – what is truly 'unconscious' in man is not the immediate opposite of consciousness, the obscure and confused 'irrational' vortex of drives, but the very founding gesture of consciousness, the act of decision by means of which I 'choose myself' – that is, combine this multitude of drives into the unity of my Self. The 'unconscious' is not the passive stuff of inert drives to be used by the creative 'synthetic' activity of the conscious Ego; the 'unconscious' in its most radical dimension is, rather, *the highest Deed of my self-positing*, or – to resort to later 'existentialist' terms – the choice of my fundamental 'project' which, in order to remain operative, must be 'repressed', kept unconscious, out of the light of day – or, to quote again from the admirable last pages of the second draft of *Weltalter*:

> The decision that is in any way the true beginning should not appear before consciousness, it should not be recalled to mind, since this, precisely, would amount to its recall. He who, apropos of a decision, reserves for himself the right to drag it again to light, will never accomplish the beginning.[32]

What we encounter here, of course, is the logic of the 'vanishing mediator': of the founding gesture of differentiation which must sink into invisibility once the difference between the 'irrational' vortex of drives and the universe of *logos* is in place.[33] In Schelling's late philosophy, this figure of the 'vanishing mediator' is conceptualized as Satan; his role is to mediate between the initial state of balanced unarticulated potentiality in which God is not yet posited as such, in a determinate content, and the actualization of the true One God who asserts Himself through the exclusion and annihilation of false gods. Satan thus stands for the paradoxical unity of actuality and potentiality: on the one hand he is the pure potentiality, the eternal lure of temptation which can never fully win, actualize itself; on the other hand, in this very capacity of temptation, Satan compels us to act and effectively to affirm the true God via the rejection of false idols. The figure of Satan thus bears witness to the fact that God Himself needs 'deviations' in order to arrive at His full actuality via their vanquishing.[34]

This passage from pure Freedom to a free Subject relies on the opposition between being and becoming, between the principle of identity and the principle of (sufficient) reason-ground. Freedom involves the principle of identity, it designates the abyss of an act of decision which breaks up the causal chain, since it is grounded only in itself (when I accomplish a truly free act, I do it for no determinate reason, simply 'because I wanted to do it'); Ground designates the existing reality as the network of causes and effects where 'nothing happens without a reason-ground'. This opposition between identity and ground overlaps with that between eternity and time: when things are conceived in the mode of identity, they appear *sub specie aeternitatis*, in their absolute contemporaneity – the way they are according to their eternal essence; when they are conceived in the mode of ground, they appear in their temporal becoming – as passing moments of the complex causal network where the past 'grounds' the present.

In this precise sense, freedom is atemporal: a flash of eternity in time. The problem Schelling is struggling with, however, is that Necessity and Freedom are also opposed as atemporal logic and temporal narrative: 'Identity' also stands for the Eleatic universe of atemporal logical necessity in which there is no free development, in which everything coexists in absolute contemporaneity; whereas actual freedom is possible only in time, as a contingent-free decision of an actual Entity in its becoming.[35] Schelling's effort here is to think freedom as the atemporal abyss of identity (the miracle of an act which is 'its own beginning', grounded only in itself) *and* as the predicate of a free Subject who decides in time. In short, he endeavours to accomplish the passage from Freedom to a free Subject, from the impersonal *Es* of 'there is Freedom' to 'Him', a God who is free.

This passage of Freedom from Subject to Predicate involves a reversal which is strictly analogous to the paradigmatic Hegelian reversal of subject and predicate (from 'determining reflection' to 'reflective determination', etc.): from Freedom's self-limitation/contraction we pass to a self-limited/contracted (i.e. actually existing) Entity which *is free*.[36] That is the ultimate mystery of Schelling's *Weltalter*, as well as of the Hegelian dialectical reversal: freedom 'in itself' is a movement of boundless expansion which cannot be constrained to any limited entity – so how can it become the predicate of precisely such a limited entity? Schelling's answer is that Freedom can become the predicate of a Subject only in so far as this Subject accomplishes the act of self-differentiation by means of which it posits itself as grounded in and simultaneously different from its contracted Substance: a free Subject has to have a Ground which is not himself, he has first to contract this Ground and then to assume a free distance towards it via the act of primordial decision which opens up time.

The divine madness

There is a subtle difference between the *Weltalter* drafts and the *Stuttgart Seminars* with respect to the divine contraction of being. In the *Weltalter* drafts, the contraction of B, the lowest 'power' (raw, formless matter), *precedes* God's self-assertion as an actual free Subject (God becomes a free Subject only later, with the emergence of the Word), so that we are compelled to surmise an 'age' when God was not yet self-illuminated, when He existed not as Himself but only 'in the power (exponent) of B', as the blind raging of unconscious drives. In implicit but clear contrast, the *Stuttgart Seminars* conceive the primordial contraction as an act which coincides with God's *Ent-Scheidung*, self-differentiation

– that is, with the act by means of which God 'deposits' the object in Himself, gets rid of it, and thus constitutes Himself as free. Contraction is thus no longer the act of catching a disease but its exact opposite: the act of healing, of expelling the foreign body in the midst of God: it now stands for the act by means of which God disturbs His original indifference, throws off that which in Him is not Himself, and thereby becomes what He truly is – it is what Kristeva would have called *abjet*; the Creation proper which follows is God's endeavour to mould this formless *abjet* into the multitude of well-shaped objects. (There is effectively an abundance of 'anal', excremental innuendo in Schelling: God secretes the '*abjet*' and then pronounces the Word in order to pull Himself out of the shit He has got into. . .).[37]

This structure of abjection clearly shows the inadequacy of the problematic of 'projective identification': its implication is that the subject originally possesses, has within himself, the entire content; then, in a second phase, he expels, projects into the Other, the part of himself with which he cannot come to terms. What lurks in the background is, of course, the old pseudo-Hegelian notion of 'disalienation' or reappropriation: the subject should fully assume the 'repressed' content projected into the Other, recognizing it as his own. In anti-Semitism, for example, the subject is supposed to project into the figure of the Jew all the aggressive, etc., drives which he is unable to acknowledge . . . . Schelling's position is far more refined and 'postmodern': it is not enough to say that the subject projects into the Jew the disavowed part of himself, since *it is only through this expulsion that a consistent Self constitutes itself in the first place* – the rejection of the 'unacceptable' content, of a traumatic foreign body which cannot be integrated into the subject's symbolic universe, is constitutive of the subject.

This key feature distinguishes Lacan's concept of alienation from its standard pseudo-Hegelian counterpart: there is no subject without some external 'prothetic' supplement which provides the minimum of his phantasmic identity – that is to say, the subject emerges via the 'externalization' of the most intimate kernel of his being (his 'fundamental fantasy'); the moment he gets too close to this traumatic content and 'internalizes' it, his very self-identity dissolves. For that reason, the assuming of fundamental fantasy and 'subjective destitution' are strictly correlative, two aspects of the same operation.

The fundamental problem of the *Stuttgart Seminars*, therefore, is that the Absolute as 'indifference' – as the abyss of primordial Freedom – is not yet a personal God: in it, freedom coincides with blind necessity, since it is not yet 'explicated', posited as such, turned into a predicate of a (free) Entity. In order to posit itself as an actual free Entity disengaged from blind necessity – in short, as a person – the Absolute has to get things straightened out, to clear up the confusion in itself, by way of acquiring a distance towards what in it is not God Himself but merely the Ground of His existence – that is, by ejecting the Ground from Himself. This process of contraction and creation is necessary if God is to clear up His own status and to posit-actualize Himself as a free Entity which is not immediately coalesced with His Ground but maintains a free distance towards it (like man who, although he is grounded in nature and can survive only in his biological body, *is* not his body but *has* it – relates freely to it and can use it as an instrument for higher purposes). What is accomplished thereby is the first step towards the idealist recuperation of Schelling's dialectical-materialist breakthrough: by reinterpreting the primordial contraction as the expelling of the object, Schelling can dispense with the divine 'age' in which egotistic 'madness' rages without constraint. However, the gap that separates the *Stuttgart Seminars* from Schelling's late 'positive philosophy' remains unbridgeable: in late Schelling, God possesses His Being in advance; the process of Creation therefore concerns another being, not the being of God Himself. As such, Creation is no longer the painful process of self-clarification and self-differentiation – one is even tempted to say: self-castration – God had to endure, but involves an activity performed from a safe distance.[38]

The critical point of *Weltalter* – and at the same time the ultimate source of its breathtaking magnitude, the sign of the absolute integrity of Schelling's thought and the feature which makes the *Weltalter* fragments the founding text of dialectical materialism – resides in the repeated failure of Schelling's desperate endeavour to avoid the terrifying intermediate stage between the pure, blissful indifference of the primordial Freedom and God as a free Creator.[39] What comes in between the primordial Freedom and God *qua* free Subject is a stage at which God is already a Subject (He becomes a Subject when, by means of contraction, He acquires reality), but not yet a *free* one. At this stage, after contracting being, God is submitted to the blind necessity of a constricted rotary motion, like an animal caught in a trap of its own making and destined endlessly to repeat the same meaningless motions. The problem is that God's Reason, His awareness of what goes on, in a sense comes too late, is behind this blind process; so that later, when He pronounces the Word and thereby attains actual freedom, He can in a sense acknowledge, accept, only what he 'contracted' not even unwillingly but in the course of a blindly spontaneous process in which his free Will simply played no part.[40] In other words, the problem is that 'one has to admit a moment of blindness, even of "madness", in the divine life', on account of which creation appears as 'a process in which God was engaged at His own risk, if one may put it this way'.[41] In the three consecutive drafts of *Weltalter*, Schelling proposes three different versions of this traumatic moment of 'short circuit' between freedom and existence – that is, of the primordial contraction which disturbs the beatitude and peace of pure Freedom, or, in terms of quantum physics, breaks the original symmetry:

- In the first draft, the primordial Freedom *qua* Will which wants nothing *'contracts' being* – condenses itself into a contracted point of material density – *of necessity*, not through an act of free decision: the primordial contraction cannot not happen, since it derives from primordial Freedom in an absolutely immediate, 'blind', non-reflected, unaccountable way. The first inner tension of the Absolute here is the tension between expansive freedom and the blind necessity of contraction.

- The second draft, which goes farthest in the direction of Freedom, endeavours to conceive *the primordial contraction itself as a free act*: as soon as the primordial Freedom actualizes itself, as soon as it turns into an actual Will, it splits into two opposed Wills, so that the tension is strictly internal to freedom; it appears as the tension between the will-to-contraction and the will-to-expansion.

- The third draft already delineates the solution adopted by Schelling's late 'positive philosophy' – in it, Schelling avoids the problem of freedom's passage to existence by conceiving the starting point of the entire processs, the primordial Freedom, as a 'synthetic principle', as the simultaneity of freedom and necessary existence. God is an Entity which exists necessarily, His existence is guaranteed in advance, and *for that very reason* the creation of the universe outside God is a contingent, truly free act, that is, an act which could also not have happened – God is not engaged in it, it is not His own being which is at stake in it. The shift, the displacement, with regard to the first two drafts is enormous: from a God who is *implicated* in the process of creation, to whom this process is His own Way of the Cross, we pass to a God who creates the universe from a safe distance of 'metalanguage'.

In a somewhat risky interpretative gesture, one is tempted to assert that the three consecutive drafts of *Weltalter* provide a condensed mirror-image of the three main stages of Schelling's entire philosophical development. Schelling$_1$ (his 'philosophy of identity') is in the power (exponent) of Being, that is, in it, necessity encompasses freedom, and freedom can reside only in the 'comprehended necessity', in our awareness of the eternal order of rational Necessity in which we participate. In short, here Schelling is a Spinozist for whom the notion of the Absolute involves the absolute contemporaneity, co-presence, of its entire content; consequently, the Absolute can be conceived only in the mode of logical deduction which renders its eternal inner articulation – temporal succession is merely an illusion of our finite point of view.[42] In contrast, Schelling$_2$ (of 'Philosophical Investigations' and *Weltalter*) is in the power (exponent) of Freedom, which is why his crucial problem is that of 'contraction': how did the abyss of primordial Freedom contract Being? Consequently, with regard to the mode of the presentation of the Absolute, logical deduction has to give way to mythical *narrative*.[43] Finally, the notion of God in Schelling$_3$ unites freedom and necessary existence, but the price is the split of philosophy into 'positive' and 'negative': negative philosophy provides the a priori deduction of the notional necessity of *what* God and the universe are; however, this *What-ness* [*Was-Sein*] can never account for the *fact that* God and the universe are – it is the task of positive philosophy to function as a kind of 'transcendental empiricism', and to 'test' the truth of rational constructions in actual life.

Schellingian politics

This distinction between the three stages of Schelling's thought – especially between the second and the third stage, the stage dominated by the *Weltalter* project and his late 'positive' philosophy – is of crucial importance if we are to comprehend Schelling's political dimension properly. What takes place in the passage from the second stage to the third – that is, in the aftermath of the breakdown of the *Weltalter* project – is a 'regression' to traditional ontology: in order to avoid the dead-lock in which he has become enmeshed, Schelling has recourse to the Aristotelian notional apparatus. In the 'positive philosophy' his entire previous ontological edifice is thus reinterpreted to suit the frame of the traditional couples of form and stuff, essence and existence, possibility and actuality, and so on. The gigantic effort of the *Weltalter* fragments to supplant the 'negative' speculative philosophy with the history of the Absolute, with the narrative of the 'ages' of divine development, makes way for a new division of labour between 'negative philosophy' (meant to deal with the formal, logical-dialectical aspect: with essences, notional truths) and 'positive philosophy' (meant to deal with the material aspect, with what is positively given – to use a typical Schellingian pun, with what is literally 'out of mind': God *qua* actually existing in opposition to the merely conceived God, to the notion of

39

God, for example) – one pretends to resolve the deadlock by simply keeping its two sides apart.

One has to be especially attentive in reading the texts in which the passage from the problematic of *Weltalter* to 'positive philosophy' takes place, since Schelling often continues to use the same terms with totally changed, sometimes even directly opposed, meanings. 'Existence', for example: in the *Freedom* essay, God's existence is identified with *Logos* (it is only through emitting a Word that God comes to exist *stricto sensu*; the pre-logical 'nature in God' is merely the obscure Ground of Existence), whereas in 'positive philosophy', existence is the pre-rational 'being-given' of a thing which cannot be deduced from its Notion; as such, it is opposed to essence (to *Logos*, which defines the universal essence-possibility of a thing), entirely in line with traditional ontology. From the unheard-of couple Ground/Existence which undermines the very foundations of traditional metaphysics, we are thus back to the traditional couple Essence/Existence.

It is the same with the couple of expansion and contraction: in *Weltalter*, 'expansion' expresses God's love, His 'giving away' of Himself; 'contraction' expresses His destructive rage, His egotistic withdrawal-into-Self; in 'positive philosophy' we again have an inversion: expansion is now identified with the destructive rage which draws every finite, limited, firmly delineated being into its formless vortex, whereas the contractive force is conceived as creative, formative, as the activity of providing things with a stable form which alone guarantees their ontological consistency. This inversion is also clearly conditioned by the reinscription of Schelling's thought into the framework of traditional ontology which operates with the notional couple of formless stuff and form as the inherent limit, the 'proper measure', of a thing (Plato's couple *peiros/apeiron*, Aristotle's entelechy).

Habermas has emphasized the political background of these three stages of Schelling's thought.[44] The Schelling of the 'philosophy of identity' is a classical bourgeois thinker who conceives the modern State and the legal order guaranteed by it as the only possible framework of human freedom: far from constraining freedom, the legal order provides its only foundation, since without the rule of law, freedom inevitably degenerates into despotic self-will. In clear contrast, the late Schelling of 'positive philosophy' is effectively 'reactionary': he fully acknowledges the 'repressive' character of State power, that is, the irreducible and constitutive antagonism between the State and its subjects; he is fully aware of how State power in the end always runs counter to the freedom of its subjects, how it remains forever a foreign power which exerts pressure on subjects, how subjects will never truly 'internalize' State power and experience it as 'their own', as an expression of their own innermost Will – in short, to put it in traditional Marxist terms, Schelling fully acknowledges the *alienated* character of the State. However, the conclusion he draws is not the revolutionary idea of the need to 'abolish' State power: he is thoroughly *in favour* of the State and of the inviolable, unconditional character of its authority. He reasons in the following way: man is a sinful being, our very existence bears the mark of the Fall of the first man, who gave preference to pride over love, and the State is precisely the *punishment* for this false pride. State power is thus literally *divine*: God's punishment for man's egotistic pride and his rebellion against His authority. With the Fall, man irreparably lost the ability to run his communal life in the spirit of humble love – if one is to prevent universal egotistic slaughter, a superior power is needed to discipline man, to bridle his egotism and false pride, and this agency is none other than the State. What we have here is a consequent theological apology for State power: the very existence of State power bears witness to the fact that man is a sinful creature, it bears witness to his inability to run his own affairs autonomously. . . .

Surprisingly, however, the 'middle' Schelling draws from these same premises the opposite, 'revolutionary' conclusion: far from acting as a pacifying agency bridling our egotism, the State is *Evil personified, materialized*, an agency which terrorizes society, a foreign power, a parasite on the social body, which is why its abolition is a *sine qua non* of a free society. This Schelling, of course, is very close to Marx: the State is an externally imposed false unity which conceals the antagonistic splitting of society; it functions as a substitute for the lack of true social unity. In contrast to Hegel, for Schelling (even for the late Schelling) the State is not an actualization of Reason but always a contingent, unauthentic substitute for the lost true unity. As Gérard Bensussan has pointed out,[45] for Schelling, the entire problematic of politics and State stands under the double sign of *inversion* and *non-achievement* (with regard to true unity): the State is an inverted, even perverted, false, violently imposed, mechanical unity, at best an imperfect indication-imitation of a true unity to come, never the accomplished unity itself. To see in the State the embodiment of rational necessity means to accept apologetically the actual order of things as necessary, and to remain blind to the fact that this order is contingent, something which could also have been different, or could not have been at all.

This means that the late 'reactionary' Schelling is also not to be easily dismissed: he clearly perceived how, owing to man's original Fall – owing, that is, to his constitutive 'out-of-jointedness', loss of the primordial organic unity – the State is a contingent substitute-formation, not a 'natural', authentic form of social unity; yet precisely as such, and for that very reason, it is *unavoidable*. Schelling thereby undermined the false alternative of either glorifying the State as ethical kingdom or endeavouring to abolish it as the instrument of oppression.[46]

The primordial dissonance

To recapitulate: the crux, the turning point, in the history of the Absolute is the divine act of *Ent-Scheidung*, the resolution which, by rejecting the vortex of drives, their 'mad dance', into the darkness of the 'eternal Past', establishes the universe of temporal 'progression' dominated by *logos*–light–desire. How does this act relate to *human* history? The relationship between the divine 'ages of the world' and human history is that of a *repetition*: first, the rotary motion of contraction and expansion, this 'divine madness', is released by the intervention of the divine Word – that is, the act of creation; however, on account of man's Fall, this shift from the timeless-eternal rotary motion to the progressive temporal line *repeats itself within human history*. Human history itself is thus divided into two great epochs, the *pagan epoch of rotary motion* (the eternal 'return of the same', the circular rise and fall of great pagan civilizations, clearly stands under the sign of pre-symbolic vortex of drives which sooner or later reduces every 'progressive' formation to dust) and the *Christian epoch of linear teleological progress* (the continuous approach to the ideal of freedom regulated by the divine *Logos* which finally, in Christ's Revelation, gets the upper hand over the destructive vortex of drives).

In so far as the same shift from the domination of rotary motion to the domination of linear progress repeats itself within Christian history in the guise of the passage from the medieval societies of the circular 'return of the same' to the modern capitalist societies of incessant progress and expansion, one is tempted, in a 'reductionist' historico-materialist vein, to anchor Schelling's mega-narrative of the divine Ages of the World to a very precise and constrained 'ontic' event: the passage from the traditional, pre-modern community to the modern capitalist society. That is to say, what Schelling proposes is a narrative of the 'ages' of the Absolute itself; this narrative, the most anti-Lyotardian, the largest possible, offers itself as the ideal testing ground for Fredric Jameson's provocative idea that all narratives are ultimately variations on one and the same theme, that of the passage from the 'closed' organic community to modern capitalist society – every narrative eventually endeavours to provide an answer to the enigma of how things got out of joint, how the old 'authentic' ties disintegrated, how the organic balance of a circular movement that characterizes traditional societies passed over to the modern, 'alienated', unbalanced individualist society we live in.

Is not the Schellingian passage from rotary motion to linear progress, therefore, this same story of the emergence of modern capitalist society elevated (or inflated) to the level of the Absolute? How is the emergence of Word connected with the pulsating 'rotation' in God, that is to say, with the interchange of expansion and contraction, of externalization and internalization? How, precisely, does the Word discharge the tension of the rotary motion, how does it mediate the antagonism between the contractive and the expansive force? The Word is a *contraction in the guise of its very opposite, of an expansion* – that is to say, in pronouncing a word, the subject contracts his being *outside* himself; he 'coagulates' the core of his being in an external *sign*. In the (verbal) sign, I – as it were – *find myself outside myself*, I posit my unity outside myself, in a signifier which represents me:

> It seems universal that every creature which cannot contain itself or draw itself together in its own fullness, draws itself together outside itself, whence, e.g., the elevated miracle of the formation of the word in the mouth belongs, which is a true creation of the full inside when it can no longer remain in itself.[47]

This notion of symbolization (of the pronunciation of Word) as the contraction of the subject outside itself, i.e. in the form of its very opposite (of expansion), announces the structural/differential notion of signifier as an element whose identity stands for its very opposite (for pure difference): we enter the symbolic order the moment a feature functions as the index of its opposite (the moment the political Leader's hatred – of the 'enemies' – is perceived by his subjects as the very form of appearance of his unlimited love for the People; the moment the apathetic indifference of a *femme fatale* is perceived by her male admirers as the token of her intense passion, etc.). For the very same reason, phallus is for Lacan the 'pure' signifier: it stands for its own opposite, i.e. it functions as the signifier of *castration*. The transition from the Real to the Symbolic, from the realm of pre-symbolic antagonism (of contraction and expansion) to the symbolic order in which the network of signifiers is correlated to the field of meaning, can only take place by means of a paradoxical 'pure' signifier, a signifier without signified: in order for the field of meaning to emerge, i.e. in order for the series of signifiers to signify *something* (to have a determinate meaning), *there must be a signifier (a 'something') which stands for 'nothing'*, a signifying element whose very presence stands for the absence of meaning (or, rather, for absence *tout court*). This 'nothing', of course, is *the subject itself*, the subject *qua* $, the empty set, the void which emerges as the result of the contraction in the form of expansion: when I contract myself outside myself, I deprive myself of my substantial content. The formation of the Word is thus the exact opposite of the primordial contraction/abjection by means of which, according to the *Stuttgart Seminars*, God expels – discharges, casts out, rejects out of Himself – His real side, the vortex of drives, and thus constitutes Himself in his Ideality, as a free subject: the primordial rejection is an act of supreme egotism, since in it God, as it were, 'gets rid of the shit in Himself' in order to purify and keep for Himself the precious spiritual essence of His being; whereas in the formation of the Word, He articulates outside Himself – He discloses, (sur)renders, this very ideal-spiritual essence of His being. In this precise sense, the formation of the Word is the supreme act and the paradigmatic case of *creation*: 'creation' means that I reveal, hand over to the Other, the innermost essence of my being.

The problem, of course, is that this second contraction, this original act of creation, this 'drawing together outside itself', is ultimately always ill-fitting, contingent – it 'betrays' the subject, represents him inadequately. Here, Schelling already announces the Lacanian problematic of a *vel*, a forced choice which is constitutive of the emergence of the subject: the subject either persists in himself, in his purity, and thereby loses himself in empty expansion, or he gets out of himself, externalizes himself, by 'contracting' or 'putting on' a signifying feature, and thereby alienates himself – that is, is no longer what he is, the void of pure $:

> . . .the subject can never grasp itself as what it is, for precisely in attracting itself [*sich-Anziehen*] it *becomes* an other; this is the basic contradiction, we can say the misfortune in all being – for either it *leaves* itself, then it is as nothing, or it attracts-contracts itself, then it is an other and not identical with itself. No longer uninhibited by being as before, but that which has inhibited itself with being, it itself feels this being as alien [*zugezogenes*] and thus contingent.[48]

Therein resides Schelling's reformulation of the classical question 'Why is there something and not nothing?': in the primordial *vel*, the subject has to decide between 'nothing' (the unground/abyss of freedom that lacks all objective being – in Lacanian mathemes: pure $) and 'something', but always irreducibly in the sense of 'something extra, something additional, something foreign/put on, in a certain respect something contingent'.[49] The dilemma is therefore the following:

either it remains still (remains *as* it is, thus pure subject), then there is no life and it is itself as nothing, or it *wants* itself, then it becomes an other, something not the same as itself, *sui dissimile.* It admittedly wants itself *as* such, but precisely this is impossible in an *immediate* way; in the very wanting itself it already becomes an other and distorts itself.[50]

Everything thus turns around the primordial act by means of which 'nothing' becomes 'something', and Schelling's entire philosophical revolution is contained, condensed, in the assertion that this act which precedes and grounds every necessity is in itself *radically contingent* – for that very reason it cannot be deduced, inferred, but only retroactively presupposed. This act involves a primordial, radical and irreducible *alienation*, a distortion of the original balance, a kind of constitutive 'out-of-jointedness': 'This whole construction therefore begins with the emergence of the first contingency – which is not identical with itself – it begins with a *dissonance,* and *must* begin this way.'[51] In order to emphasize the non-spontaneous, 'artificial', 'corrupted' character of this act, Schelling plays on the multiple meanings of the German verb *anziehen*: being attracted, drawn to something; contracting a disease; putting on clothes; acting in a false, pretentious way – apropos of this last feature, Schelling directly evokes what was later conceptualized (by Jon Elster) as 'states which are essentially by-products':

> There are certain moral and other qualities that one has only precisely to the extent that one does not have them – as the German language splendidly expresses it, to the extent to which one does not put on [*sich anzieht*] those qualities. E.g., true charm is possible only precisely if it does not know about itself, whereas a person who knows of his charm, who puts it on, immediately stops being charming, and if he conducts himself *as* being charming will instead become the opposite.[52]

The implications of this are very radical and far-reaching: fake is original, that is, every positive feature, every 'something' that we are, is ultimately 'put on'.

At this point, it is customary to oppose Schelling to Hegel, to the Hegelian logical necessity of the immanent self-deployment of the absolute Idea; before yielding to this commonplace, however, it would be worth pausing to consider the fact that Hegel develops an analogous *vel* in his *Phenomenology of Spirit,* apropos of the Beautiful Soul and the act. The choice that confronts the subject here is: either inactivity or an act which is by definition contingent, branded with a merely subjective content. This contingency of the act disturbs the balance of the (social) Substance in which the subject is embedded; the reaction of the Substance thereby set in motion inexorably leads to the failure of the subject's enterprise.[53] The true critical 'materialist' supplement to Schelling is to be sought elsewhere: in Marx who, in his dialectics of the commodity-form, also starts from the need of the abstract-universal Value to embody itself in a contingent use-value, to 'put on' a use-value dress, to appear in the form of a use-value; as he is quick to add, however, *at least two* use-values (commodities) are needed if a Value is to express itself, so that the use-value of the first commodity gives body to the Value of the second. And Lacan's definition of the signifier as that which 'represents the subject for another signifier' ultimately amounts to the same assertion of an irreducible duality: if a subject is to be represented by a signifier, there must be a minimal chain of two signifiers, one of which represents the subject for the other.

'Symbolic castration'

The crucial point not to be missed here is that in so far as we are dealing with *Subject*, the 'contraction' in question is no longer the primordial contraction by means of which the original Freedom catches being and thereby gets caught in the rotary motion of contraction and expansion, but the contraction of the subject outside himself, in an external sign, which resolves the tension, the 'inner dispute', of contraction and expansion. The paradox of the Word is therefore that its emergence resolves the tension of the pre-symbolic antagonism, but at a price: the Word, the contraction of the Self outside the Self, involves an irretrievable externalization-alienation – with the emergence of the Word, we pass from *antagonism* to the Hegelian *contradiction* between $ and S_1, between the subject and its inadequate symbolic representation. This 'contingency' of the contraction in the Word points towards what, in good old structuralist terms, is called 'the arbitrary of the signifier': Schelling asserts the irreducible gap between the subject and a signifier which the subject has to 'contract' if he is to acquire (symbolic) existence: the subject *qua* $ is never adequately represented in a signifier.[54] This 'contradiction' between the subject and his (necessarily, constitutively inadequate) symbolic representation provides the context for Schelling's 'Lacanian' formulation according to which God-Absolute *becomes inexpressible at the very moment He expresses Himself, that is, pronounces a Word.* Prior to his symbolic externalization, the subject cannot be said to be 'inexpressible', since the medium of expression itself is not yet given – or, to invoke Lacan's precise formulation, desire is *non-articulable* precisely as always-already *articulated* in a signifying chain.

In short, by means of the Word, the subject finally *finds* himself, comes to himself: he is no longer a mere obscure longing for himself since, in the Word, he directly attains himself, posits himself as such. The price, however, is the irretrievable *loss* of the subject's self-identity: the verbal sign that stands for the subject – in which the subject posits himself as self-identical – bears the mark of an irreducible dissonance; it never 'fits' the subject. This paradoxical necessity on account of which the act of returning-to-oneself, of finding oneself, immediately, in its very actualization, assumes the form of its opposite, of the radical loss of one's self-identity, displays the structure of what Lacan calls 'symbolic castration'. This castration involved in the passage to the Word can also be formulated as the redoubling, the splitting, of an element into itself and its place in the structure.

Apropos of the Word, Schelling refers to the medieval logic in which *reduplicatio* designated the operation by means of which a term is no longer conceived *simpliciter* but is posited *as such*: *reduplicatio* points towards the minimal, constitutive gap that forever separates an element from its re-marking in the symbolic network; here Hogrebe[55] invokes the difference between an element and its place [*Platz*] in an anonymous structure. Because of this structure of castration, Spirit is super-natural or extra-natural, although it grew out of Nature: Nature has an ineradicable tendency to 'speak itself out', it is caught in the search for a Speaker [*die Suche nach dem Sprecher*] whose Word would posit it as such; this Speaker, however, can only be an entity which is itself not natural, not part of Nature, but Nature's Other. Or – to put it in a slightly different way – Nature is searching for itself, it strives for itself, but it can 'find itself', attain itself, only *outside itself*, in a medium which is itself not natural. The moment Nature becomes *ein Aussprechliches* (something that can be spoken of in meaningful propositions), it ceases to be the *Aussprechendes* (that which is speaking):[56] the speaking agency is the Spirit *qua* $, the substanceless void of non-Nature, Nature's distance towards itself.

In short, the fundamental paradox of symbolization – the paradox the term 'symbolic castration' aims at recapturing – is that Nature can attain itself, its self-identity, only at the price of radical decentrement: it can find itself only in a medium outside itself. A father becomes father 'as such', the bearer of symbolic authority, only in so far as he assumes his 'castration', the difference between himself in the immediate reality of his being and the place in the symbolic structure which guarantees his authority: the father's authority is radically 'decentred' with regard to father *qua* flesh-and-blood person – that is, it is the anonymous structure of the symbolic Law which speaks through him.

This paradox, of course, can also be formulated in terms of the Hegelian opposition of In- and For-itself: in so far as an object is 'in itself', it is *not yet* fully itself, has not yet found itself, achieved its self-identity; however, it can become 'for itself' only via a decentring *reduplicatio* – that is to say, the price of achieving full self-identity is that the object in question is *no longer* just itself but itself *plus* a supplementary re-mark which is essential if self-identity is to be accomplished. The opposition In-itself/For-itself thus involves the paradoxical logic of a failed encounter, the splitting of identity into a 'not yet' and a 'no longer'. In order to elucidate this point, suffice it to recall the Derridean problematic of gift:[57] the moment a gift is recognized by the other 'as such', as gift, it is no longer a pure gift but already caught in the logic of exchange – so gift is always in-between, it is either not yet a gift, a gift only 'in itself', or no longer a gift, since this recognition (its positing as a gift 'for itself', 'as such') makes it lose the status of gift. The same goes for the 'invention' of something new: in order to be fully actualized as invention, the act of invention has to be acknowledged as such by the field of existing knowledge, integrated into it, recognized as invention – but the moment this occurs, invention is no longer pure invention but becomes part of established knowledge.[58]

This Schellingian distinction between the rotary motion of drives and the universe of logos, of symbolic identity-and-difference, also provides the proper background for Lacan's concept of identification: identification takes place at the level of logos, it is always identification with a signifier; as such, it *comes after* the 'impossible' relationship between a drive *qua* real and its object, *objet petit a* (a drive is doomed to circle for ever around its object-cause; that is to say, it can only encircle it, its place, without ever attaining it). In other words, symbolic identification (ultimately identification with the Master-Signifier that represents the subject) compensates for the 'impossibility', the structural failure, of the subject's traumatic relationship towards *objet a*: the subject who identifies (with a signifying feature) is always-already in himself split in his relationship to *a*, and he identifies with a signifier in order to resolve (or at least obfuscate) the deadlock of the radically ambiguous attraction/repulsion of his relationship to *a*.

The problem with identification is that this concept is usually conceived in too narrow a sense. That is to say, the discussion of identification in the political field is generally centred on what Freud defines in his *Group Psychology* as the first form of identification: the vertical identification with the object *qua* Leader that constitutes the horizontal link between subjects. Yet the other two forms of identification (brought together by Lacan under a common concept) are perhaps far more interesting. Freud mentions a group of girls in a college who identify with the hysterical outbursts of their fellow-student in love; in this way, through this particular feature, they identify with being-in-love, with the love relationship. A similar metonymical mechanism is at work in the dream with the apparently sad content that Freud quotes in his *Interpretation of Dreams*: the dreamer dreams that he is at a funeral. The key to this dream: at the funeral, where the dreamer had actually been the previous day, he re-encountered, after a long time, his great love, who had married another man; what we find in this dream is therefore no masochism, no death drive, but a simple displacement from the true cause – the loved person. The same logic accounts for the great popularity of the problematic of 'alienation in developed capitalism' (consumerism, the lack of authentic communication, etc.) in late-Socialist societies – this particular detour, this 'compassion' for the anxieties of those living in developed capitalism, enabled identification with them, like the poor man who is always willing to sympathize with the anxieties of a millionaire worried to death about the fate of his investments. . . .

Lacan's further point is that symbolic identification is always identification with *le trait unaire*, the unary feature. Let us recall Lacan's own example from the Seminar on identification (which actually originates in Saussure): the 10.45 train from Paris to Lyon. Although, materially, the train is not 'the same' (carriages and the locomotive probably change every couple of days), it is symbolically counted as 'the same', namely 'the 10.45 to Lyon'. And even when the train is late (when, say, due to a mechanical failure, it actually leaves at 11.05), it is still the same '10.45 to Lyon' which, unfortunately, is late. . . . *Le trait unaire* is therefore the ideal feature that enables us to identify the train as 'the same' even if it does not fit the material features contained in its designation. As such, *le trait unaire* dwells on the borderline between the Imaginary and the Symbolic: it is an image which, by being cut out of the continuity of 'reality', has started to function as a symbol. This borderline is perhaps best illustrated by the notion of *insignia*: an image that functions as a symbol, as a 'trademark' – it stands for its bearer, although he no longer possesses the property it designates. One must be very careful here not to miss the difference between this concept of *trait unaire* and the standard idealist or Gestaltist notion of ideal unity which repeats itself as identical in the diversity of its empirical realizations: the point of (Saussure's and) Lacan's example of the train is that the feature '10.45 to Lyon' remains valid even when it is 'falsified' – when the train actually leaves, say, at 11.07.[59]

The paradox of reflection

This Schellingian problematic of the primordial dissonance in the process of the subject's representation also enables us to avoid the fatal trap of accepting too hastily the so-called 'critique of the reflective model of consciousness': according to this *doxa*, we cannot ground our direct, immediate experience of the Sense of Being in notional reflection, there is always some remainder which cannot be accounted for by means of reflection, so we have to presuppose an original pre-reflective 'opening to the world' or 'self-acquaintance' which precedes reflective self-consciousness. . . . The first thing to note here is that Schelling himself, to whom this critique usually refers as its principal forerunner, in the very gesture of asserting, against Hegel, the primacy of Being – that is, the necessary failure of every attempt to reduce Being to reflection – emphasizes again and again that this primacy is thoroughly 'empty'. As we have just seen, Schelling's point is that if the subject is effectively to 'attain itself', to 'posit itself as such' and acquire a minimum of self-acquaintance, it has to alienate-externalize itself, to 'put on' a contingent clothing. An even more important point, however, is that this critique of reflection inevitably becomes enmeshed in aporias which are none other than the good old Hegelian aporias of reflection (one usually tends to forget the key underlying claim of Hegel's logic of reflection: every attempt of reflection to accomplish the complete mediation of an immediate content fails in so far as it produces its own surplus of non-reflected immediacy). To prove this point, let us turn to Maurice Merleau-Ponty, who developed the critique of reflection with an unparalleled stringency decades ago, long before it became fashionable:

> The search for the conditions of possibility is in principle posterior to an actual experience, and from this it follows that even if subsequently one determines rigorously the *sine qua non* of that experience, it can never be washed of the original stain of having been discovered *post festum* nor ever become what positively founds that experience. . . . Never, therefore, will the philosophy of reflection be able to install itself in the mind it discloses, whence to see the world as its correlative. Precisely because it is reflection, re-turn, re-conquest, or recovery, it cannot flatter itself that it would simply coincide with a constitutive principle already at work in the spectacle of the world, that, starting with this spectacle, it would travel the very route that the constitutive principle had followed in the opposite direction. But this is what it would have to do if it is really a *return*, that is, if its point of arrival were also the starting point.[60]

Here we have the classic motif of a primordial pre-reflective world-experience which can never be recuperated by reflection – or so it seems. That is to say: what, strictly speaking, eludes reflective recuperation? The philosophical rigour of Merleau-Ponty is attested by the fact that he avoided the temptation to 'reify' this unrecuperable surplus into a positive pre-reflective In-itself, and provided the only adequate answer: what ultimately eludes reflection is *its own act*:

> The movement of recovery, of recuperation, of return to self, the progression toward internal adequation, the very effort to coincide with a *naturans* which is already ourselves and which is supposed to unfold the things and the world before itself – precisely inasmuch as they are a return of a reconquest, these operations of reconstitution or of reestablishment which come second, cannot by principle be the mirror image of its internal constitution and its establishment . . . the reflection recuperates everything except itself as an effort of recuperation, it clarifies everything except its own role.[61]

And again, this aporia, far from posing a threat to Hegel (as Merleau-Ponty tends to think), was explicitly formulated by Hegel himself in the guise of the opposition between 'external' and 'positing' reflection: in the passage from positing to external reflection, the locus of the immediacy which eludes reflective recuperation shifts from reflection itself to its external presupposition/starting point.

As the term itself suggests, the premiss of 'positing' reflection is that every given positive content can be 'mediated', reduced to something 'posited', recuperated by reflective activity; there is something, however, that eludes the power of this universal reflection – itself, its own act. When reflection becomes aware of this inherent limitation to its activity, we revert to immediacy – that is to say, reflection necessarily (mis)perceives its own act in a 'reified' form, as the In-itself of an external presupposition. What is crucial for the impasse of reflection is this very *oscillation of the locus of its unrecuperable kernel between the In-itself which precedes reflective activity and the reflective activity itself* – and the Hegelian 'trick', of course, consists in resolving the deadlock by simply assuming the *identity* of these two irrecuperable kernels: the In-itself reflection endeavours vainly to catch up with, like Achilles with the tortoise, *coincides with reflective activity itself* – the unfathomable X of the immediate life-experience reflection is after, as it were, its own tail. . . .[62] In other words, the way to break out of the vicious cycle of reflection is not to lay one's hands on some positive-immediate pre-reflective support exempted from the reflective whirlpool, but, on the contrary, to call into question this very external starting point of reflection, the immediate life-experience which allegedly eludes reflective recuperation: this immediate life-experience is 'always-already' tainted by reflection: to repeat Hegel's precise formula from his *Great Logic*, the (reflective-recuperative) return to the immediacy *creates what it returns to*. Or – to put it in Schelling's terms – one should always bear in mind that the Real, the 'indivisible remainder' which resists its reflective idealization, is not a kind of external kernel which idealization/symbolization is unable to 'swallow', to internalize, but the 'irrationality', the unaccountable 'madness', of the very founding gesture of idealization/symbolization.

The virtual reality of Ideas

There is another strange, yet profoundly justified intermediate stage in the self-deployment of the Schellingian Absolute. The shift from the rotary motion of drives to the universe of Light, of spoken Word – in short, of actual creation – does not occur directly: in between the two, prior to the pronouncement of the Word yet after the rotary motion, Schelling situates the ethereal universe of what he calls 'ideas'. As early as his *Essay on Freedom*, Schelling claims that God, prior to the actual creation of the world, pronounces a Word *in Himself*[63] – what, exactly, does he have in mind here? As is often the case with him, a reference to intimate personal experience instantly illuminates an otherwise obscure and weird notion: at the outset of a temptation, before I yield to it and actively will the object I am tempted with – that is, before I posit this willing as effectively *mine* – I experience it as a 'no-man's-willing', as a passive-impersonal intention, neither mine nor somebody else's, which tempts me with its seductive images. In an analogous way, God, before creating actual things, plays in His mind with the possibility of things, with their ideas. Ideas are thus things in a state of indifference, when they are not yet posited as actual – their existence in ideas is timeless, but in the sense of a dream-like phantasmagoria, a spectral pseudo-existence.

Here again we encounter Schelling's anti-Platonism: as to their ontological status, timeless ideas are *less* than things that belong to temporal reality, they can best be imagined as a kind of prenatal nightly glimmering which has not yet been brought to the light of day – one has to presuppose such a magical life of things which precedes their actual existence. Or – if we are to venture into a risky comparison with quantum physics – 'ideas' designate a kind of virtual reality of things in which multiple, incompatible possibilities coexist prior to the 'collapse' of the wave function which brings about the actual existence of things. In Lacanian terms, we are dealing here with the free floating of a multitude of signifiers prior to their *capitonnage* – that is, before a subjective resolution converts this multitude into a unified structured field of meaning (or, as Kant would have put it: actual existence takes place through the synthetic act of the subject).

This notion of a phantasmic life of things prior to their actual creation, of course, refers to the Leibnizean notion of a multitude of possible worlds out of which God chooses and then realizes the best one. Schelling, however, gives a specific twist to this notion; in order to render this twist visible, suffice it to recall *Groundhog Day*, a film in which the hero (Bill Murray) gets 'stuck in time': every consecutive morning he awakens on the same day, so that he lives this day again and again with his memory of the previous 'same' days intact (he knows in advance whom he will encounter outside the hotel where he is staying, etc.). When the initial shock is over, the hero, a slick and cynical TV reporter, takes advantage of the situation to get to know his love (Andie MacDowell) thoroughly, so that finally, after much trial and error, he is able to seduce her in one day, although at the beginning of that day she feels nothing but contempt for his superficial cynical attitude. The 'Schellingian' dimension of the film resides in its anti-Platonic depreciation of eternity and immortality: as long as the hero knows that he is immortal, caught in the 'eternal return of the same' – that the same day will dawn again and again – his life bears the mark of the 'unbearable lightness of being', of an insipid and shallow game in which events have a kind of ethereal pseudo-existence; he falls back into temporal reality only and precisely when his attachment to the girl grows into true love. Eternity is a false, insipid game: an authentic encounter with the Other in which 'things are for real' necessarily entails a return to temporal reality.

The ascent from Eternity to Time

It should be clear, then, from what we have said, why Schelling has to venture into speculations on the *Ungrund* of the Absolute *qua* primordial Freedom. His fundamental problem is human freedom, its possibility: without the abyss of primordial Freedom which precedes the vortex of the Real, it would be impossible to account for the emergence of human freedom in the heart of the realm of natural necessity. The chain of natural necessity can be torn asunder, the Light of freedom can break out of the vicious cycle of natural drives and illuminate the obscure Ground of being, only if natural necessity itself is not the original fact but results from the contraction of the primordial abyss of Freedom, of a Willing which wills nothing – that is to say, only if this primordial Freedom which, by means of its contraction, gets entrapped into the vicious cycle of its own self-imposed chains, in man blows these chains asunder and regains itself. In other words: human freedom is actual, not just an illusion due to our ignorance of the necessity that effectively governs our lives, only if man is not a mere epiphenomenon of the universe but a 'being of the Centre', a being in whom the abyss of the primordial Freedom breaks through in the midst of the created universe. In this way, Schelling is able to think human freedom as actual *and* man as a finite, mortal being, subordinated to the Absolute – he is able, that is, to avoid both extremes: the notion of man as an epiphenomenon whose freedom is an illusion grounded in his ignorance, and the false elevation of man to the subject of all being with no Absolute above him.

In Schelling's 'philosophy of identity', freedom is still conceived in the classical idealist way: as the capacity of the Absolute to deploy its content, to actualize its potential, according to its inherent necessity, unconstrained by any external impediment; from this standpoint of the Absolute *qua* Identity, it is not possible to provide a satisfactory solution to the key problem of how the infinite Absolute passes to the finite multitude of temporal entities. It is only when Schelling breaks the constraints of the 'philosophy of identity' with his specification of freedom as the 'concrete' freedom of a living person that he can solve the problem of creation: of the 'descent from infinite to finite', this symptomatic point of failure of the 'philosophy of identity'. That is to say, in his identity-philosophy Schelling provides three incompatible versions of this 'descent',[64] thereby becoming entangled in the paradoxical argumentation of the 'borrowed copper pan', of listing mutually exclusive arguments, evoked by Freud (I didn't borrow the pan from you; the pan was already broken when I borrowed it . . .) – the argumentation which, of course, indirectly confirms what it endeavours to deny (that I broke the pan I borrowed from you – or, in the case of Schelling, that God is fully responsible for the emergence of Evil):

- *the finite is itself responsible for its fall from the Absolute*: the positive cause of the finite is not God Himself but the broken link between God and His creature – that is, the creature's *fall* from God – which is why finitude as such is Evil. This position should not be confused with the classical position (advocated by St Augustine and Leibniz, among others) according to which Evil is merely negative, a lack, a deficiency of some positive feature: in clear contrast, Schelling emphasizes the active gesture of ontological apostasy, of egotistic assertion of one's autonomy in the face of God, of a deliberate falling away from the Absolute, which provides the finite with its false freedom.

- *the finite results indirectly from the divine positing of ideas*: ideas are posited in God as infinite, that is, as direct moments of His infinite being; it is only when an idea is 'reflected-into-self' – comprehended in-and-for-itself, as an autonomous entity and no longer as it is relatively, with respect to God – that it becomes finite . . .

- *the finite is created by God so that it may become infinite through its own efforts*: God did create the finite, but in order for a being to emerge in the midst of the finite which will be God's *Gegen-Bild*, that is, will participate in God's infinite freedom – the goal of creation is the emergence of man, in whom the finite returns to the infinite.

What we have here is thus a gradual retreat from God's immaculate-ness: (1) God *has no responsibility* for the finite *qua* Evil; the responsibility falls on finite creatures themselves which have actively forsaken God; (2) God *is responsible for the finite, but only indirectly*, by articulating ideas in Himself; (3) God *is fully responsible* for the finite, He created it, but with the purpose of giving birth to man as His *Gegen-Bild*.

With Schelling's shift from the 'philosophy of identity' to *Weltalter*, however, the status of the finite appears in a wholly new light: the emergence of the finite is now grounded in an antagonism which dwells in the midst of God Himself. The passage from the infinite to the finite, from eternity to the temporal reality of finite entities, is no longer characterized as the Fall or Descent from the Absolute; the creation of the universe of finite temporal entities is, on the contrary, conceived as 'ascent': it designates the process by means of which God endeavours to 'find Himself', to regain his mind by curing Himself of the rotary motion of drives, of this 'divine madness'. This, then, is how Schelling solves the problem of the 'Fall' of eternity into time: this 'Fall' is actually not a fall at all but a *Beginning* in the precise sense of relief from an unbearable tension, a *resolution* – that is, the act of resolving an acute, debilitating deadlock. By means of positing finite-temporal reality, God breaks out of the vicious cycle of drives, He accomplishes the passage from the drive's self-enclosed pulsating which can never stabilize itself into firm reality to the actual world of differentiated objects, from pre-symbolic antagonism to symbolic difference.[65]

The 'enchainment'

There, in this endeavour to think 'system' and 'freedom' together, resides Schelling's unique place in the history of philosophy: man is a subordinated moment of the Absolute, a link in the 'great chain of being'; he emerged from nature, and nature remains for ever the Ground of his being; yet he is simultaneously a free being which, as such, is self-centred, an End-in-itself, directly rejoining the Absolute. How, precisely, are we to think these two sides together? Schelling resorts here to his key notion of 'powers [*Potenzen*]': in the hierarchically ordered 'great chain of being', the same structural-formal relationship *repeats itself* in different powers: what is *gravitation* for inert matter (the striving to rejoin the outside centre of gravity) is *melancholy* for man *qua* finite, mortal being separated from the Absolute and longing to rejoin it; a *plant* is to an *animal* what *woman* is to *man*; and so on.

The crucial point not to be missed is the *self-relating* character of this repetition: when a given relationship between the two poles (between 'A' and 'B', the ideal and the real pole) is raised to a higher power, one of the two poles is posited as the form, the neutral medium, of the new, higher polarity. The polarity of plant and animal, for example, has as its neutral medium *life* (i.e. the domain of life is structured along the polar axis of vegetable and animal life); life raised to a higher power is *animal life*, and within the animal domain, the polarity of plant and animal is repeated in the guise of the polarity of female and male. It is because of this self-referentiality that we are dealing here not with the same form repeating itself in different material domains, but with an incessant interchange between form and content: part of the content of a lower level becomes the formal principle of a higher level. We can now see why Schelling uses the term 'enchainment [*Verkettung*]' to designate the hierarchical succession of polarities: these polarities are literally 'enchained' in so far as one pole of the lower level becomes the global, formal principle encompassing both poles of the higher level. In short, this enchainment of powers displays the structure of *mise en abîme*.[66]

What, then, do we get at the two extremes of this process of self-relating elevation to a higher and higher power? At the lowest end, of course, *das Ding*, the ineffable Real of the Thing; at the opposite end, the substanceless void of $, the pure subject; what sets in motion this process in which one and the same polarity reappears in different 'powers' again and again is the fact that at any given level, in any given 'power', the subordination of the real under the ideal pole (of darkness under light, of female under male...) never comes out without a remainder which, of course, is the Lacanian *objet petit a*. This reference to Lacan enables us to interpret the Schellingian polar tension of A and B as the minimal signifying dyad of S_1 and S_2, while the 'impossible' relationship between $ and a ($ \lozenge a$) designates the strict correlation between the remainder which eludes the signifying couple and the subject: for Lacan (as well as for Schelling) the subject *qua* $ is neither a thing nor a state of things but an *event* which occurs when the symbolic enchainment fails in its endeavour to absorb the Real of the Thing without remainder ... in short, the repetition of the dyad A:B in ever new 'powers' is *stricto sensu* the symbolic repetition which constitutes a signifying chain. And in so far as the relationship A:B invokes the sexual difference (between masculine and feminine principles: in Schelling, the sexual connotation of A:B is explicit), its repetition in higher and higher powers bears witness to the fact that 'there is no sexual relationship': every formulation of A:B entails-produces a remainder which, of course, is the *objet a* as asexual.

How does this repetition of the antagonistic-'impossible' relationship between A and B lead to the emergence of man? According to Schelling, man's position is radically problematic, marked by a maximum gap between possibility and actuality: as for his place in the enchainment of powers, man is *in potentia* the crown of creation, yet his actuality is that of a shattering Fall, so that Schelling even characterizes the appearance of man as a 'blockage in development'. In man, the development (the increase of powers) is destined finally to reach a turning point and to bring about the crucial reversal in the relationship between A and B: the predominance of A (the ideal, spiritual principle of expansion) over B (the real, bodily principle of contraction). That is to say, in nature, the relationship A:B stands under the power of B: Spirit gradually reveals itself, yet it remains constrained by the inertia of Matter, enveloped in it; in man, on the contrary, B should subordinate itself to A – that is, Spirit should get the upper hand and take control directly, while corporeality should get rid of its inertia and transform itself into an ethereal, transparent medium of the shining of Spirit. It is thus easy to imagine the great chain of development as a continuous progression from lower (inorganic) to higher (organic) forms of nature, and finally to man – yet with man as the 'crown of creation', an unexpected complication arises: instead of the simple shift from B to A as the predominant principle, B itself, the contractive principle, profits from the illuminating power of A to gain full awareness of itself; it comes to light, is posited as such, emancipates itself and asserts itself as the egotistic evil Spirit – this is what the 'Fall' is about.

Therein resides the paradox of man: if the progression of nature were to continue unperturbed in him, a new angelic entity would appear dwelling in the power of A, an entity for whom matter would lose its inertia and turn into a transparent medium of A. On account of his Fall, however, man is a radically split entity: on the one hand he lacks his proper place, unable as he is to find a home in nature – that is to say, he is aware that he 'doesn't really belong here', that he is a stranger on earth, that his terrestrial life is a spectacle of horrors; on the other hand, the true world, the world of spirits, appears to him as a spectral, unattainable Beyond, as the ultimate enigma, the radical uncertainty of what will happen after death. Instead of the subordination of natural life to spiritual life already in man's terrestrial existence, the two lives are kept apart by the barrier of death, so that one succeeds the other – for man, the true life can be imagined only in the guise of the *afterlife*. In short, here Schelling provides one of the most forceful formulations of the paradigmatic modern notion of man's radical, constitutive *displacement*, of the lack of his or her 'proper place'.

'Selfhood as such is spirit'

The paradox, therefore, is that Spirit and Matter, contrary to what one is led to expect, are harmoniously co-ordinated in nature, whereas the Fall of man perverts their proper relationship and entails their irreducible discord: the true stumbling block to the idealization of the Real is not in nature but in man – it is with man that the hierarchical scale of progression, of intensification of powers, stumbles. Nature is a picture of a harmonious progression of life-forms, whereas the universe of man, of human history, offers the sad spectacle of a degenerate, poisoned nature, caught in a vicious cycle – man's world is full of ruins. Significantly, teleological descriptions refer as a rule to the purposefulness of nature – it is easy to present nature as a purposeful totality in which every organism unknowingly serves some higher End; human history, on the contrary, is a place of horrors and misfortunes, of enterprises gone astray, a place where our gaze can discern nothing but ruins and traces of senseless suffering and destruction, with hardly any progress. Therein resides the ultimate paradox of teleology: it is easy to discover hidden Purposes in nature, which acts blindly, as a purposeless mechanism; whereas man – who, in his activity, consciously pursues goals – gets involved in a meaningless expenditure of his potential. . . .[67] Man hampers the free circulation of nature, he is a kind of embolism in the upward flow of natural energies, and – as Schelling puts it, with his unique naivety – it is as if nature possesses an obscure presentiment of this fact and takes its revenge by bringing upon man natural catastrophes: earthquakes, droughts, floods. . . .

The first task of the 'materialist' reading of Schelling, of course, is to demonstrate how non-human nature appears as a meaningful, harmonious, purposeful totality *only from the standpoint of man as the locus of senseless destruction and purposeless expenditure of forces*: the point from which everything appears as meaningful must itself be the point of the suspension of meaning. The second task of such a reading is to acknowledge fully *the structural necessity of the 'stagnation' of natural progress in man*: this stagnation is not an unfortunate accident, since the *'egotistic' perversion of the Spirit is constitutive of spirituality*:

> That principle which is raised from the ground of nature, and by which man is divided from God, is man's selfhood, but this becomes *spirit* because of its unity with the ideal principle. Selfhood as such is spirit; or man as selfish, particular being (divided from God) is spirit; it is precisely this combination which constitutes the personality. But by being spirit, selfhood is raised from the creaturely to the super-creaturely; it is will beholding itself in complete freedom, no longer the instrument of the universal will creating in nature, but above and outside all nature. Spirit is above light, just as in nature it raises itself above the unity of light and the dark principle. Thus by being spirit, selfhood is free from both principles.[68]

In man as a living, actual spirit, his selfhood – which, in an animal, is merely a blind egotistic striving – comes to light. By means of this self-illumination, I become aware of myself, I 'posit' my Self in the radical exclusion of all otherness. That which, in me, resists the blissful submergence in the Good is therefore not my inert biological nature but the very kernel of my *spiritual* selfhood, the awareness that, beyond all particular physical and psychical features, I am 'me', a unique *person*, an absolutely singular point of spiritual self-reference. In this precise sense, 'selfhood as such is spirit': the Spirit in its actuality is the contraction of Light itself *against* nature ('above and outside all nature'). In other words, if man were to dwell in the Good, he would have to renounce that very unity which makes him an individual person, and be submerged in the universal medium of Light.

This contraction of the Light itself (of the spiritual principle of love) into a concrete living person is unthinkable for the standard idealism which is able to deal only with the impersonal kingdom of Ideas, never with the *actual, personal existence* of the ideal principle. By means of this contraction-into-self, the Spirit – although it is nothing but the self-illuminated ground, the unity of the two principles (A and B) – 'disconnects/unties/uncouples the band' of A and B, and thereby acquires a distance towards both of them; this distance, of course, is freedom as the predicate of an actual, living subject bound neither by his material, bodily environs nor by the determinate spiritual content of his being – that is, he is able to transcend both. Neither in nature nor in God is this band disconnected: in nature, Light remains entrapped, enchained within the Ground; whereas in God, Ground turns into an ethereal, non-resistant medium of Light – only man has the freedom of the actual choice between the two principles. We can see now how *freedom hinges on man's finitude*: only a finite creature 'raised from the creaturely to the super-creaturely' can disconnect the band of the two principles and behave freely towards them. Freedom *qua* the untied band is, of course, another name for the Fall: if the band were not disconnected, we would have the harmonious 'great chain of being', the teleological order running from inanimate matter through animals to the ethereal angelic selfless Spirits bathing in their bliss.

The vision of a state of reconciliation in which the natural progress (the gradual spiritualization of nature) would fulfil itself, reach its peak, find its completion in the full predominance of the ideal principle – in which, that is, corporeality would get rid of its inertia and transform itself into an ethereal medium of the shining of Spirit – is thus a fantasy which obfuscates the fact that the World of Spirits has to remain for ever a spectral apparition; that the barrier which separates it from our terrestrial reality is insurmountable. The paradox lies in the fact that 'less is more': man is free precisely and only in so far as he is 'out of joint', displaced, hampered, 'not at home in this world'; the obstacle which prevents him from leaving the misery of his terrestrial life behind and entering the ethereal spiritual existence is the positive condition of his freedom. This structure of finitude also accounts for the possibility of the symbolic *reduplicatio*: finitude is the very limit which prevents a thing from becoming fully itself, from attaining its self-identity, so that either a thing is *not yet* itself and dwells in the state of virtual proto-existence, or it becomes itself, is 'posited as such', but this positing is achieved by the supplement of the Word – that is, the thing is already re-marked, *no longer* merely itself. No wonder, then, that we encounter here, apropos of the Word, the inversion which characterizes the dislocation of man: that which should be 'more', the spiritual *meaning of things,* is experienced as 'less', as the transitory *meaning of words,* the pale copy-shadow of actual things (in strict analogy to the fact that the true world, the world of spirits, appears to man as a spectral, unattainable Beyond).

It is therefore misleading to conceive the constitutive displacement of man as the division between the finitude of his bodily existence and the infinity of the Spirit: the Infinite becomes actual, living Spirit only when it 'attains itself', when it becomes aware of itself, in a finite creature 'raised from the creaturely to the super-creaturely'. That is to say: what is Spirit? The domain of signification, of the symbolic; as such, it can emerge only in a creature which is neither constrained to its bodily finitude nor directly infinite (i.e. no longer anchored to terrestrial Ground) but in between, a finite entity in which the Infinite resounds in the guise of a shadowy phantasmagoria, a presentiment of Another World. The domain of the Spirit is thus inherently anamorphic: it can exist only in the guise of an anticipation of itself; the moment we 'look it straight in the face' its spell is broken, it dissolves into vulgar positivity. For that reason, only a finite entity can speak: God *qua* infinite does not speak, since in Him no distance which separates 'words' from 'things' can occur. In other words, God's Word necessarily implies His finitude – and perhaps Schelling was the only one fully to assume this uncanny consequence of the fact that God pronounces a Word.

Existence and its Ground

This 'egotistic' perversion of the Spirit which is inherent to the very notion of actually existing Spirit forms the core of Schelling's conception of Evil, at which he arrived by the radicalization of Kant's notion of 'radical Evil' in *Religion Within the Limits of Reason Alone.* Schelling's starting point is the repudiation of the traditional philosophical *topos* according to which the possibility of Evil is grounded in man's finitude, in his deficiency in comparison to divine perfection – in the fact that he is split between the material and the spiritual world: Schelling literally turns this *topos* round and asserts that the root of Evil, on the contrary, lies in man's *perfection*, his advantage over other finite creatures and, on the other hand, in a certain split in *God Himself.* That is to say: the central tenet of 'Philosophical Investigations' is that if one is to account for the possibility of Evil, one has to presuppose a split of the Absolute itself into God in so far as He fully exists and the obscure, impenetrable Ground of his Existence – with the speculative audacity characteristic of his mode of thinking, Schelling locates the split which opens up the possibility of Evil in God Himself. This distinction between God's Existence and its Ground, between the Absolute in so far as it fully exists – in so far as it is posited as such, illuminated by the Light of Reason – and the Absolute *qua* obscure longing [*Sehnsucht*] which strives for something outside itself without possessing a clear notion of what it actually strives for, means that God is not fully 'Himself' – that there is something in God which is not God.

In 'Philosophical Investigations', this relationship between the obscure Will of the Ground and the illuminated, effectively existing Will is not yet thought through, so that Schelling's position is, strictly speaking, contradictory. That is to say, his answer to the question 'What does the obscure Will aspire to?' is: it strives after illumination, it yearns for the Word to be pronounced. If, however, the obscure Will of the

Ground itself aspires to *logos*, in what precise sense is it then *opposed* to it? *Weltalter* resolves this contradiction by qualifying the first Will as the divine *Selbstheit*, the contractive force which actively opposes the Light of Reason, and thereby serves as the necessary ground of the latter's expansion.[69] As early as 'Philosophical Investigations', however, Schelling's position is more subtle than it may appear: this obscure-impenetrable side of God, the Ground of His Existence, is *not* to be conceived as a positive Base, the true foundation of Being, with Reason as its parasitic accident: the Ground is in itself ontologically hindered, hampered; its status is, in a radical sense, *pre-ontological*: it 'is' only *sous rature*, in the mode of its own withdrawal. The only true Substance is the Spirit, that is, God in His actual Existence; and *Grund* is ultimately a name for God's self-deferral, for that elusive X which lacks any proper ontological consistency, yet on account of which God is never fully Himself, can never attain full self-identity. God needs this foreign body at its heart, since without this minimum of contractive force He would not be 'Himself' – what, paradoxically, forever prevents God from attaining full self-identity is the very impenetrable kernel of his *Selbstheit*. . . .

This tension in the midst of the Absolute itself is, therefore, far more enigmatic than it may appear, since it is thoroughly incompatible with the oppositions which define the space of traditional ontology: the opposition between Ground and Existence does not overlap with the opposition between mere possibility and actuality (if it did, Ground could not corrode the self-identity of actual Existence from within); it is not simply a new name for the duality of the Real and the Ideal in Schelling's early philosophy – that is, for the symmetrical polarity of two ontological principles (the Ground is 'less' than Existence, it lacks full ontological consistency); it definitely does not imply that Ground is in any way the 'true substance' or 'foundation' of Reason. The enigma resides in the fact that Ground is ontologically non-accomplished, 'less' than Existence, but it is precisely as such that it corrodes the consistency of the ontological edifice of Existence from within. In other words, Schelling first opposes Existence (the fully actual God) and the mere Ground of Existence (the blind striving which lacks actuality) as the Perfect and the Imperfect, then goes on to treat the two as complementary, and to conceive the true completeness as the unity of the two, as if the Perfect needs the Imperfect in order to assert itself. *This is why there is Evil in the world: on account of the Perfect's perverse need for the Imperfect,* as if the intersection of the Perfect and the Imperfect were more perfect than the Perfect itself. . . .

Evil as the perverted unity of Existence and Ground

How, then, is the emergence of Evil related to this distinction between Ground and Existence? Schelling's basic definition of Evil as the *Verkehrung* (perversion or, rather, distorting inversion) of the proper relationship between Ground and Existence is misleading in so far as it leaves open the door to two traditional misconceptions against which the thrust of his entire argumentation is directed: the notion of Evil as the split itself (between Existence and Ground, between the Infinite and the Finite) – as, that is, the fall of the Finite from the Infinite (in contrast to Good as the unity of the Finite and the Infinite) – and the notion of Evil as the assertion of the Ground to the detriment of Existence, of the Finite to the detriment of the Infinite – that is to say, the predominance of Ground over Existence (in contrast to Good as the predominance of Existence over Ground, of Reason over obscure drives).

Schelling's thesis here is much more subtle: both Good and Evil are modes of the *unity* of Ground and Existence; *in the case of Evil, this unity is false, inverted* – how? Suffice it to recall today's ecological crisis: its possibility is opened up by man's split nature – by the fact that man is simultaneously a living organism (and, as such, part of nature) and a spiritual entity (and, as such, elevated above nature). If man were only one of the two, the crisis could not occur: as part of nature, man would be an organism living in symbiosis with his environment, a predator exploiting other animals and plants yet, for that very reason, included in nature's circuit and unable to pose a fundamental threat to it; as a spiritual being, man would entertain towards nature a relationship of contemplative comprehension with no need to intervene actively in it for the purpose of material exploitation. What renders man's existence so explosive is *the combination of the two features*: in man's striving to dominate nature, to put it to work for his purposes, 'normal' animal egotism – the attitude of a natural-living organism engaged in the struggle for survival in a hostile environment – is 'self-illuminated', posited as such, raised to the power of Spirit, and thereby exacerbated, universalized into a propensity for absolute domination which no longer serves the end of survival but turns into an end-in-itself.[70] This is the true 'perversion' of Evil: in it, 'normal' animal egotism is 'spiritualized', it expresses itself in the medium of Word – we are no longer dealing with an obscure drive but with a Will which, finally, 'found itself'.

We can now see how far we are from the traditional notion of lack, privation or imperfection as the ground of Evil; as Schelling points out: 'the simple consideration that man, the most perfect of all visible creatures, is alone capable of evil, shows that the ground of evil could by no means lie in defect or privation'.[71] Evil does not reside in finitude as such, in its deficiency with regard to the infinite God – it can emerge only in a finite creature which again rejoins the Infinite – that is, when the unity of Finite and Infinite is re-established in man *qua* finite, but free being.[72] The problem of Evil could then be restated as follows: how is the *false* unity of Ground and Existence possible?

The first thing to emphasize here is the elementary dialectical point that man is the *unity* of Ground and Existence precisely in so far as it is only in him that their *difference* is finally explicated, posited as such: only man is aware of being split between the obscure vortex of natural drives and the spiritual bliss of *logos*; that is to say, his psychical life is the battleground of two principles or Wills, whereas in nature, the Light of Existence remains implicit, 'contained' in the Ground.[73] Man is the only creature which can elevate itself to this duality and sustain it: he is the highest paradox of *universal singularity* – the point of utmost contraction, the all-exclusive One of self-consciousness, *and* the embracing All – a singular being (the vanishing point of *cogito*) which is able to comprehend/mirror the entire universe. In God prior to Creation, the two principles are still in a state of indifference; in the realm of nature, the second principle – A, the Spirit – can appear only under the domination or in the power of B (as the implicit, secret spiritual content of nature); this, again, means that their difference is not yet posited as such, that the two cannot yet come up against each other. When, however, with the emergence of man, the two principles – Existence and its Ground – are posited in their distinction, they are not merely opposed to each other: *their unity also has to be posited* – that is to say, each of them is in the same breath posited as united with its opposite, as its opposite's inherent constituent. In other words, from the previous *indifference* of the two principles we pass to their *unity* – and it is here that we encounter freedom as freedom for Good and Evil, since this unity can take two forms, the form of the true or of the perverted unity. On the one hand, nature can spiritualize itself, it can turn into the medium of Spirit's self-manifestation; on the other hand, with the emergence of the Word, the obscure principle of Ground and Selfhood which hitherto acted as an anonymous, impersonal, blind force is itself spiritualized, illuminated; it becomes a Person aware of itself, so that we are now dealing with an Evil which, in full awareness of itself, *wills itself as Evil* – which is not merely indifference towards the Good but an active striving for Evil.[74]

The domain of ideologico-political struggle exemplifies perfectly how *'Evil' is not particularity as such but its erroneous, 'perverted' unity with the Universal*: not 'egotism' as such, but egotism in the guise of its opposite.

When a political agent (Party, etc.) claims to represent the universal interest of the State or Nation – in contrast to its opponents who, of course, are accused of pursuing only their narrow power-seeking goals – it thereby structures the discursive space so that every attack on it – on this particular political subject – is *eo ipso* an attack on the Nation itself. 'Evil' in its most elementary form is such a 'short circuit' between the Particular and the Universal, such a presumption to believe that my words and deeds are directly words and deeds of the big Other (Nation, Culture, State, God), a presumption which 'inverts' the proper relationship between the Particular and the Universal: when I proclaim myself the immediate 'functionary of Humanity' (or Nation or Culture), I thereby effectively accomplish the exact opposite of what I claim to be doing – that is, I degrade the Universal dimension to which I refer (Humanity, Nation, State) to my own particularity, since it is my own particular point of view which decides on the content of Humanity. I am thereby caught in the infernal cycle of 'the purer you are, the dirtier you are': the more I refer to the Universal in order to legitimate my acts, the more I effectively abase it to a means of my own self-assertion.[75]

We can see now why, according to Schelling, the status of the philosophy of nature is introductory or, more precisely, preparatory: only in man, in whom both principles are finally posited as such, 'things are for real'; in man, for the first time, everything – the fate of the entire universe, the success or failure of Creation – is truly at stake. Here Schelling is radically 'anthropocentric': the whole of nature, the universe as such, was created in order to serve as the setting for man's ethical struggle, for the battle between Good and Evil.[76] Consequently, Schelling can claim that God loves and wills nature, the universe, His entire Creation, only on behalf of man and in man. In this way, he can also account for the strange feeling we have when we encounter an evil deed of enormous dimensions: it is as if this deed concerns not only human beings but the entire universe – as if, in it and through it, the universe as such has gone awry, been perverted, thrown off the rails (see, for example, the scenes of nature run amok – earthquakes, solar eclipse – which accompanied the Crucifixion). In this precise sense, man is for Schelling the 'being of the Centre' – perhaps the reference to a specific Hitchcockian technique can be of some help here: in a series of his films we have a shot which, on account of its connection with the preceding shots, is perceived by the spectators as a subjective (point-of-view) shot; then, while the camera remains immobile, the very subject whose point of view this shot was supposed to represent enters it – that is, *enters*, as it were, *his own picture/frame*. This is what the 'centrality' of man is about: in a sense man has 'his own centre in himself', unlike natural-material objects whose 'centre of gravity' is located outside themselves (which is why, precisely, matter is subordinated to the force of gravitation).[77]

To recapitulate: in human Evil, the *Selbstheit* of the Ground is self-illuminated, elevated to the Spirit; it takes over as the *spiritual* principle of egotism which strives to instrumentalize and subordinate to itself every Otherness. Pure Evil is the egotism of Spirit which cuts all its links with nature; as such, it is – as Schelling emphasizes again and again – far more spiritual than the Good, since the true spiritual Good does not aim to dominate nature, but lets it be in its Otherness. In short, the true 'diabolical' Evil consists in the contraction of the Spirit *against* Nature: in it, the Spirit, as it were, provides itself with a Ground of its own, outside its 'natural' surroundings, with a footing from which it can oppose itself to the world and set out to conquer it. For that reason it is misleading simply to assert that in Good, Ground is dominated by Reason, whereas in Evil, Reason is dominated by Ground: in Evil, Ground *qua* natural base of Reason is brutally enslaved by the egotistically perverted Reason-Light – by the principle of *Selbstheit* that wills itself in the full awareness of itself.[78]

The emergence of Evil can also be accounted for by means of the Lacanian '(symbolic) castration' – that is, the difference between a formal structure and the elements which fill out its places: the possibility of Evil is opened up by the minimal distance between the structure (Centre versus its inferior base or its periphery) and the elements (Reason, Ground) – on account of this distance, Reason is no longer automatically in the Centre: that is to say, it is possible that this 'natural' situation is perverted, and that Ground places itself in the centre. (The paradox is, of course, that Reason *is* Centre: Centre is simply Reason itself in its *reduplicatio*, as 're-marked'. The logic here is the same as that of the Name-of-the-Father: the moment 'father' becomes a symbolic title, it no longer immediately coincides with the empirical person of the father, so that it is possible for a person who is not a 'real father' effectively to 'function' as one, and vice versa. For that precise reason, *Evil can occur only within the symbolic universe*: it designates the gap between a real entity and its symbolic *reduplicatio*, so that it can best be defined as a *perturbed tautology* – in Evil, 'father is no longer Father' or 'Centre is no longer in the centre'.[79])

This inversion can occur only in man, since man is the only creature which has in itself the 'power of the centre' and can use it freely, by positing in the centre either Reason – the 'Centre itself' – or Ground. God also has in Himself the 'power of the centre', but since His nature is perfect, it is meaningless to define His freedom as the freedom to do Good *or* Evil – in Him, the formal structure of Centre directly overlaps with the reign of the Light of Reason *qua* the true Centre – that is to say, He, as it were, automatically uses His freedom to choose the Good; animal creatures, on the other hand, lack the 'power of the centre', their will is not self-illuminated, they gravitate towards a centre which is external to them. This imbalance between form and content accounts for the inherent *instability* of Evil, for its self-destructive nature: the evil Will 'wants it all', it strives to dominate the universe, but it inevitably collapses, since it is based on an 'unnatural' inversion of the proper relationship between different elements and/or powers.

The unavoidable conclusion of 'Philosophical Investigations' is therefore that God, in so far as He is himself engaged in the process of Creation, becomes actual God only through man's free decision for Him – it is not difficult to discern here the echoes of the old theosophical idea sustained by, among others, Meister Eckhart, according to which God Himself is born through man. Man gives birth to the living God from within himself – that is to say, he accomplishes the passage of the impersonal, anonymous divinity into the personal God. This, of course, charges man with the burden of a terrible responsibility: the fate of the entire universe – and, ultimately, of God Himself – depends on his acts. Every human victory over Evil, every emergence of a community of believers, contributes to the formation of the mystical body of God Himself; and, vice versa, man's choice of Evil asserts God's *Selbstheit*, His contractive force – Schelling describes Hell as the 'consuming fire of the divine egotism'. Here he inscribes himself in the lineage of the revolutionary messianic theology whose most outspoken representative in Marxism is Walter Benjamin (see his *Theses on the Philosophy of History*): history is an 'open' process, a succession of empty signs, of traces which point towards the eschatological moment to come in which 'all accounts will be settled', all (symbolic) debts will be set off, all signs will acquire their full meaning; the coming of this moment is not guaranteed in advance, but depends on our freedom. The outcome of the struggle for freedom will determine the meaning of the past itself: in it, it will be decided what things 'truly were'. We can see how only a thin, barely perceptible line separates this messianic revolutionary logic from the most extreme fatalism according to which everything has already happened and things, in their temporal process of becoming, merely become what they always-already were: the past itself is not fixed, it 'will have been' – that is to say, through the deliverance-to-come, *it will become what it always-already was*.

The three levels of freedom

To recapitulate again: in what consists, according to Schelling, the Fall of Man? When man emerges as self-consciousness, he posits himself as a self-centred being, as a subject who reduces all other entities to a medium of his self-assertion, to mere objects to be appropriated and exploited. The unthinkable paradox for this self-centred attitude is that my self-consciousness is not simply 'mine', the consciousness of myself as the subject – as self-consciousness, I am always-already 'decentred', a medium in which a transcendent Object (the Absolute) attains consciousness, becomes aware of itself. It is not possible for me to comprehend this Object, since it transcends me – I can apprehend its dimension only by means of ecstatic yielding. The price the active-appropriative consciousness pays for its false pretence to be its own Centre is that the world it inhabits necessarily assumes the appearance of a foreign, hostile, superior Power indifferent to its plight. Here we encounter an exemplary case of what Hegel calls 'reflective determination': in my perception of objective reality as the Kingdom of Satan, as the place of misery and sorrow, I perceive my own egotistic, self-centred attitude towards this same reality in an 'objectivized', 'reified' form – or, in Lacanese, I receive my own message in its inverted form.

Therein resides the crucial political 'sting' of Schelling: the more individuals experience themselves as self-responsible and self-centred subjects pursuing their autonomous, self-posited goals, the more the State opposes itself to them in the guise of a foreign, hostile agency which frustrates their projects – that is to say: the more they are unable to recognize themselves, their own spiritual substance, in the State. In a utopian perspective (utopian, since false pride is inherent in man) the State would be discarded in favour of a religious community founded in the ecstatic relationship to the transcendent Other. This ecstatic relationship is the highest freedom accessible to man; that is to say, Schelling distinguishes three levels of freedom:

• The common notion of freedom conceives it as the freedom to choose, to decide 'freely' after pondering the *pro et contra*, disregarding any external coercion: for dessert I've chosen apple pie rather than cherry pie because apple pie gives me more pleasure, not because I was forced to do so under the pressure of some authority (parents, peers . . .). This is the level of utilitarianism: in his behaviour, man follows the 'felicific calculus', so if one knows and is able to manipulate stimuli which arouse pleasure or pain, one can control his behaviour, and thus dominate him. If this were all, however, man would act like the proverbial Buridan's ass and starve to death between two equal piles of hay.

• The next, higher level of freedom is therefore the fathomless, groundless decision, a decision based on no positive reasons but only in itself; the paradigmatic case, of course, is the primordial act by means of which I choose my eternal character. Such an act casts a horrifying spell on weak-willed people – what one encounters here is the terrifying persistence of the Will on its own, irrespective of the reasons *pro et contra* – as if, for a brief moment, the chain of causal connections has been torn asunder. The paradigmatic case of freedom is not a person who, yielding to 'pathological' temptations, forsakes his duty, but a person who, with 'irrational' obstinacy, follows his path even if it clearly runs against his material interests (suffice it to recall Orson Welles's favourite story about the scorpion who stung the frog on whose back he was crossing the river, although he knew that as a consequence of his act he would drown) – this alone is Evil *qua* spiritual, the demoniac, diabolical Evil of which Schelling says that it is incomparably more spiritual, remote from sensual *Genuss*, than the Good.[80] The Good always involves a harmonious unity of sensual and spiritual – it is a Spirit which penetrates and illuminates nature from within and, without forcing itself upon it, renders it ethereal, deprives it of its impenetrable inertia; whereas true 'diabolical' Evil is a pale, bloodless, fanatical spiritualism which despises sensuality and is bent on violently dominating and exploiting it. This diabolical spiritualism, a perversion of the true spirituality, is the obscure Ground which has 'attained itself', its selfhood – that is to say, has reached the Light and posited itself as such.[81]

• This freedom as the groundless act of decision, as the vertiginous obstinacy of an actual Will which disregards reasons, is not yet, however, the highest; what stands even higher is my submerging myself in the primordial abyss [*Ungrund*] of the Absolute, in the primordial Will which wills nothing – a state in which activity and passivity, being-active and being-acted-upon, harmoniously overlap (the paradigmatic case, of course, is the mystical experience of Love). Against this background, Schelling gives a specific twist to the distinction between *Vernunft* and *Verstand*, Reason and Understanding, which plays a crucial role in German Idealism: '*Vernunft* is nothing but *Verstand* in its subordination to the highest, the soul.'[82] *Verstand* is man's intellect as active, as the power of active seizing and deciding by means of which man asserts himself as a fully autonomous Subject; however, man reaches his acme when he turns his very subjectivity into the Predicate of an ever higher Power (in the mathematical sense of the term) – when he, as it were, yields to the Other, 'depersonalizes' his most intense activity and performs it as if some other, higher Power is acting through him, using him as its medium – like an artist who, in the highest frenzy of creativity, experiences himself as a medium through which some more substantial, impersonal Power expresses itself.

The materialist notion of subject

This tripartite categorization of freedom is founded upon the distinction between the abyss of pure Freedom and God *qua* Entity [*Seiendes*] which is no longer *freedom itself* but *is free*: pure Freedom is not yet the personal God but the impersonal Deity [*Gottheit*]. Freedom can become a predicate only if we are already dealing with the duality of Existence and its Ground: God *qua* actual person who is free must possess a contracted ground of His being which is not directly accessible but can be inferred only from God's activity as its reclusive, withdrawing base. Reality as such (inclusive of the psychical reality of a person) involves contraction: without contraction, it bursts asunder in unconstrained expansion. . . . Hogrebe is therefore right again: Schelling's crucial problem concerns the 'impossible' relationship between Subject and Predicate. What takes place in this passage from freedom as subject to freedom as predicate – to an entity which is not freedom itself but is a free being – is the 'disciplining' of freedom: the transformation of freedom into a predicate renders it bearable, neutralizes its traumatic impact, since as long as freedom remains its own subject, and not a predicate, it can effectuate itself only in the guise of a destructive vortex which devours every determinate content, a fire which dissolves every fixed shape.

In the last pages of *Liberté et existence*, Jean-François Marquet provides a clear outline of the enigma of freedom Schelling is trying to cope with.[83] Schelling interprets Parmenides' 'thinking and being are the same' as the unity of *Das-Sein* and *Was-Sein*: everything which *is* must be *something*, it has to possess a *notion* which renders it *thinkable* in its *Was-Sein*, in what it is – what is at stake here is precisely the notion, not a mere name. However, as Schelling points out, when we are dealing with a person, the relationship between notion and name is the opposite of what it is with regard to a thing: the notion of a thing provides some minimal information about it, tells me what this thing is, whereas its name tells me nothing; in the case of a person, on the contrary, I cannot say that I really 'know her' when I know *that* she exists and *what* she is (her positive features) – I effectively 'know' a person only when I conceive both her existence (the fact that she exists) and her notion (what she is) as the two 'predicates' of the I, of the person as such, of the unfathomable kernel of her freedom: what I have to know about a person in order to claim that I know her is not merely *what* she is but, above all, *who* she is – 'what she wants' as a free being.[84]

True freedom means not only that I am not fully determined by my surroundings but also that I am not fully determined by *myself* (by my own notion, by what I am, by my positive features): a person relates freely both to her existence and to her notion – that is to say, she is not fully determined by them but can transcend them (she can put at stake, risk, her existence as well as transform the bundle of features which make up her identity). The fact that Another Person is for me originally an enigma, an abyss beyond her positive features, accounts for the key role of the symbolic *obligation* and *debt*, of this desperate attempt to bind the Other, in intersubjective relations: since I cannot take hold of the Other, of the abyss which forms the elusive centre of her being, directly, I can only take her at her Word. And Schelling simply took seriously and literally the fact that God Himself, this absolute Other, is also a free person: as such, He also could become free only by gaining a distance towards the Ground of His being, by relating freely to this Ground, by not being wholly determined by it. The paradox (sacrilegious from the orthodox point of view, of course) is that this free relationship towards the Ground presupposes, is the obverse of, dependency on the Ground: God's Light, the creative emanation of His *Logos*, is, as Schelling puts it, a 'regulated madness' which draws its energy from the vortex of drives, as with a human person who is truly free not by opposing his drives but by adroitly exploiting their energy, regulating their madness. . . .

Paradoxical as it may sound, with this specific notion of freedom as the subject's free relating to her existence and notion Schelling was the first to delineate the contours of a *materialist* notion of subject. In the standard (idealist and materialist) version of the philosophical opposition of subject and object, materiality is always on the side of the object: the object is dense, impenetrable and inert, whereas the subject stands for the transparency of the Thought to itself; within this horizon, the only way to assert a 'materialist' position is by trying to demonstrate how the subject is always-already an object (like the Derridean endeavour to demonstrate that the voice is always-already a writing, that it always-already contains some material trace which introduces into it the minimum of self-deferral, of non-coincidence with itself).

In clear contrast to this standard version, the materialist notion of subject outlined by Schelling (but also by Hegel, in his deservedly famous description of the struggle for recognition between the (future) Master and Servant – not to mention Lacan, of course) focuses on the fundamental 'impenetrability', the inert density, which always pertains to our encounter with Another Subject – which distinguishes this encounter from the encounter with an ordinary object. Again, paradoxical as it may sound, ordinary objects are in this precise sense *less* 'material' than Another Subject, since they lack the opacity characteristic of the Other's desire, the eternal enigma of '*Che vuoi?*', of what does the Other want from me? One is led by this to assert that the Freudian–Lacanian (and already Kantian) *Ding* is originally the Other Subject, not a mere non-subjective thing – an ordinary material object is in the end always transparent, it lacks the enigma which would render it effectively opaque. . . . This original violence of the Other, the violence constitutive of what Heidegger called *Mit-Sein*, our relating to another human being, is what gets completely lost in the Habermasian ideology of the free space of intersubjective dialogue – perhaps even Heidegger's otherwise exemplary analysis of *Mit-Sein* in *Being and Time* passes too quickly over this traumatic dimension.[85]

It is against the background of this materialist notion of subject that one can comprehend the limit of Schelling's philosophical enterprise, and thereby the cause of the failure of the *Weltalter* project. As we have already indicated, the criticism of Schelling which seems to impose itself from a Lacanian standpoint concerns his inability to 'traverse the fantasy': does not Schelling remain caught in the phantasmic loop? Does not the Schellingian problematic of a timeless act which is always-already accomplished and thereby *precedes its own temporal genesis* – that is, is present prior to its actual emergence – involve the structure of fantasy at its purest? And, furthermore, is not this presupposition of such an eternal act also the elementary matrix of *ideology*? So is not the most one can say about Schelling that he states openly the constitutive paradox (the temporal loop, the 'always-already') of ideology? Does he not thereby evade the true 'materialist' question: how does a material-temporal process retroactively engender its own phantasmic foundation?

The answer is no: what, according to Schelling, precedes the material-temporal process is not an eternal ideal order, and so on, but the pure void/abyss [*Ungrund*] of Freedom, and Schelling's point is precisely that if Freedom is to actualize itself – that is, to become the predicate of a free Entity – it has to 'contract' the opaque Ground. The problem is, rather, that Schelling formulates the 'out-of-jointedness', the imbalance involved in this primordial contraction, as the ontological condition of the universe ('there is something and not nothing' only through a primordial catastrophe, only in so far as things are out of joint. . .), in the very terms of the pre-modern mythology of a sexualized universe (of the primordial balance to be re-established, etc.). Here his ambiguity is radical and irreducible: the logic of his thought compels him to assert the inevitability of the 'out-of-jointedness' and of man's Fall – at the very point at which A should prevail over B, things *have* to go wrong – but the same logic leads him to maintain the dream of final reconciliation – it should be possible to heal the wound and to reinstate the lost balance, that is, the harmonious line of development of the 'great chain of being' from the lower to the higher stages (see, for example, the dialogue *Clara*, contemporaneous with *Weltalter*, in which death is reduced to the passage from the lower, terrestrial life to the higher 'world of Spirits [*Geisterwelt*]'). We are therefore back where we started: error cannot simply be subtracted from Truth – that is to say, it was possible for Schelling to accomplish the unheard-of step to radical contingency only in the guise of a 'regression' to the pre-modern mythology of a sexualized universe. This very 'regression' enabled him to formulate the materialist concept of subject (the opaque-enigmatic Otherness of freedom) in contrast to the purely spiritual 'idealist' subject: the materialist subject as the point at which nature 'runs amok' and goes off the rails. . . .

The Absolute 'out of mind'

One of the fundamental themes of Schelling's later thought is the original ex-stasis, *Ausser-sich-gesetzt-werden*, of the Spirit: the predicative activity of Understanding is founded upon a pre-predicative reference to a 'constitutive Outside' – that is to say, the Spirit is constitutively 'outside itself'; a kind of umbilical cord connects it to a traumatic kernel which is simultaneously its condition of possibility (the well from which the Spirit draws its resources) and its condition of impossibility (the abyss whose all-destructive vortex continuously threatens to swallow the Spirit). In the best tradition of Hegelian puns, Schelling reactivates here the literal meaning of 'out of one's mind', the standard expression for the state of madness: the constitutive 'madness' of the human mind resides in the fact that it is originally 'out of mind', ex-static with regard to itself. In this way he can provide a persuasive answer to the Kantian criticism according to which his ruminations about the Absolute involve a 'regression' to pre-critical metaphysics – an illegitimate foray into the noumenal domain, a forbidden leap from the mere notion of God to His actual existence.

From Schelling's standpoint, the terms of the traditional problem of the ontological proof of God had to be inverted: what is truly problematic is not God's existence but his notion. Since the Spirit itself is originally not 'within itself' but 'outside itself', the true question is not how we can progress from the mere notion of God to God's actual existence, but the exact opposite – what comes first, what is always-already here, is the experience of a 'senseless', pre-predicative, pre-semantic existence, and the true problem for philosophy is how we can accomplish the passage from this senseless existence to Reason – that is, how did our universe get caught in the cobweb of Reason in the first place ...

This is where Schelling parts with philosophical Idealism which is not ready to admit the dependence of *logos* on its Ground. Idealism is fully justified in its claim that one cannot reduce Culture, the domain of spiritual Meanings, to a simple prolongation of nature – to a more differentiated, 'intelligent', means of biological survival: Spirit *is* an End-in-itself for whom its physical and biological environs serves as its Ground. The paradox one must sustain, however, is that the universe of 'spiritual' products is none the less rooted in its Ground. The present threat of a global ecological catastrophe provides the ultimate proof: the universe of human culture hinges on an unstable balance of our ecosphere; the slightest variation – the depletion of the ozone layer, global warming, not to mention the possibility of a giant comet hitting earth – can sweep the ground from under the feet of the human race, and entail the end of civilization.

The status of our 'spiritual' universe is thus far more fragile than it may appear: the natural environment within which our civilization can thrive is the product of a radically contingent set of circumstances, so that at any moment, owing to the unforeseen consequences of man's industrial activity or to its own unforeseeable logic, nature can 'run amok' and go off the rails. What is more, humanity itself lives off the debris of gigantic past catastrophes (our main sources of energy, oil and coal, bear direct witness to global catastrophes of almost inconceivable proportions) and, to add insult to injury, the most probable hypothesis about the origins of man is that the stimulus which incited *Homo sapiens* to distinguish itself from the realm of animal life was again some global ecological turmoil. In short, the comet we are all afraid of *has already hit Earth* – we, humans, are the living proof! So, again, the loop is closed – that is to say, the structure of our fear of the ultimate catastrophe that awaits us in the future is clearly phantasmic: this catastrophe *has already taken place*; what we fear is our own 'eternally past' origins.

Here Schelling is the exact opposite of Kant: Reason is originally 'ecstatic', outside itself; it never begins in itself; its activity is never founded in itself, but always triggered by some traumatic encounter, some collision which provides the impulse to the thought – this collision, this encounter with the real, distinguishes an actual experience from the mere possibility of experience. On the contrary,

Kant, like a good compulsive neurotic, proceeds in the opposite direction: he sets up the network of the conditions of possible experience in order to make sure that the actual experience of the real, the encounter with the Thing, will never take place, so that everything the subject will effectively encounter will be the already gentrified-domesticated reality of representations. . . .[86]

This Schelling, of course, instantly gives rise to a series of 'postmodern' associations: Reason can thrive only on a foreign, 'irrational' Ground of the rotary motion of drives from which it draws its life-force; but it has simultaneously to maintain a proper distance towards it – if it goes too close to the vortex of drives, it runs the danger of losing its identity and going mad:

> Following the eternal act of self-revelation, all is rule, order, and form in the world as we now see it. But the ruleless still lies in the ground as if it could break through once again, and nowhere does it appear as though order and form were original, but rather as if something initially ruleless had been brought to order. This is the incomprehensible basis of reality in things, the indivisible remainder, that which with the greatest exertion cannot be resolved in the understanding, but rather remains eternally in the ground. From this non-understanding is born understanding in the true sense. Without this preceding darkness there is no reality of the creature; the gloom is its necessary inheritance.[87]

This Ground is rather like the figure of woman in David Lynch's films: the traumatic Thing, the point of simultaneous attraction and repulsion, which stands for the vortex of Life itself threatening to draw us into its depressive abyss. And does not this pre-predicative vortex of the Real point directly towards the Lacanian *jouissance*? Does not Schelling himself determine the Real [*das Reale*] as the circular movement of 'irrational' (i.e. pre-logical, pre-symbolic) drives which find satisfaction in the very 'meaningless' repetition of their circular path?[88] For Schelling (as well as for Lacan) this Real is the Limit, the ultimate obstacle on account of which every 'semantic idealism', every attempt to deploy the Absolute as a self-enclosed matrix generating all possible significations of Being, is destined to fail. For both Schelling and Lacan, the most radical version of this 'semantic idealism' is, of course, Hegel's system, which is therefore the principal target of their critique: the symbolic order can never achieve its full completion and close its circle, since its very constitution involves a point at which Meaning stumbles upon its boundary and suspends itself in Enjoy-Meant [*Jouis-sense*].

The 'formula of the world'

Appealing as it may sound to our 'postmodern' receptivity, such a reading is none the less off the mark: it falls short of the *Grundoperation* of German Idealism common to Schelling and Hegel, since it fails to bring the duality Reason and its Ground to the point of self-reference. That is to say: what has to fall is the last barrier which separates Reason from its 'irrational' Ground: the most difficult task, the highest effort, of philosophical speculation is to bring to light *the 'madness* [*Wahnsinn*]' *of the very gesture of instituting the domain of Sinn.* Every Organization of Sense, every universal conceptual scheme by means of which we endeavour to comprehend reality, is in itself – at its most fundamental, for structural reasons and not merely due to contingent circumstances – biased, out of balance, 'crazy', minimally 'paranoiac' (as the early Lacan would have put it): its imposition disturbs the 'natural order of things' and throws the universe off balance. In other words, there is no neutral Universality: every Universality, every attempt at All, at a global comprehension, bears the indelible mark of a 'pathological' exclusiveness of One – that is, it hinges on the 'partiality' of its position of enunciation.[89] So, again, it is not sufficient to say that no conceptual structure is perfectly neutral, that it fails to comprehend reality in a truly impartial way; the point is, rather, that the status of this 'bias' is a priori, structural.

We are dealing here with the inherent constituent of the emergence of a formal structure – in short, with the *condition of the structure's consistency*: but for this exclusive base in a One – but for this partiality and distortion sustained by a minimum of Egotism – the structure disintegrates, loses its consistency in the dispersed plurality. When we repeat after Schelling that every Order arises on the basis of and has its roots in a general Disorder, we are therefore not making the usual relativist point that man's ordering activity is limited to local attempts to introduce a minimum of Order into the wide ocean of primordial chaos – to attempts which, as such, are ultimately doomed to fail; our point is, rather, that the very imposition of an Order is an act of supreme violence – *Order is a violent imposition which throws the universe out of joint.*[90] Disorder is the condition of possibility of Order not only in the sense that the very notion of Order is conceivable only against the background of general Disorder, as a series of local attempts to limit the Disorder – *the highest Disorder, the highest violation of 'natural balance', is the very imposition of a (biased) Order.* So we are back at our starting point: the 'unconscious' is not primarily the Real in its opposition to the Ideal; in its most radical dimension, the 'unconscious' is, rather, the very act of decision/differentiation by means of which the Ideal establishes itself in its opposition to the Real and imposes its Order on to the Real, the act by means of which the Present differs from the Past – that is to say, by means of which the rotary motion of drives is 'repressed' into the eternal past. Is this not clearly indicated in Schelling's 'formula of the world [*Weltformel*]' from *Weltalter III*?[91]:

$$\left(\frac{A^3}{A^2 = (A = B)} \right) B$$

– the ever-increasing 'sublation [*Aufhebung*]' of the Real (B) in the Ideal (A), the progressive subordination of the Real to the Ideal, relies on the exception of a B which, as the excluded ground of the process of sublation, guarantees its consistency. This supplementary B which brackets/encloses the progressive 'sublation' of B by A provides a minimal definition of *dialectical materialism*: the fundamental materialist thesis is that a Universal can become 'for-itself', be 'posited as such', only in so far as a kind of umbilical cord links it to a particular element which, in terms of its 'official' place, is merely one species of the Universal. In other words, the elementary idealist illusion resides in belief in the possibility of a purely neutral Universal, a Universal which is not 'anchored' to a particular material locus (or, with regard to language, the belief in a pure enunciated which does not involve a particular/partial subjective position of enunciation).

Hogrebe is thus fully justified in supplementing Hegel's '*Das Wahre is das Ganze*' into '*Das Wahre ist so das Ganze bis auf Eins, dafür steht das B neben dem Klammerausdruck* (The True is the Whole up to One, which is why B stands outside the brackets)'.[92] Is not Hegel also, however, at a different level, aware of this? Is not this precisely the point of his theory of the Monarch: in order to actualize itself as the structure of the universal-rational mediation of all particular social content, the State has to be enclosed, grounded in an 'irrational' exception – that is, in the Monarch, who introduces the element of contingent personal whimsy and egotism and who, as such, clearly pertains to the power of 'B'? Reason's condition of possibility is the condition of its impossibility – or, as Lacan would have put it, 'there's One [*y'a de l'Un*]': a consistent rational structure has to be anchored to an 'irrational' exception of One which, in its very capacity as exception, guarantees the structure's consistency. For *that* reason – and again, everything hinges on this point – 'repression' is always *double*: not only is the Real 'repressed' – mediated, sublated, domesticated – by the Ideal, pressed into the service of the Ideal, but the Ideal Order itself emerges only in so far as its own 'madness' – the violent act of its imposition, or, in Kierkegaardian terms: its own 'becoming' – is 'repressed'. In short, the obscure Ground is not merely the basis, the background, of the Light of Reason, but primarily the dark spot of the very gesture which gives rise to Light as opposed to Darkness. The unconscious act, the decision which breaks up the drives' 'irrational' rotary motion, is itself radically contingent, groundless – in short: 'irrational'.

It is as if Schelling is caught here in a radical ambiguity: again and again he succumbs to temptation and reduces the 'madness' of the *self-relating* act by means of which the obscure Ground imposes on to itself the network of Reason to the *external* relationship of Reason to its obscure Ground from which it draws its life-force, yet towards which it has to maintain a proper distance. In the last pages of *Weltalter III*, which irradiate an almost horrifying poetic power, Schelling struggles to demonstrate how, on account of man's finitude, the split between Ground and Reason condemns him to *Wahnsinn*: what creeps in and inserts itself between the natural *Un-Sinn*, the senseless fact of physical existence, and the Divine, blissful *Sinn*, is *Wahn-Sinn* (madness, or, literally: the delirious Sense, the Sense which goes astray and roams around). These pages instantly recall the famous fragment from Hegel's *Jenaer Realphilosophie* on the pure Self as the pre-symbolic 'night of the world' in which horrifying apparitions haunt the mind ('here shoots a bloody head – there another white ghastly apparition'), awaiting the dawn of the Word to dispel them.

Sinn, true spiritual freedom, appears to man only in a flash, in the guise of a traumatic encounter whose sudden dazzle throws him off the rails: man is anchored to his egotistic Ground to such an extent that he cannot endure the direct sight of the light of *Sinn*, but can only *imitate* Sense, under the constant threat of slipping back into the rotary motion of Ground. (This is Schelling's way of asserting the fundamentally *hysterical* nature of human subjectivity: the hysterical – feminine – subject merely 'imitates' morality, symbolic order, and so on; she merely 'puts on [*anziehen*]' morality without effectively identifying with it.) Is it enough, however, to concede that this *Wahn-Sinn* is the eternal, constitutive supplement of *Sinn*, the Ground from which *Sinn* draws its life-force, the source of the perpetual renewal and discovery of new horizons of *Sinn*? Is not the notion of man's *Wahn-Sinn* which inserts itself between the natural *Un-Sinn* and the divine *Sinn* deficient and misleading, in so far as it renders invisible the *wahnsinnig* ('crazy') nature of the very gesture by means of which *Sinn* emerges out of *Un-Sinn*? So it is not sufficient to assert that Reason is nothing but 'regulated madness': *the very gesture of regulating madness is stricto sensu mad.* Or – to put it in yet another way: it is not sufficient to assert that Reason discerns the islands of Necessity in the sea of

Chaos – the very gesture of instituting Necessity is in itself radically contingent.

To recapitulate: two things are worth bearing in mind apropos of Schelling's *Weltformel.* First, this formula enables us to draw the demarcation line which effectively separates dialectical materialism from idealism: the assertion that the progressive movement of sublation–mediation of B by A is itself framed in B, that it can occur only in so far as it has a foothold in B, provides the minimal definition of dialectical materialism. In other words, the full sublation of B in A, the accomplished spiritualization of matter by means of which matter would lose its inert-impenetrable character and turn into an ethereal medium of A, is nothing but an idealist phantasm – in a way, Hegel was already aware of this, which is why he denounced the idea of another ethereal, spiritualized matter as an empty notion of Understanding. Secondly, however, one should bear in mind a dangerous trap which lurks here: if we simply assert that A is always framed in B, do we not expose ourselves to the danger of espousing a version of *Lebensphilosophie* according to which Reason is always 'at the service of passion'? And, accordingly, does not our claim that there is no neutral universality, that every scheme of Reason is a partial-violent imposition, point towards Nietzschean perspectivism?

This, however, is not Schelling's position. To put it in a somewhat simplified way: his main point is precisely that 'B is not everything' – the vortex of the Real is not the ultimate fact, since it is preceded by the abyss of pure Freedom as the absolute indifference of A and B. Schelling's point is *not,* therefore, that A is ultimately bound to serve B; rather, it resides in the *irreducible gap between pure Freedom ($) and every symbolic scheme of Reason, every determinate symbolic representation of the subject in A, in the ideal medium.* The leap from $ (pure Freedom) to A is possible only via a detour through B, in the medium of B; in other words, it is radically contingent: if the subject ($) is to represent-express itself in A, it has to rely on B, on a contracted element which eludes idealization. In Lacanian terms: there is no symbolic representation without fantasy, that is, the subject ($) is constitutively split between S_1 and a; it can represent itself in S_1, in a signifier, only in so far as the phantasmic consistency of the signifying network is guaranteed by a reference to *objet petit a.*

Notes

1. F.W.J. Schelling, *Die Weltalter. Fragmente. In den Urfassungen von 1811 und 1813,* ed. Manfred Schröter, Munich: Biederstein 1946 (reprint 1979), p. 4; quoted in Andrew

Bowie, *Schelling and Modern European Philosophy*, New York and London: Routledge 1993, p. 101.

2. F.W.J. Schelling, *Grundlegung der positiven Philosophie*, Turin 1972, p. 222 (quoted in Wolfram Hogrebe, *Prädikation und Genesis*, Frankfurt: Suhrkamp 1989, p. 39).

3. F.W.J. Schelling, 'Philosophical Investigations into the Essence of Human Freedom and Related Matters', in *Philosophy of German Idealism*, ed. Ernst Behler, New York: Continuum 1987, p. 260.

4. Ibid., pp. 260–61.

5. More precisely, here Schelling merely explicates what is 'in itself' already in Fichte: is not the ultimate paradox of Fichte's *Selbst-Dewusstsein*, of this pure act of self-positing, of this performative which grounds itself absolutely, that it is totally beyond reach for the finite-temporal-subjective consciousness and therefore, in a sense, radically *unconscious*?

6. One can also formulate this in terms of the relationship between *guilt* and *freedom*. Our common-sense notion involves the co-dependence, overlapping even, of these two terms: only a free being can be guilty. In a first approach, Schelling appears to undermine this notion by claiming that *man can be guilty even if he is not free*: he can be guilty, i.e. held responsible, for what he was not even free to choose, since he made his fundamental choice prior to his phenomenal existence – his guilt is the trace of this 'repressed' primordial free choice of his eternal character which now exerts its hold over him with an inexorable necessity. One can therefore say that, in a sense, Schelling and Kant are here at the very opposite of the Nietzschean liberating assertion of the *Unschuld des Werdens*, of a freedom unconstrained by any guilt and/or responsibility: the paradox of the Schellingian subject is that he is fully responsible and guilty, although (in his phenomenal existence) he never had the chance to choose freely, i.e. to commit an act that would afflict him with guilt.

7. F.W.J. Schelling, 'Philosophical Investigations into the Essence of Human Freedom and Related Matters', p. 259.

8. Ibid., *Die Weltalter*, pp. 183–4.

9. Ibid., p. 184.

10. A parallel imposes itself here between the Lacanian triad of *symbolic identification (Ideal Ego)*, *superego* and *the Real of radical freedom* on the one hand, and Schelling on the other: in a manner strictly analogous to Lacan's assertion that the symbolic identification with the Ego Ideal which involves us in the 'service of goods' is necessarily preceded by the ferocious and 'evil' superego, whereas the ethical attitude proper ('do not compromise your desire') enables us to break out of this vicious circle of Ego Ideal and superego by fully assuming the 'burden of desire', Schelling enables us to discern the contours of the pulsating Real of drives which precedes the ideal existence as its unfathomable *Grund*, as well as – prior to both – the indifference of the Absolute as the primordial Freedom which does not have being at all, but merely enjoys its non-being.

11. F.W.J. Schelling, *Die Weltalter*, p. 134.

12. This acme of philosophical speculation at its most daring and 'crazy' fits perfectly the very real subjective experience of the subject's own non-being, the experience which is the price the subject has to pay for his access to the radical freedom beyond the enchainment of entities. In his autobiography, Louis Althusser writes that he was persecuted all his adult life by the notion that he didn't exist, by the fear that others would become aware of his nonexistence – i.e. of the fact that he was an impostor who only pretended to exist. For example, his great fear after the publication of *Reading Capital* was that some perspicacious critic would reveal the scandalous fact that the main author of this book didn't exist. . . . In a sense, this is what Schelling aims at and, also, what psychoanalysis is about: the psychoanalytic cure is effectively over when the subject loses this fear and *freely assumes his own nonexistence*.

13. F.W.J. Schelling, *Die Weltalter*, p. 13; quoted in Bowie, p. 105.

14. F.W.J. Schelling, *Sämtliche Werke*, ed. K.F.A. Schelling, Stuttgart: Cotta 1856–61, vol. VIII, p. 43.

15. Ibid., p. 715.

16. Ibid., p. 712.

17. Therein resides the anti-Hegelian 'sting' of Schelling's aesthetics: for Schelling, art

is not primarily the 'sensible appearing of the Idea [*das sinnliche Scheinen der Idee*]' (even if we conceive this 'Idea' as phantasmic in the psychoanalytic sense of the term) but, rather, the 'sensible appearing of a *disturbance* of/in the Idea [*das sinnliche Scheinen der VERSTÖRUNG der Idee*]', i.e. the appearance of what Schelling calls the 'power B', of the unfathomable-chaotic Ground which is simultaneously the condition of possibility and the condition of impossibility of the Idea – that is to say, always puts an obstacle in the path of the full realization of the Idea. In short, far from representing the suprasensible Idea in a sensible medium, the power of great art resides in the *opposite* achievement of evoking, within the very 'Apolloniac' domain of ethereal, idealized form, the formless vortex of the Real – or, as Rilke put it in his famous dictum, 'the Beautiful is the veil of the Horrible', of the chaotic primordial vortex of the Real.

In his *Discours, figure* (Paris: Klinsieck 1971), Jean-François Lyotard implicitly refers to this anti-Hegelian notion of Schelling when he asks a simple but none the less crucial question: if a work of art always originates in some phantasmic matrix, if it 'stages' unconscious desires organized, structured, in fantasies (the classical Freudian *topos*), why isn't it, then, reducible to a clinical symptom? The standard answer according to which a work of art renders unconscious fantasies in a way acceptable to the big Other of the public symbolic space, not in a direct, obscene way, is clearly unsatisfactory, since an ordinary symptom is also a compromise formation which expresses an illicit desire in an 'aseptic' and acceptable form, and is no less 'clinical' for that reason. Lyotard's answer is that a work of art, by activating the death drive, stages the *non-fulfilment* of the desire and its phantasmic matrix. In Lacanian terms, we could say that a work of art always contains a minimum of the 'going-through fantasy [*la traversée du fantasme*]': the very transposition of the fantasy into the form of art implies a distance towards the phantasmic content. The *doxa* according to which art merely transposes illicit fantasies into a socially acceptable form must therefore be inverted: a work of art, rather, renders visible what the phantasmic content conceals, what it is its function to conceal.

18. See Wolfram Hogrebe, *Prädikation und Genesis*, p. 100.

19. Ibid., p. 90.

20. F.W.J. Schelling, *Sämtliche Werke*, vol. VIII, p. 600.

21. See *Hegel's Philosophy of Mind*, Oxford: Clarendon Press 1992, paras 409–10.

22. Perhaps the most 'palpable' example of this dependence of expansion on contraction is provided by *love*: the profession of universal love for humanity as such necessarily strikes us as an exercise in shallow, insipid and ineffective sentimental humanism – if I am to love something in a truly passionate, active way, if I want to give myself to it with all the power of expansion, I must first contract-condense this 'something' into a particular object whom I love 'more than anything else'. . . .

23. Jacques Derrida, 'Before the Law', in *Acts of Literature*, New York: Routledge 1992, p. 211.

24. What we have here is also an exemplary case of the difference between historical and dialectical materialism: the historical-materialist analysis of *Speed* attains its limit in pinpointing the ideology of the 'production of the couple' as the ultimate point of reference which underlies the film's narrative, while dialectical materialism is able to reach beyond (or, rather, beneath) this social dimension, and to discern in the wild run of the bus a metaphor for life itself.

25. Althusser and some of his followers (including Etienne Balibar) refer to this very Marxian concept of a 'tendency' to exemplify the difference between Hegel and Marx: the Hegelian 'contradiction' automatically leads to its self-cancelling, to its 'sublation [*Aufhebung*]', a 'reconcilation' at a higher level; whereas Marx's materialist 'contradiction' is best exemplified by the obscure but crucial concept of 'tendency': a 'tendency' begets out of itself its counter-tendency, actualizes itself in the guise of an antagonistic relationship within which no teleological necessity guarantees the final victory of the tendency over the counter-tendency – the outcome depends on the overdetermined concrete network of contingent conditions.

Suffice it to recall the already-mentioned example of the 'tendency' of the profit rate to fall: this very tendency induces Capital to modify the material and social conditions of production so as to raise the profit rate. The (always precarious) outcome of this struggle is contingent on the power of organized labour, the rhythm of technological change, differences in the profit rate in different countries, etc.; due to this complex interaction of factors, the immediate result of the profit rate's tendency to fall can well be a temporary *rise* (or, to take another example, the immediate result of the class struggle can be 'class peace').

Is all this, however, effectively an argument *against* Hegel? Is not the Marxian notion of tendency, on the contrary, an exemplary case of the properly dialectical necessity to 'recognize our own essence in the force we are fighting against', whose exemplary case is provided by the dialectic of the Beautiful Soul? 'Reconciliation' occurs when the subject recognizes its condition of possibility in what first appeared to it as its condition of impossibility, as the impediment to its full realization. The Beautiful Soul is thus compelled to recognize, in the very disorder and injustice of the world, the positive condition of its own attitude of deploring the wicked ways of the world: it needs these corrupted environs if it is to retain its consistency – the moment this external hindrance disappears, the Beautiful Soul loses its footing. Hegel articulated this dialectic while he was still young, apropos of Crime *qua* transgression of the mores of Community and their ensuing reconciliation by way of which each of the two recognizes its own essence in its Other: the criminal recognizes in his community his substantial truth; the community recognizes in the criminal's act its own necessary offspring.

26. See Jacqueline Rose, 'Negativity in the Work of Melanie Klein', in *Why War?*, Oxford: Blackwell 1993, esp. pp. 167–8. Incidentally, an analogous concept of 'contradiction' was elaborated by Etienne Balibar apropos of Spinoza. See Etienne Balibar, 'Spinoza, the Anti-Orwell: The Fear of the Masses', in *Masses, Classes, Ideas*, New York: Routledge 1994.

27. A further example of such paradoxical antagonistic causality is the way explicit rules of constraint affect sexual arousal. The 'politically correct' rules in sexual interplay with a woman (before every subsequent step, one has to ask the partner for explicit permission – 'May I unbutton your blouse?', etc.) can thoroughly spoil the game, depriving it of all the excitement; or, on the contrary, they can stir up arousal in so far as they add a supplementary 'turn of the screw' to the erotic double entendre. It is the same with the opposite procedure, 'non-PC' brutal and reckless treatment of the partner: it can terrorize and repel the partner, or it can become erotically cathected and thus provide supplementary stimulus – the situation is radically ambiguous, there are no laws that guarantee the effect in advance.

28. Therein resides the paradox of the Lacanian notion of symbolic causality: in contrast to the standard defence of freedom which grounds it in the *deficiency* of the causal network, i.e. in its insufficiency to explain the emergence of free subjectivity, Lacan grounds freedom in the *excess* of causes. There are always too many causes; an excessive multitude of them, as it were, floats around in search of effects – they are causes, but it is not clear *what they are causes of*; the *capitonnage* then structures this multitude into a stable causal network.

29. This logic of antagonism also helps us to clarify Lacan's notion of *hainamoration*: what Lacan aims at here is not the standard theme of the 'ambiguity' of love and hate, of their polar co-dependence, of how the one pole continually passes over into its opposite, so that there is no love without hate, etc.; his point is, rather, that hate is – from within, as it were – buckled on love. That is to say: the object of love is always split into itself and what is in it more than itself, the *objet a*, and I endeavour to annihilate you precisely in order to distil from you what I truly love in you. . . . The exemplary case of this love–hate tension is the attitude towards the Lady in courtly love: when the chivalrous poet sets the beloved woman on a pedestal and glorifies her as the inaccessible-sublime Lady, what he effectively fears is that the beloved woman will *step down* from the pedestal and behave like an active sexual being, plying him with demands to satisfy her sexually – in short, the poetic elevation of the woman conceals the fear of feminine sexuality, of the woman as an active sexual subject. For that reason, the poetic elevation of the Lady is the obverse of the hatred for a sexually active woman who is dismissed as 'vulgar' and can easily become the victim of extremely violent outbursts.

The logic of antagonism should not, therefore, be confused with the dialectical *coincidentia oppositorum*; as an exemplary case of the latter, suffice it to mention the opposition between the feminism which focuses on women *qua* victims of patriarchal domination and the 'aggressive' feminism which tells women to stop moaning and take full advantage of their sexual and emotional hold over men – however, is not assuming the role of victim the most efficient way to gain power and to disarm the opponent? When I claim to speak from the position of victim, do I not devalue any counter-argument in advance, and secure the 'authenticity' of my speech? Is this not the most effective aggressive–manipulative attitude?

30. What we encounter here again is the profound anti-Heideggerian 'sting' of Schelling: as Hogrebe points out (see Hogrebe, p. 58), Schelling rejects ontological dualism (the dualism of ontic and ontological, inner-worldly entities and their ontological horizon, genesis and value, physical processes and ideal truths, body and soul, Real and Ideal, object and subject, etc.); instead he asserts a 'pre-worldly', *purely ontic* dualism of drives in God (contraction and expansion, i.e. egotism and love). This shift accounts for the uncanny feeling Schelling's philosophy inevitably gives rise to in a reader trained in standard philosophy: notwithstanding his official monism, Schelling's position seems to involve a dualism far more radical than any traditional philosophical version of it. . . .

31. One can see here again how, in man as well as in God, the act of decision involves the distinction between *identity* and *ground*: at the level of essential identity, everything is here, opposites coincide, in pure, timeless simultaneity (freedom is not yet antagonistic to necessity, it fully coincides with the ability of an entity to deploy its potential according to its inherent necessity; the Will itself is not yet an actual will but coincides with its opposite in the guise of a Will which wants nothing); when the Will actualizes itself via the act of decision, and becomes a Will which effectively wants something, the original indifference is broken, time is instituted, i.e. one of the two terms of the antagonism is repressed into the Past as the Ground of the other.

32. F.W.J. Schelling, *Die Weltalter*, p. 184.

33. The category of 'vanishing mediator', one of the fundamental categories of dialectical materialism, was introduced by Fredric Jameson apropos of Max Weber (see Fredric Jameson, 'The Vanishing Mediator; or, Max Weber as Storyteller', in *The Ideologies of Theory*, vol. 2, Minneapolis: University of Minnesota Press 1988; for a Lacanian reading of it, see Chapter 5 of Slavoj Žižek, *For They Know Not What They Do*, London: Verso 1991; and Chapter 3 of Slavoj Žižek, *Enjoy Your Symptom!*, New York: Routledge 1992).

As the exemplary case of an analysis which relies on the logic of 'vanishing mediator', suffice it to recall Charles Rosen's great musicological study *Classical Style*: what Rosen renders visible is the sonata form 'in its becoming', when it still had a 'scandalous' impact, i.e. before it established itself as the hegemonic norm; in other words, he renders visible the radically contingent, 'open' process of formation of what we perceive today as the standard. In political theory, the exemplary case of a 'vanishing mediator' is provided by the Hegelian notion of the historical *hero* who resolves the deadlock of the passage from the 'natural state' of violence to the civil state of peace guaranteed by legitimate power. This passage cannot take place directly, in a continuous line, since there is no common ground, no intersection, between the state of natural violence and the state of civil peace; what is needed, therefore, is a paradoxical agent who, by means of violence itself, overcomes violence, i.e. the paradox of an act which retroactively establishes the conditions of its own legitimacy and thereby obliterates its violent character, transforming itself into a solemn 'founding act'.

34. In order to clarify this logic of Satan, suffice it to recall the Stalinist discourse in which the role of Satan is imputed to the 'traitor' (in Stalinist caricatures, Trotsky, the arch-traitor, was regularly portrayed as the Devil). In the Stalinist universe, the Party progresses, asserts the correct line, through the repeated exclusion of revisionist-deviationist enemies – it is the Traitor, the 'enemy within', who again and again disturbs our complacent balance and instigates our decision, our *passage à l'acte*. Like Schelling's Satan, the Stalinist 'traitor' thus stands for the eternal temptation of 'deviation' in all its multiple forms (right-wing deviation, left-wing-deviation, even – why not? – 'opportunist' Centrist deviation): as such – i.e. as the pure *potentiality* of temptation – he repeatedly forces the Party to *actualize* its correct line by purging deviationists from its ranks. On this

role of Satan in Schelling, see Lidia Procesi, 'Unicité et pluralité de Dieu: la contradiction et le diable chez Schelling', in J.-F. Courtine and J.-F. Marquet, *Le dernier Schelling*, Paris: Vrin 1994, pp. 101–15.

35. This double, crosswise relationship of the opposition freedom/necessity to the opposition time/eternity bears witness to Schelling's far-reaching displacement of the edifice of classical philosophical idealism, a displacement which can also be articulated in terms of a Greimasian semiotic square: Schelling supplements the fundamental opposition of idealism, that between the Ideal and the Real, with the opposition between expansion and contraction which does *not* overlap with the first one, so that we obtain, on the one hand, the 'soul', i.e. the ideal Spirit which has 'contracted' and therefore effectively exists as a person; and, on the other, the Real in the mode of expansion (light in nature as opposed to matter, etc.).

36. This reversal of determining reflection into reflective determination finds a precise analogy in Lacan's reversal of the *ego ideal* into the *ideal ego*: the ego ideal (the ideal of the ego) is a virtual symbolic point from which the ego observes itself in order to find itself likeable, whereas the ideal ego is an imaginary positive entity in which the ideal is realized. In the domain of epistemology, the crucial distinction between the ideal of science and the ideal science follows the same logic: the ideal of science is a virtual point which concrete sciences endeavour to approach; the ideal science is an existing science which acts as a model for other sciences (physics among natural sciences, linguistics in 'structuralism').

Here again we are dealing with the opposition between *becoming* and *being*: the ideal of science sets in motion the endless process of becoming of sciences, whereas the ideal science refers to an entity in the mode of being, i.e. to an actually existing science. In political theory, the French distinction between *le politique* (the political) and *la politique* (politics) plays the same structural role: the 'political' designates the process of becoming (of 'ordering') of a political order, its 'invention', its generative movement; whereas 'politics' refers to a constituted domain of social being. . . . The royal example – the 'mother of all examples' – of course, is provided by the passage of materialist dialectics (the process of dialectical analysis) into dialectical materialism as a positive philosophical system.

37. See 'Stuttgart Seminars', in *Idealism and the Endgame of Theory: Three Essays by F.W.J. Schelling*, Albany, NY: SUNY Press 1994.

38. More precisely, in Schelling's late works the act of creation is also not simply external to God but concerns His own being: by creating the universe outside Himself, God in a way *suspends His own (actual) being*, i.e. shifts it to mere potentiality. See Miklos Veto, 'L'unicité de Dieu selon Schelling', in J.-F. Courtine and J.-F. Marquet, *Le dernier Schelling*, pp. 96–7.

39. See Jean-François Marquet, *Liberté et existence. étude sur la formation de la philosophie de Schelling*, Paris: Gallimard 1973, probably *the* book on the development of Schelling's philosophy.

40. Ibid., p. 464.

41. Ibid., pp. 541–2.

42. Is not Einstein's space–time continuum – i.e. his notion of a timeless static universe in which everything exists simultaneously, and temporal succession is a mere illusion of the observer, of his limited view – analogous to Schelling's Absolute in which everything is also absolutely contemporaneous, and there is temporal succession only for man's finite gaze?

43. In this second phase philosophy turns into a 'transcendental historiography', a narrative of the Absolute: its form is no longer the logical deduction (of a system) but a *dialogue*. Philosophy as a narrative is the process of *remembering* the past of the Absolute; as such, it involves a Socratic split into the 'knowledge which doesn't know' (Socrates) and the 'ignorance which knows' (the partner subjected to questions): the knowing one questions the partner in order to draw from the obscure depths to the light of day the hidden knowledge the partner possesses, but is unaware of. It is like trying to recall a forgotten name: part of us (the part which doesn't know) is searching for the name in the other part where we know the name is hidden.

84

There is a great temptation here to conceive along the same lines the relationship between analyst and analysand in the psychoanalytic process: is not the analyst's position characterized by the same 'knowing ignorance'; and, on the other hand, is not the fundamental presupposition of psychoanalysis the presence, in the analysand's unconscious, of a knowledge which does not know itself? Schelling, of course, links these two poles to sexual difference: woman possesses an obscure, passive, silent, intuitive knowledge which dwells in the unfathomable depths of the Earth – she 'knows more than she is aware of', is unaware of knowing – whereas it is man's task to probe actively into these depths from above, and to unearth the Wisdom concealed down there.... This difference overlaps with the couple of Truth and Knowledge: Truth is a woman (as Nietzsche already knew), whereas man endeavours to bring this Truth to the light of day – i.e. to explicit knowledge – by means of dialogical probing. (In an analogous way, Richard Wagner 'sexualized' the relationship between music and poetry: a poet is a man whose task is to fecundate the feminine music....)

No wonder, then, that – apropos of the analogous couple art and science – Schelling wrote the first version of Freud's *Wo es war, soll ich werden*: where art was (with its intuitive insight), there science (with its conceptual articulation) should arrive. In order to dispel the mistaken impression that we are dealing here only with obscurantist variations on the theme of the unfathomable depths of Truth which our knowledge can only approach asymptotically, never fully attain, suffice it to recall Alain Badiou's Marxist version: where the confused spontaneous mass ideology was, there the Communist Party should arrive to organize class consciousness.

44. See Jürgen Habermas, 'Dialektischer Idealismus im übergang zum Materialismus – Geschichtsphilosophische Folgerungen aus Schellings Idee einer Contraction Gottes', in *Theorie und Praxis*, Berlin: Luchterhand 1969, pp. 108–61.

45. See Gérard Bensussan, 'Schelling – une politique négative', in *Le dernier Schelling*, pp. 71–86.

46. We must be careful here not to confuse Schelling's position with the liberal commonplace according to which no State is perfect, so that we can only approach the ideal and gradually improve the existing form of the State: this liberal distinction between the inaccessible perfect State and its imperfect empirical approximations should be abandoned for a more pertinent distinction between the existing State and the process of its becoming, 'state-ing' (in the sense in which Heidegger distinguishes between 'world' and its 'worlding [*Weltung*]', or Ernesto Laclau between the order and its 'ordering') – what gets lost in the State *qua* positive, existing institution is the radically contingent process of its becoming.

47. F.W.J. Schelling, *Die Weltalter*, pp. 56–7; quoted in Bowie, p. 115.

48. F.W.J. Schelling, *On the History of Modern Philosophy*, Cambridge: Cambridge University Press 1994, p. 115.

49. Ibid.

50. Ibid., p. 116.

51. Ibid.

52. Ibid., p. 115.

53. On a more general level, the Hegelian counterpart to Schelling's splitting between the pure subject ($) and the artificial-contingent feature the subject 'puts on' is *contradiction* itself: in Hegel, 'contradiction' designates the fact that the subject 'is' a feature which defines its identity, and simultaneously the negation of this feature. Consequently, when Hegel asserts against Aristotle that S can be *in the same respect* 'P and non-P', one should be careful not to miss his point: we are not dealing here with a fixed, self-identical S – the passage from P to non-P changes the status of S, splitting it from within. In so far as P (the predicate) is always a symbolic feature, the Lacanian version of the contradiction is: '$ is simultaneously, in the same respect, S_1 and a' – the subject is simultaneously the signifier which represents it and the object which fills in the gap of the failure of the (symbolic) representation. (As for the Hegelian 'contradiction', see Chapter 4 of Slavoj Žižek, *Tarrying with the Negative*, Durham, NC: Duke University Press 1993.)

On a somewhat different level, a perfect example of the Hegelian contradiction is provided by the dialectic of social Cause: contradiction does not reside in the fact that individuals posit/sustain their Cause (God, Nation, State . . . a State or a Nation is alive only in so far as individuals are engaged on its behalf) and are simultaneously posited by it (individuals are actual social beings only as members of some spiritual community which is their effective Substance); it resides, rather, in the fact that individuals *posit their Cause as independent of themselves, of their activity*, i.e. *as an In-itself* – the 'In-itself' of a Cause is always in-itself 'for us', for a subject.

Suffice it to recall the example of nature and its exploitation by man: nature appears as an effective 'In-itself' – as a mechanism obeying its objective laws – only 'for us', for the subject who is no longer fully embedded in the determinate context of its surroundings, but is able to surmount its particular life-interests and to assume towards nature the distance of 'disinterested' theoretical observation. For an animal, nature is not 'in-itself' but a living environment, a collection of entities which arouse its interest in so far as they satisfy some of its needs or pose a threat to it: nature can be perceived as 'independent' only by man, who is *not* directly part of it but elevated above it. This distance renders possible the exploitation of nature by means of the 'cunning of reason': here we are also dealing with 'contradiction', since we can exploit nature for our own purposes, reduce it to our means, only in so far as we acknowledge it in its 'In-itself' and conceive it as a mechanism which goes its own way irrespective of us and our needs.

54. Bowie (pp. 156–7) concludes from this failure that the philosophical matrix of reflection is inadequate, since it presupposes a 'successful' mirroring-representation of the subject in its sign. However, does not the ultimate paradox of the Hegelian absolute reflection reside in the fact that it 'succeeds' in its very failure? Does not this very failure to find an adequate representation sustain the subject; is it not this very failure which accounts for the transformation of S to $, of the 'pathological', full, substantial subject to the subject *qua* pure negativity, empty point of self-relating? See Chapter 2 of Slavoj Žižek, *For They Know Not What They Do*, London: Verso 1991.

55. See Wolfram Hogrebe, *Prädikation und Genesis*, pp. 102–3.

56. F.W.J. Schelling, *Sämtliche Werke*, vol. VIII, p. 629.

57. See Jacques Derrida, *Given Time I: Counterfeit Money*, Chicago and London: University of Chicago Press 1992.

58. What about the third term, 'In- and For-itself'? 'For-itself' remains caught in the reflective illusion according to which its gesture of *reduplicatio* merely 'remarks' (ascertains, takes note of) some pre-existing In-itself; the 'In- and For-itself' occurs when this illusion is dispelled, i.e. when it becomes clear that the reflective *reduplicatio* retroactively 'posits', brings forth, the In-itself which gets lost with the entry of reflection – it is the (reflective) loss itself which constitutes the lost object. . . .

59. At a different level, the unary feature *qua* Master-Signifier is the gesture of decision that solves the uncertain status of 'arguments': arguments always abound, yet it is never clear in advance what they are arguments for. A woman, for example, laughs in a certain way, makes certain characteristic gestures, etc. – these features can function as something that makes her attractive or as something that makes her repellent. (The end of a love affair is at hand when we are repelled by the very features that once made the beloved person irresistible.) And the Master-Signifier is the signifier, the feature, that *determines how all other features will affect us*. See Chapter 4 of Slavoj Žižek, *Tarrying with the Negative*.

60. Maurice Merleau-Ponty, *The Visible and the Invisible*, Evanston, IL: Northwestern University Press 1968, pp. 44–5.

61. Ibid., p. 33.

62. Among recent popular films, Kenneth Branagh's *Frankenstein* provides an exemplary case of such reflective inscription of the formal frame into the diegetic content. It is quite appropriate that in this film the role of Dr Frankenstein, who patches the monster together from bits and pieces of different corpses, is played by the director himself. That is to say, the film is undoubtedly a confused bric-à-brac of phantasmic fragments from a multitude of early-nineteenth-century literary universes: on the skeleton of Mary Shelley's novel are grafted fragments from Emily Brontë, Charles Dickens, etc., etc., so that what the spectator is confronted with is an artificially resuscitated inconsistent

composite – in short, an entity exactly like Dr Frankenstein's monster, who thus represents within the diegetic space the very structuring principle of the film. . . .

63. F.W.J. Schelling, 'Philosophical Investigations into the Essence of Human Freedom and Related Matters', p. 239.

64. See Alan White, *Schelling: An Introduction to the System of Freedom*, New Haven, CT and London: Yale University Press 1983, p. 94.

65. An exemplary case of how one achieves full actuality only by means of a 'fall' into temporal reality is, in Wagner's *Walküre*, Brünnhilde's decision to renounce her divine immortality for the sake of love, and to become an ordinary mortal woman: what appears as a 'minus' (the deficiency of terrestrial existence, of inhabiting a world of mortality and lack) is effectively a 'plus', i.e. the only way fully to realize one's desire – Brünnhilde's 'fall' is effectively her access to a full-blooded passion inaccessible to gods in their bloodless, ethereal existence. And does this not bring us to Schelling's most audacious thought: God Himself is in a sense 'less actual', 'less effective [*wirklich*]', than man? One should not confuse this with the usual claim of atheism: Schelling's point is not that there is no God, that God is merely a product of human imagination. There definitely are gods, yet – as Lacan would have put it – they 'belong to the (pre-symbolic) real', i.e. in themselves, they are not yet explicated, posited as such – only in man does God become *wirklich*, actual.

66. In *The Truth in Painting* (see Jacques Derrida, *The Truth in Painting*, Chicago: University of Chicago Press 1987, pp. 33–4), Derrida points out the weak point of the logic of *mise en abîme*: it avoids the very thing into which it pretends to plunge us, i.e. it opens up a gap of what is beyond representation, yet it fills up this gap again and again, and thus remains caught in the alternation between opening the gap and filling it up (the Hegelian 'spurious/bad infinity'). Perhaps one should read Hegel's depiction of the Monarch in his *Philosophy of Right* as a kind of inversion of the structure of *mise en abîme*: the Monarch is an element whose very presence 'stands in' for the gap, for its opening, and thus points towards a dimension beyond presence.

67. The structure here, of course, is more complex: in accordance with Schelling's notion of beginning as the opposite of the process that follows it, the beginning of history is necessarily the Fall, and the history of humankind is the teleological process of the gradual rise from the depths of this primordial catastrophe which occurs in three main stages: the pagan era, the Christian era, and the reconciliation to come. Schelling locates his own philosophy in this process, at the very doorstep of the third era, as the announcement of a total politico-spiritual transmutation by means of which humanity will redeem itself and God will fully reveal Himself. However, this outcome is by no means assured: new disasters lurk in the atmosphere all the time, threatening to blot out all progress hitherto, and to throw us back into the original barbarity. . . .

68. F.W.J. Schelling, 'Philosophical Investigations into the Essence of Human Freedom and Related Matters', p. 242.

69. Even this blatant contradiction in 'Philosophical Investigations', however, bespeaks a deeper truth: this very obscure yearning [*Sehnsucht*] of the Ground to attain existence – i.e. to illuminate itself, to posit itself as such – is the greatest enemy of Light, since in it we are dealing with the striving of the Ground to illuminate itself, to posit itself *as such*, i.e. as Ground in contrast to the (already existing) Light – as we have already seen, 'Evil' is not simply Ground *qua* opposed to the Light of Existence but the Ground which illuminates itself, attains full actuality and posits itself *as Ground*. The Ground of Existence is a beneficent force in so far as it modestly keeps itself in the background of Light, acting as a kind of catalyst of its shining; it turns into the force of Evil when it actualizes itself and posits itself as such. Or – to put it in yet another way – the most perfidious betrayal of Truth is to opt for the endless search for Truth, since the true aim of this search is not the attainment of its professed goal – the Truth – but the perpetuation of the process of search itself. This same 'economical paradox' is the distinctive feature of the Freudian concept of *drive*: the obscure yearning of the Schellingian Ground is another name for the drive whose true aim is the endless reproduction of its circular movement.

70. Here I rely on Vittorio Hösle, *Praktische Philosophie in der modernen Welt*, Munich: Beck 1992, pp. 166–97. Incidentally, this reference to ecology allows us to appreciate fully

the subtlety of Schelling's position. One would expect Schelling's determination of man as the 'being of the Centre', of nature as the mere background for man's ethical struggle, to condemn him to an old-fashioned anthropocentric attitude out of touch with our times, which demand a more 'cosmocentric' view. For Schelling, however, it is the very fact that man is the 'being of the Centre' which confers upon him the proper responsibility and humility – it is the ordinary materialist attitude of reducing man to an insignificant species on a small planet in a distant galaxy which effectively involves the subjective attitude of domination over nature and its ruthless exploitation.

71. F.W.J. Schelling, 'Philosophical Investigations into the Essence of Human Freedom and Related Matters', p. 245.

72. Therein consists the link between Evil and freedom: Evil cannot depend upon necessity or chance (an outcome of necessity or mere chance, by definition, does not involve the moral responsibility contained in the notion of Evil), it can result only from a free-autonomous act, that is to say, an act accomplished by a creature which, on account of its freedom, directly participates in God's nature.

Owing to this unique position of man among the creatures, he is God's *Gegen-Bild* and, as such, the mediator between God and Nature. However, owing to man's Fall, this mediation fails, so that another is needed between God and man *qua* first mediator: Christ, the 'second man'. Apropos of Christianity, Schelling is fully justified in pointing out that Christ was not a mythical entity like Zeus but a real, flesh-and-blood, living man. In pre-Christian religions, we are dealing either with ethereal incarnations of the Divinity which lack full corporeal materiality (mythical entities or spectral apparitions *personifying* divine Powers) or with real, flesh-and-blood human people who are representatives or Messengers of God: what is unthinkable here is an actual, flesh-and-blood person who is not merely God's representative but *is directly God*. In clear contrast to the New Age spiritualism which conceives Christ as one in a series of the many personifications of Divinity, along with Hindu gods, Buddha, Muhammad, and others, Christianity is a 'revealed Religion': it is only in Christ that the distance of representation which separates Divinity from its terrestrial incarnation is surmounted. Here we have another – the ultimate – example of how the 'Fall into temporality' is not a fall at all but the acquisition of full actuality: Christ is the actual and true God precisely and only in so far as he was a real (suffering, mortal) human person.

73. In his 'Philosophical Investigations', Schelling even takes a step further and claims that true Evil can emerge only in the wake of Christianity as revealed Truth. In the pagan universe, Wisdom comes 'from below', it originates in the obscure, unfathomable depths; i.e. pagan civilizations are 'natural formations', caught in the cycle of corruption and generation, while Christian Wisdom comes 'from above', it originates in the eternal Light exempted from the circuit of drives. And it is only in contrast to this Light, against its background, that Evil can assert itself as such: the decadence and horrors of the late Roman Empire bear witness to an Evil which aggressively asserts itself as such, in a gesture of defiance against the revealed Truth. . . .

74. In the domain of social life, for example, the supreme case of the false, perverted unity is the *State*: like a true forerunner of Marx, Schelling consistently denounces the State as inherently evil, since it is a false, mechanical, coercive, external unity of the people, a unity imposed from above, not their organic unity which would spring up 'from below'.

75. The clearest example, of course, was the good old 'totalitarian' Communist Party, which claimed to stand directly for the liberation of the whole of humanity (in contrast to all other political agents, who stood for narrow class interests): any attack on it equalled an attack on all that was progressive in the entire cumulative history of humankind. . . .

76. In this respect Heidegger's procedure in *Being and Time* is the very opposite of Schelling's. Schelling (and, among others who follow in his footsteps, Otto Weininger) proposes an '*ethical' reading of ontology* (the very fact of reality, the fact that the universe exists, involves an ethical decision; it is a proof that, in God, Good got the upper hand over Evil, expansion over contraction); whereas Heidegger is in the habit of taking a category whose 'ethical' connotation in our common language is indelible (guilt [*Schuld*], the opposition of 'authentic' and 'unauthentic' existence) and then depriving it of this

connotation, i.e. offering it as a neutral description of man's ontological predicament (*Schuld* as the designation of the fact that man, due to his finitude, has to opt for a limited set of possibilities, sacrificing all the others, etc.). This denial of the 'ethical' connotation, of course, provides an exemplary case of the Freudian *Verneinung*: the whole power of Heidegger's argument relies on the fact that the denied ethical dimension maintains its underground efficiency.

77. Vittorio Hösle (in *Praktische Philosophie in der modernen Welt*, p. 44) provides an extremely ingenious solution to the contradiction between Kant's thesis, taken over by Schelling, according to which the world was created in order to become the battleground for the moral conflict between Good and Evil, the conflict whose happy outcome – i.e. the final victory of the Good – is guaranteed by God as the necessary postulate of pure reason, and today's threat of humanity's self-destruction by means of a nuclear or ecological catastrophe: the *necessary existence of extraterrestrial intelligence*. That is to say, if the possibility of this catastrophe is serious, does not this render the universe meaningless, and thus expose the impotence (or, even worse, perversity) of God's act of Creation?

The only consequent solution is to take seriously and literally Kant's repeated insistence that the moral imperative holds not only for humans but for all other finite rational beings which perhaps, unbeknown to us, exist on other planets, and to draw the conclusion that these ETs, which will prolong the battle for morality in the event of humanity's self-destruction, *have to exist.* . . . The way to avoid this conclusion is to abandon its key premiss, absolute determinism: according to Hösle, God is all-powerful, He foresaw everything, including humanity's (eventual) self-destruction – in this case, of course, the creation of the universe and of humanity with the full foreknowledge of its future self-destruction is a meaningless, perverse act. Schelling, on the contrary, remains radically 'anthropocentric': man's fate is open; he *can* – but *not necessarily* – sink into self-destruction, and thus bring about the regression of the universe to the rotary motion prior to *Ent-Scheidung*; consequently, what is at stake in man's struggle for the Good is the fate of God Himself, the success or failure of His act of Creation.

78. From a Hegelian perspective, we should emphasize here the ambiguity of Schelling's notion of Evil as the principle of Ground raised to the power of Reason-Light: is not this the very definition of Reason? Is not Reason itself the 'illuminated Ground'?

79. Jean-Luc Godard's famous witticism 'Every film ought to have a beginning, a middle and an end, although not necessarily in that order' relies on this very gap of *reduplicatio* that forever separates 'what effectively takes place at the beginning' from the beginning 'as such' (the formal determination of Beginning): it may well happen that the beginning 'as such' is not at the beginning. . . .

80. F.W.J. Schelling, *Sämtliche Werke*, vol. VII, p. 468.

81. For a proper understanding of Schelling's claim that Evil is *das reinste Geistige*, much more spiritual than Good, a reference to the Lacanian formula of symbolic castration (–*phi*: enjoyment – *phi* – is permitted, but only in so far as it incorporates the 'minus' of castration, i.e. in so far as it is domesticated, 'phallicized', submitted to the paternal metaphor) might be of some help. As Jacques-Alain Miller has pointed out, it is possible for the two elements of the formula, – and *phi*, to separate, to part from each other, so that on the one side we obtain the pure (–), the Symbolic bereft of the life-substance of enjoyment and thus rendered sterile – i.e. the radical erasure of enjoyment – and on the other *phi*, the enjoyment which is, as it were, set free, and wanders around at liberty outside the Symbolic. The price, of course, is that this enjoyment is no longer experienced as 'healthy', liberating and satisfying, but is branded as something putrid, damp and oppressive.

Suffice it to recall Lenin's incisive description of the 'spiritual' state of Russia after the crackdown of the revolution of 1905: an atmosphere of pure, mystical spirituality, of the violent denial of corporeality, accompanied by an obsession with pornography and sexual perversion. . . . The lesson is that so-called 'healthy' sexuality, far from being a 'natural' state of things which only occasionally gets perturbed, hangs in a fragile balance, a combination of two elements (– and *phi*), which can disintegrate into its two components at any moment.

82. F.W.J. Schelling, *Sämtliche Werke*, vol. VII, p. 472.

83. Jean-François Marquet, *Liberté et existence. étude sur la formation de la philosophie de Schelling*, pp. 569–70.

84. One should relate all this to Lacan's reading of the Freudian notion of *Vorstellungs-Repräsentanz*: not simply 'a representation that acts as a representative of the organic drive' but 'a (signifier-)representative of the (missing) representation'. The *name* of a person is such a *Vorstellungs-Repräsentanz*: what it aims at, what it encircles without signifying, is precisely that abyss in another person which eludes representations [*Vorstellungen*], that 'irrepresentable' X beyond positive properties, beyond 'what I positively am', which makes me a person. And, incidentally, all this also enables us to discern the Kantian background of psychoanalysis: not only the rather obvious point that the drive *qua* Thing-in-itself [*Ding-an-sich*] is accessible only via its psychic *Vorstellungen* but, above all, the not-so-obvious fact that the Kantian *Ding* is, in its most fundamental dimension, another subject, not a physical object.

85. At a different level, the same traumatic dimension is also obfuscated by the Althusserian concept of interpellation: when Althusser defines interpellation as the subject's constitutive (mis)recognition in the Other's call – i.e. as the act of identification with the big Other – he thereby circumvents the intermediate, transitory but necessary moment of 'interpellation prior to identification' in which the subject is confronted with an opaque call of the Other to which no discernible meaning can be attributed and which, therefore, precludes any possibility of identification; see Chapter 3 of Slavoj Žižek, *The Metastases of Enjoyment*, London: Verso 1994.

86. At a closer glance, things are none the less more ambiguous: by means of this negative gesture – i.e. of his delimitation of the Real (of the Thing-in-itself) from the phenomenal domain of mere representations – Kant opens up, circumscribes, the place of the Real which is then 'peopled' by Schelling.

87. F.W.J. Schelling, 'Philosophical Investigations into the Essence of Human Freedom and Related Matters', pp. 238–9. Schelling's determination of the *object* as the 'indivisible remainder' is Lacanian *avant la lettre*, in so far as it runs against the *doxa* of the indivisible *subject* (the 'individual', his/her indivisible unity, in contrast to the object that can be divided *ad infinitum*). According to Lacan, the subject is not only divisible, but effectively *divided*: it is the product of the operation of signifying division, whereas the object is the indivisible remainder, the 'fallout', of this same operation. Lacan's 'matheme' of fantasy which expresses this link between subject and object ($ \lozenge a$) is therefore a formula which designates the encounter of two radically heterogeneous entities: $ qua$ the void of the distance between the signifiers in a chain, and the inert remainder of the real which resists symbolization. The Lacanian 'matheme' is therefore the very opposite of the inherent deployment of the notional content: it expresses a properly inconceivable collision of two elements whose nature is radically heterogeneous.

88. Incidentally, Schelling chose for his seal the sphinx on the 'eternal Wheel', the ancient symbol of nature's rotary motion.

89. This thesis, according to which a Universal is always marked by some stain of particularity, is never truly neutral, it always implies a particular point of view from which the All is disclosed (every universal notion of philosophy always involves the position of a particular philosophy, for example), is, of course, merely another way of asserting that every Master-Signifier (S_1) is 'branded', stigmatized, by a, by the absolute particularity of an objectal leftover.

An exemplary case of this One which sustains the All of Universality is provided by a quick glance at any manual of philosophy: it becomes clear how every universal, all-encompassing notion of philosophy is rooted in a particular philosophy, how it involves the standpoint of *One*, of a particular philosophy. There is no neutral notion of philosophy to be divided into analytical philosophy, hermeneutic philosophy, etc.; every particular philosophy encompasses itself and (its view on) all other philosophies. Or – as Hegel put it in his *Lessons on the History of Philosophy* – every epochal philosophy is in a way the whole of philosophy, it is not a subdivision of the Whole but this Whole itself apprehended in a specific modality. What we have here is thus not a simple reduction of the Universal to the Particular but, rather, a kind of *surplus* of the Universal: no single Universal encompasses the entire particular content, since each Particular has *its own* Universal, i.e. it contains a specific perspective on the entire field. If, then, Evil resides in the 'contracted' subjective position involved in our allegedly neutral view on the entire universal field, how are we to step out of it? The point, of course, is that the reference to universality is unavoidable, since it is inherent to speech as such: the moment we speak, a kind of universal dimension is always involved. So the thing to do is not to claim or openly admit that we speak only from our particular position (this assertion already involves a view of totality within which our particular position is located), but to admit the irreducible plurality of the Universals themselves: the discord is already at the level of the Universal, so that the only true self-restraint is to admit the particularity of one's own Universal. . . .

90. Does not Wagner's *Ring* bear witness to a similar foreboding? Wotan's universe of *logos*, of symbolic contracts and laws, is founded upon a primordial *breach* and as such is destined to fall into ruins. . . .

91. *Sämtliche Werke*, vol. VIII, p. 688.

92. Hogrebe, p. 112.

2

Schelling-for-Hegel:
The 'Vanishing Mediator'

From subjectivization to subjective destitution

The notion of Schelling's *Grundoperation* – the 'vanishing mediation' between the two poles (the Real and the Ideal, B and A) – opens up the possibility of establishing a connection with Hegelian dialectics: the founding gesture 'repressed' by the formal envelope of the 'panlogicist' Hegel is *the same* as the gesture which is 'repressed' by the formal envelope of the 'obscurantist' Schelling, yet which simultaneously serves as its unacknowledged ground. What I have in mind, of course, is the gesture delineated by Schelling in the last pages of the second draft of *Weltalter*, where he dwells on how what is truly 'unconscious' is not so much the rotary motion of drives 'repressed' by the primordial act of decision but, rather, *this act itself*, that is, the act of assuming a distance towards the rotary motion, of distinguishing the past of the drives from the present of the Word. One is tempted to go even a step further: is not this same gesture, or at least its structural place, forecast already in Kant, in his problematic notion of 'diabolical Evil', of an Evil which is accomplished 'out of principle', just for the sake of it, for no 'pathological' gain, and is as such formally indistinguishable from the Good? This 'diabolical Evil' effectively functions as the 'vanishing mediator', whose disappearance renders possible the establishment of the opposition between the Good and 'normal', merely 'pathological' Evil. Does this gesture of 'vanishing mediation' not point, therefore, towards what, following some German interpreters, one could call the *Grundoperation des Deutschen Idealismus*, the fundamental, elementary operation of German Idealism?

It is our endeavour to articulate clearly the *Grundoperation* of German Idealism which necessitates reference to Lacan; that is to say, our premiss is that the 'royal road' to this *Grundoperation* involves reading German Idealism through the prism of Lacanian psychoanalytic theory. However, in order to gain access to this *Grundoperation*, one has first to invalidate the predominant 'philosophical' reading of Lacan: the notion of Lacan as the 'philosopher of language' who emphasized the price the subject has to pay in order to gain access to the symbolic order – all the false poetry of 'castration', of some primordial act of sacrifice and renunciation, of *jouissance* as impossible; the notion that, at the end of the psychoanalytic cure, the analysand has to assume symbolic castration, to accept a fundamental, constitutive loss or lack; and so on. To such an approach one has to oppose its obverse, which is usually passed over in silence: the trouble with *jouissance* is not that it is unattainable, that it always eludes our grasp, but, rather, that *one can never get rid of it*, that its stain drags along for ever – therein resides the point of Lacan's concept of surplus-enjoyment: the very renunciation of *jouissance* brings about a remainder/surplus of *jouissance*. (Critiques of psychoanalysis according to which Freud intended to 'besmirch everything' and to discern the traces of enjoyment even in the highest ethical acts therefore possess a grain of truth.)

Incidentally, this surplus-enjoyment complicates the problem of responsibility. The subject can exonerate himself from responsibility with regard to the symbolic network of tradition which overdetermines his speech; he is justified in claiming: 'I am not the true author of my statements, since I merely repeat the performative patterns I grew into – it is the big Other which effectively speaks through me' (someone who makes a racist remark, for example, can always evoke the network of historical sedimentations in which his speech act is embedded). However, the subject is fully responsible for the little bit of enjoyment he derives from his aggressive racist outburst. The same goes for the reverse case of a victim: my description of the circumstances whose victim I was can be entirely truthful and accurate; the catch is that my narrative is always embedded in a present constellation within which it provides me with a surplus-enjoyment (the report on my victimization by means of which I impute the guilt to others and present myself as an innocent, passive victim of circumstances always provides a deep libidinal satisfaction), and for this enjoyment contained in my subjective position of enunciation, while I report on my victimization, I am fully responsible. The line of separation thus runs along the axis Other–*jouissance*: with regard to the 'big Other', I am not the author of my speech acts, they are (over)determined by their symbolic context, so I can escape my responsibility; however, I remain fully responsible for the fragment of *jouissance* which adheres to all my speech acts.

The predominant 'philosophical' reading of Lacan is not a simple misreading, external to what Lacan effectively accomplished: there certainly is an entire stratum of Lacanian theory which corresponds to this reading; the easiest way to isolate this stratum is to focus on the shifts in Lacan's formulas of the conclusion of the psychoanalytic cure. Crucial here is the shift from *subjectivization* to *subjective destitution*. In so far as the status of the subject as such involves a certain guilt and/or indebtedness – the philosophical *topos* from Kierkegaard to Heidegger readily accepted by Lacan in the 1950s – the gesture of 'subjectivization' at the conclusion of the cure means that the subject has to assume fully his constitutive guilt and/or debt, obfuscated in his 'inauthentic' everyday existence; inversely, 'subjective destitution' at the conclusion of the cure means that the subject has to do away with his guilt and/or debt.

In this way we arrive at two opposed readings of Freud's *Wo es war, soll ich werden.*[1] 'Subjectivization' *qua* the assumption of guilt implies that the analysand 'subjectivizes', fully assumes, 'internalizes', his contingent fate – that is, it points towards a tragic/heroic gesture of *amor fati*, whose exemplary case in literature is provided by Oedipus: although Oedipus was not guilty of his crime – his acts were predetermined by the contingency of fate well before his birth – he none the less heroically assumed full responsibility for his horrible deeds – that is to say, he took his fate upon himself, 'internalized' it and lived it to its bitter end. . . . 'Subjectivization' thus consists in the purely formal gesture of symbolic conversion by means of which the subject integrates into his symbolic universe – turns into part and parcel of his life-narrative, provides with meaning – the meaningless contingency of his destiny. In clear contrast, 'subjective destitution' involves the opposite gesture: at the end of the psychoanalytic cure, the analysand has to suspend the urge to symbolize/internalize, to interpret, to search for a 'deeper meaning'; he has to accept that the traumatic encounters which traced out the itinerary of his life were utterly contingent and indifferent, that they bear no 'deeper message'.

Against this background, one can determine the ambiguous role of love in the psychoanalytic cure: although the psychoanalyst has to manipulate transferential love deftly, he must certainly not give way to its lure – why? At its most elementary, love involves the internalization of an external, meaningless encounter or collision: on the one hand, the event of love is radically contingent, one can never foresee its occurrence, it offers the supreme example of *tyche*; on the other hand, when we encounter our 'true love', it seems as if this is what we have been waiting for all our life; as if, in some mysterious way, all our previous life has led to this encounter . . . 'love' is one of the names for the already-mentioned purely formal act of conversion by means of which a meaningless external contingency of the Real is 'internalized', symbolized, provided with Meaning. The main ethical injunction of psychoanalysis is therefore not to yield to the temptation of symbolization/internalization: in the psychoanalytic cure the analysand, as it were, *passes through falling in love backwards*: at the moment of 'exit from transference' which marks the end of the cure, the subject is able to perceive the events around which his life story is crystallized into a meaningful Whole in their senseless contingency. . . .

Desire versus drive

The paradoxical stakes of our strategy are now becoming somewhat clearer: precisely in so far as our aim is to elevate Lacan to the dignity of an author who provides the key to the *Grundoperation* of German Idealism, perhaps the acme of the entire history of philosophy, our main opponent is a typical 'philosophical' reading of Lacan, a *doxa* on Lacan which reduces his teaching to the framework of traditional philosophy. Far from being a simple case of false reading, this *doxa* definitely has support in Lacan: Lacan himself often yields to its temptation, since this *doxa* is a kind of 'spontaneous philosophy of (Lacanian) psychoanalysis'. What, then, are its basic contours?

The moment we enter the symbolic order, the immediacy of the pre-symbolic Real is lost for ever, the true object of desire ('mother') becomes impossible-unattainable. Every positive object we encounter in reality is already a substitute for this lost original, the incestuous *Ding* rendered inaccessible by the very fact of language – that is 'symbolic castration'. The very existence of man *qua* being-of-language stands thus under the sign of an irreducible and constitutive lack: we are submerged in the universe of signs which forever prevent us from attaining the Thing; so-called 'external reality' itself is already 'structured like a language', that is, its meaning is always-already overdetermined by the symbolic framework which structures our perception of reality. The symbolic agency of the paternal prohibition (the 'Name-of-the-Father') merely personifies, gives body to, the impossibility which is co-substantial with the very fact of the symbolic order – '*jouissance* is forbidden to him who speaks as such'.[2]

This gap that forever separates the lost Thing from symbolic semblances which are never '*that*' defines the contours of the ethics of desire: 'do not compromise your desire' can only mean 'do not put up with any of the substitutes for the Thing, keep the gap of desire open'. The analogy with Kant's philosophy is crucial here: in Kant one has to avoid two traps: not only the simple utilitarian-pragmatic limitation of our interest to the object of phenomenal experience, but also the obscurantist *Schwärmerei*, the dream of a direct contact with the Thing beyond phenomenal reality; in an analogous way, the ethics of pure desire compels us to avoid not only debilitating contentment with the pleasures provided by the objects of phenomenal reality but also the danger of yielding to fascination with the Thing, and being drawn into its lethal vortex, which can only end in psychosis or suicidal *passage à l'acte.*

In our everyday lives, we constantly fall prey to imaginary lures which promise the healing of the original/constitutive wound of symbolization, from Woman with whom full sexual relationship will be possible to the totalitarian political ideal of a fully realized community. In contrast, the fundamental maxim of the ethics of desire is simply desire as such: one has to maintain desire in its dissatisfaction. What we have here is a kind of heroism of the lack: the aim of the psychoanalytic cure is to induce the subject heroically to assume his constitutive lack, to endure the splitting which propels desire. A productive way out of this deadlock is provided by the possibility of *sublimation*: when one picks out an empirical, positive object and 'elevates it to the dignity of the Thing' – turns it into a kind of stand-in for the impossible Thing – one thereby remains faithful to one's desire without getting drawn into the deadly vortex of the Thing. . . . Such a (mis)reading of Lacan led Rudolf Bernet[3] to interpret Antigone's clinging to her desire as a *negative* attitude, that is, as the exemplary case of the lethal obsession with the Thing which cannot achieve sublimation and therefore gets lost in a suicidal abyss – as if the whole point of Lacan's reading of *Antigone* is not to present her as an exemplary case of the psychoanalytic ethics of 'not compromising one's desire'!

Bernard Baas[4] draws political consequences from this reading of Lacan: the field of the political is characterized by the radically ambiguous relationship of the subjects towards the public Thing [*res publica*], the kernel of the Real around which the life of a community revolves. The subject, *qua* member of a community, is split not only between his 'pathological' urges and his relationship to the Thing – his relationship to the Thing is also split: on the one hand, the law of desire orders us to neglect our pathological interests and to follow our Thing; on the other, an even higher law (Baas writes it with a capital L) enjoins us to maintain a minimal distance towards our Thing – to bear in mind, apropos of every political action which purports to realize our Cause, that 'this is not that [*ce n'est pas ça*]'. The Thing can appear only in its retreat, as the obscure Ground which motivates our activity, but dissipates the moment we endeavour to grasp it in its positive ontological consistency: if we neglect this Law, sooner or later we get caught in the 'totalitarian' self-destructive vicious cycle. . . . What is lurking in the background, of course, is the Kantian distinction between the constitutive and the regulative aspect: the Thing (freedom, for example) has to remain a regulative ideal – any attempt at its full realization can lead only to the most terrifying tyranny. (It is easy to discern here the contours of Kant's criticism of the perversion of the French Revolution in the revolutionary terror of the Jacobins.) And how can we avoid recognizing a reference to the contemporary political landscape, with its two extremes of unprincipled liberal pragmatism and fundamentalist fanaticism?

On a first approach, this reading of Lacan cannot but appear convincing, almost a matter of course – yet it is the very ease of this translation of Lacanian concepts into the modern structuralist and/or existentialist philosophemes of constitutive lack, and so on, which should render it suspect. To put it somewhat bluntly, we are dealing here with an 'idealist' distortion of Lacan; to this 'idealist' problematic of desire, its constitutive lack, and so on, one has to oppose the 'materialist' problematic of the Real of drives. That is to say: for Lacan the 'Real' is *not*, in the Kantian mode, a purely negative category, a designation of a limit without any specification of what lies beyond – the Real *qua* drive is, on the contrary, the *agens*, the 'driving force', of desiring.[5]

This 'active' (and not purely negative) status of drives, of the pre-symbolic 'libido', induces Lacan to elaborate the highly Schellingian myth of 'lamella': in it, he deploys – in the form of a mythical narrative, not of a conceptual articulation – the 'real genesis', that is, what had to occur *prior* to symbolization, *prior* to the emergence of the symbolic order.[6] In short, Lacan's point here is that the passage from the radically 'impossible' Real (the maternal Thing-Body which can be apprehended only in a negative way) to the reign of the symbolic Law, to desire which is regulated by Law, sustained by the fundamental Prohibition, is not direct: something happens *between* 'pure', 'pre-human' nature and the order of symbolic exchanges, and this 'something' is precisely the Real of drives – *no longer* the 'closed circuit' of instincts and their innate rhythm of satisfaction (drives are already 'derailed nature'), but *not yet* the symbolic desire sustained by Prohibition. The Lacanian Thing is not simply the 'impossible' Real which withdraws into the dim recesses of the Unattainable with the entry of the symbolic order, it is the very universe of drives.[7] Here, the reference to Schelling is of crucial importance, since Schelling was the first to accomplish an analogous step within the domain of philosophy: his mythical narrative on the 'ages of the world' focuses on a process in God which precedes the actuality of the divine *Logos*, and, as we have already seen, this process is described in terms which clearly pave the way for Lacan's notion of the Real of drives.

The philosophical consequences of this shift are far-reaching: it compels us to call into question one of commonplaces of philosophical discourse, from Kant through Heidegger to (early) Lacan: namely, the notion of man as an entity who is structurally – at a formal–transcendental level – 'guilty', indebted, in default with respect to his ethical determination. (As we have just seen, man regresses to a most horrible Evil at the very moment he endeavours fully to recover his 'ontological indebtedness' by directly realizing his noumenal ethical determination.) Here one has to accomplish 'another turn of the screw' and to transpose the lack of the subject (his inability to comply fully with the big Other's ethical injunction) into a *lack of this Other itself*: as Schelling emphasizes, the Absolute itself is split into its true Existence and the impenetrable Ground of its Existence, so that God Himself, in an unheard-of way, seems to resist the full actualization of the Ideal – this displacement of the split into the Absolute itself, of course, delivers us from guilt.

Hegel goes even a step further; if one were to formulate his position in Schelling's terms, one would have to say that Hegel posits identity between God Himself and the Ground of his Existence: their difference is purely formal, that is, it involves a shift in the point of view from which we observe the Absolute. The difference between Good and Evil, for example, is not simply an attribute of the object of our perception; it is always dialectically mediated by a different attitude of the observing subject itself towards the object perceived as 'good' or 'evil' – as Hegel puts it, what is effectively evil is ultimately the gaze itself which perceives a state of things as evil. However, this paradox is not to be reduced to the standard theological commonplace according to which things appear as evil only from our limited, finite perspective, whereas from the standpoint of totality they are 'good' in the sense that they contribute to the harmony of the Whole (take the famous comparison of our finite view with an individual who observes a beautiful painting from too close: what appear to him as blurred stains are, if one steps back and grasps the picture in its entirety, elements which contribute to its beauty and harmony). Hegel's point is, rather, the exact opposite of this theological commonplace – in so far as the Woman that exists is one of the names of God, one is tempted to evoke here Chandler's famous male-chauvinist wisecrack from *The High Window*: 'From thirty feet away she looked like a lot of class. From ten feet away she looked like something made up to be seen from thirty feet away.'[8] Things are somewhat similar with the Absolute itself: if it is to continue to give rise to sublime awe, one has to maintain a proper distance towards it – like the castle from Kafka's novel of the same name which looks majestic from the valley below, but when the land-surveyor K.

climbs the hill and gets close to it, he suddenly notices that the castle, this mysterious seat of Power, is actually just a bunch of old decaying barracks. . . .

'The voice is a voice'

After Schelling, then, Hegel: how are we to penetrate *his* 'formal envelope of error'? As I have already indicated, through Lacan – in so far as we do not reduce Lacan to one more 'deconstructionist'. Let us elaborate this crucial point apropos of the Derridean couple supplement/centre. In a way reminiscent of the Foucauldian endless variations on the complex heterogeneity of power relations (they run upwards, downwards, laterally . . .), Derrida also likes to indulge heavily in exuberant variations on the paradoxical character of the supplement (the excessive element which is neither inside nor outside; it sticks out of the series it belongs to and simultaneously completes it, etc.). Lacan, on the contrary – by means of a gesture which for Derrida, of course, would undoubtedly signal reinscription into traditional philosophical discourse – *directly offers a concept of this element*, namely the concept of the Master-Signifier, S_1, in relation to S_2, the 'ordinary' chain of knowledge. This concept is not a simple unambiguous concept, but the concept of the structural ambiguity itself; that is to say, Lacan reunites in one and the same concept what Derrida keeps apart: in Lacan, S_1 stands for the supplement – the trait which sticks out, but is as such, in its very excess, unavoidable – and, simultaneously, for the totalizing Master-Signifier. Therein, in this 'speculative identity' of supplement and Centre, resides Lacan's implicit 'Hegelian' move: the Centre Derrida endeavours to 'deconstruct' is ultimately the very supplement which threatens to disrupt its totalizing power – or, to put it in Kierkegaardese, supplement is the Centre itself 'in its becoming'. In this precise sense, supplement is both the condition of possibility *and* the condition of impossibility of the Centre.

Mutatis mutandis, the same goes for the couple voice/writing: voice provides an exemplary case of Hegelian self-identity. In his 'deconstruction' of Western logo-phono-centrism, Derrida proposed the idea that the 'metaphysics of presence' is ultimately founded upon the illusion of 'hearing-oneself-speaking [*s'entendre-parler*]', upon the illusory experience of the Voice as the transparent medium that enables and guarantees the speaker's immediate self-presence. In his psychoanalytic theory of voice as a partial object (on a par with other such objects: breasts, faeces . . .), Lacan supplements Derrida with the Hegelian identity as the coincidence of the opposites. True, the experience of *s'entendre-parler* serves to ground the illusion of the transparent self-presence of the speaking subject; however, is not the voice *at the same time* that which undermines most radically the subject's self-presence and self-transparence? Not writing, which undermines the voice as it were from without, from a minimal distance, but the voice itself: one is tempted to say the voice *as such* in its uncanny presence – I hear myself speaking, yet what I hear is never fully myself but a parasite, a foreign body in my very heart. In short, voice is that on account of which 'I can't hear myself think', so that the subject's basic plea to his or her voice is: 'Would you please shut up, I can't hear myself think!'

This stranger *in myself* acquires positive existence in different guises, from the voice of conscience and the opaque voice of the hypnotist to the persecutor in paranoia. The voice's 'self-identity' resides in the fact that the voice *qua* medium of transparent self-presence *coincides with* the voice *qua* foreign body which undercuts my self-presence 'from within'. In the antagonistic tension between signifier and object, voice is thus on the side of the object: voice, in its fundamental dimension, is not the ideal (totally transparent, pliant, self-effacing) signifier, but its exact opposite, the opaque inertia of an objectal remainder. With regard to this inner friction of the voice, the tension between voice and writing is already secondary: in it, this inner friction is, as it were, displaced into the relationship of the voice to writing *qua* its *external* Other.[9]

Consequently, the status of voice in Lacan does not amount to a simple symmetrical reversal of the Derridean notion of writing as supplement – that is to say, it is not that instead of writing supplementing the voice, it is now the voice's turn to supplement writing – the very logic of the relationship is different in each case.[10] In Lacan, voice prior to writing (and to the movement of *différance*) is a drive and, as such, caught in the antagonism of a closed circular movement; by the expulsion of its own opaque materiality into the 'externality' of writing, voice establishes itself as the ideal medium of self-transparency. The passage from this inner antagonism of the voice to the 'external' relationship between voice and writing is thus strictly analogous to the Schellingian passsage from the 'closed' rotary motion of drives to the 'opening' of the difference that resolves the tension of the drives' pulsation. Perhaps therein resides the abyss that forever separates the Real of an antagonism from Derrida's *différance*: *différance* points towards the constant and constitutive deferral of impossible self-identity, whereas in Lacan, what the movement of symbolic deferral-substitution forever fails to attain is not Identity but the Real of an antagonism. (In social life, for example, what the multitude of [ideological] symbolizations-narrativizations fails to render is not society's *self-identity* but its *antagonism*, the constitutive splitting of the 'body politic'.)

To recapitulate: in Derrida, voice is the medium of illusory self-transparency; consequently, the fact that voice, for structural reasons, always fails to deliver this self-transparency means that voice is always-already tainted with writing, that it always-already contains the minimal materiality of a trace which introduces an interspace, a gap, into the voice's pure self-presence.... In Lacan's 'graph of desire', however, voice is the remainder of the signifying operation, that is, the meaningless piece of the real which stays behind once the operation of 'quilting [*capitonnage*]' responsible for the stabilization of meaning is performed – *voice is that which, in the signifier, resists meaning*, it stands for the opaque inertia which cannot be recuperated by meaning. It is only the dimension of writing which accounts for the stability of meaning – or, to quote the immortal words of Samuel Goldwyn: 'A verbal agreement isn't worth the paper it's written on.' As such, voice is neither dead nor alive: its status, rather, is that of a 'living dead', of a spectral apparition which somehow survives its own death – the eclipse of meaning. In other words, it is true that the life of a voice can be opposed to the dead letter of writing, but this life is the uncanny life of an 'undead' monster, not a 'healthy' living self-presence of Meaning .... It is against this background that one should conceive the Lacanian notion of the 'second death': what expires in it is the very spectre which survived the 'first', physical, death – that is to say, in it, 'only the place itself takes place', to paraphrase Mallarmé – for a brief moment, the subject is confronted with the *void* filled out by the spectral presence.

As I have already hinted, one could also formulate this paradoxical status of voice in terms of the Hegelian notion of tautology as the highest contradiction. 'Voice is voice' in *s'entendre-parler* is a tautology analogous to 'God is ... God': the first voice ('Voice is ... ') is the medium of self-transparent presence, whereas the second voice (' ... voice') is the opaque stain which decentres me from within, a strange body in my very midst – the form of identity contains utter heterogeneity. My self-identity is sustained by its 'condition of impossibility', by a 'spectral' foreign body in my very heart. 'Supplement is the Centre', on the contrary, has to be read as an 'infinite judgement' in the Hegelian sense of the term: instead of the tautology giving form to the radical antagonism between the two appearances of the same term, the very juxtaposition of two terms which seem incompatible renders visible their 'speculative identity' – 'the Spirit is a bone', for example.

The ultimate Lacanian 'infinite judgement', of course, is his formula of fantasy $\$ \lozenge a$, positing the co-dependence of the pure void of subjectivity and the formless remainder of the Real which, precisely, resists subjectivization: *objet a* is not merely the objectal correlative to the subject, it is the subject itself in its 'impossible' objectal existence, a kind of objectal stand-in for the subject. And it is the same with 'Supplement is the Centre': the point is not merely that there is no Centre without the supplement, that it is only the supplement which, retroactively, constitutes the Centre; the Centre itself is nothing but the supplement perceived from a certain perspective – the shift from the Centre to its supplement concerns the point of view, not the 'thing itself'. We are dealing here with a purely topological shift, analogous to the shift in the status of low-class popular food brought about by the development of industrialized mass food: the cheapest and most elementary kind of food (dark wholemeal bread, for example) gradually disappears from the market, forced out by industrially produced square white loaves or hamburger buns, only to return triumphantly as the most expensive 'natural', 'home-made' speciality....[11] The fight against the opaque Voice is therefore the fight against transparent self-identity itself; in endeavouring to contain the supplement, the Centre undermines its own foundations.

To put it in yet another way: Lacan subverts the 'metaphysics of presence' at the very point at which, by equating voice with subjectivity, he seems to succumb to one of its basic premisses: to the horror and/or delight of the deconstructionists, he claims that a signifying chain subjectivizes itself through the voice – there is no subject prior to the voice. Writing is in itself non-subjective, it involves no subjective position of enunciation, no difference between the enunciated content and its process of enunciation. However, the voice through which the signifying chain subjectivizes itself is not the voice *qua* the medium of the transparent self-presence of Meaning, but the voice *qua* a dark spot of non-subjectivizable remainder, the point of the eclipse of meaning, the point at which meaning slides into *jouis-sense*. Or – to put it even more pointedly – we have a chain of (written) signs which transparently designate their signified – when does this chain subjectivize itself, how is its 'flat' meaning (denotation in which no subjectivity reverberates) transformed into Sense? Only when a nonsensical vocal dark spot which, in its very opaqueness, functions as the stand-in for the subject, is added to it.

The Lacanian paradox is therefore that if one is to transform (objective-denotative) Meaning into (subjective-expressive) Sense, one has simply to supplement it with a senseless vocal stain: *Sense = meaning + nonsense*. The presence of this impenetrable vocal supplement effectuates the magic transmutation of a written chain of signifiers into 'subjectivized' speech in which one can discern, beyond its denotative meaning, the reverberation of a subjective position of enunciation – in this precise sense, Lacan can assert that the voice accounts for the minimal *passage à l'acte* of the signifying chain. Suffice it to recall the example of 'hate speech' – speech acts in which the very intention-to-signify, the intention to 'say something', is eclipsed by the intention to attain and destroy the kernel of the real, *objet a*, in the Other (victim) – it is crucial that the term used is 'hate speech', not 'hate writing'.

'And' as a category

It seems that Schelling, in contrast to this (Lacanian and) Hegelian matrix of self-identity, insists on an irreducible and irrecuperable Otherness (in the guise of the obscure Ground which eludes the grasp of *Logos*, etc.); this, then, inevitably leads him to conceive the Absolute as Third with respect to the polar opposites of the Ideal and the Real, of *Logos* and its Ground: the Absolute is primarily the 'absolute indifference' providing the neutral medium for the coexistence of the polar opposites.[12] Hegel's premiss is that there is no need for this Third: an element can well be a 'part of itself', that is, the encompassing unity of itself and its Otherness – this is what notional self-relating is about. Philosophical common sense's reaction here is that of course Hegel doesn't need a Third, the common medium of the opposites, since the Spirit *already is* the unity of itself and its Otherness – but the whole point of Schelling is that one cannot reduce the Real to the Ideal, contingency to notional necessity. . . . [13] However, is such a reading the only one possible?

What is at stake here could also be formulated as the problem of the status of 'and' as a category. In Althusser, 'and' functions as a precise theoretical category: when an 'and' appears in the title of some of his essays, this little word unmistakably signals the confrontation of some general ideological notion (or, more precisely, of a neutral, ambiguous notion that oscillates between its ideological actuality and its scientific potentiality) with its specification which tells us how we are to concretize this notion so that it begins to function as non-ideological, as a strict theoretical concept. 'And' thus *splits up* the ambiguous starting unity, introduces into it the difference between ideology and science. Suffice it to mention two examples. 'Ideology *and* Ideological State Apparatuses': ISAs designate the concrete network of the material conditions of existence of an ideological edifice, that is, that which ideology itself has to misrecognize in its 'normal' functioning. 'Contradiction *and* Overdetermination': in so far as the concept of overdetermination designates the undecidable complex totality *qua* the mode of existence of contradiction, it enables us to discard the idealist-teleological burden that usually weighs upon the notion of contradiction (the teleological necessity that guarantees in advance the 'sublation' of the contradiction in a higher unity).[14] Perhaps the first exemplary case of such an 'and' is Marx's famous 'freedom, equality, *and Bentham*' from *Capital*: the supplementary 'Bentham' stands for the social circumstances that provide the concrete content of the pathetic phrases on freedom and equality – commodity exchange, market bargaining, utilitarian egotism. . . . And do we not encounter an analogous conjunction in Heidegger's *Being and Time*? 'Being' designates the fundamental theme of philosophy in its abstract universality, whereas 'time' stands for the concrete horizon of the sense of being.

'And' is thus, in a sense, *tautological*: it conjoins the same content in its two modalities – first in its ideological evidence, then in the extra-ideological conditions of its existence. For that reason, no third term is needed here to designate the medium itself in which the two terms, conjoined by means of the 'and', encounter each other: this third term is already the second term itself which stands for the network (the 'medium') of the concrete existence of an ideological universality. In contrast to this dialectico-materialist 'and', the idealist-ideological 'and' functions precisely as this third term, as the common medium of the polarity or plurality of elements. Therein resides the gap that separates for ever Freud's and Jung's respective notions of libido: Jung conceives of libido as a kind of neutral energy, with its concrete forms (sexual, creative, destructive libido) as its different 'metamorphoses'; whereas Freud insists that libido in its concrete existence is irreducibly *sexual* – all other forms of libido are forms of 'ideological' mis-recognition of this sexual content. And is not the same operation to be repeated apropos of 'man *and* woman'? Ideology compels us to assume 'humanity' as the neutral medium within which 'man' and 'woman' are posited as the two complementary poles – against this ideological evidence, one could maintain that 'woman' stands for the aspect of concrete existence and 'man' for the empty-ambiguous universality. The paradox (of a profoundly Hegelian nature) is that 'woman' – that is, the moment of specific difference – functions as the encompassing ground that accounts for the emergence of the universality of man.

The difference between these two 'and's – the 'idealist' one which stands for the medium of the coexistence of the two poles, and the 'materialist' one in which the second term designates the concrete medium of existence of the first (of the ideological universality) – renders Schelling's radical ambiguity clearly perceptible. In a materialist perspective, the 'and' in Schelling's qualification of freedom in its actuality as 'the freedom for good *and* evil' points towards the uncanny fact that *Evil is the concrete existence of the Good.* Freedom is not the neutral 'and' between Evil and Good, but, in its concrete existence, the freedom of a living, finite human person, Evil itself, the pure form of Evil – this, perhaps, is what Schelling tried to conceal from himself by taking refuge in suspicious ideological formulas on the 'inversion of the natural relationship'. . . .

There, in these two versions of the 'and', resides the ultimate difference between Schelling and Hegel, as well as Schelling's crucial limitation: when Schelling asserts the irrational Ground of *Logos* as the indelible remainder of the primordial chaotic Thing which forever threatens to draw us back into its whirlpool – 'What we call understanding, if it is real, living, active understanding, is really nothing but *regulated madness*. Understanding can manifest itself, show itself, only in its opposite, thus in what lacks understanding'[15] – he is exposed to the permanent temptation of conceiving Ground and *Logos*, the Real and the Ideal principle, as complementary. This limitation of Schelling becomes patently obvious when he is compelled to tackle the eternal 'naive' question of how the divine Absolute contracts the 'false note' of dissonance and egotism: all too often he resorts to common-sense 'wisdoms' about the impenetrable Ground as the only base upon which the edifice of Reason can be built – there is no warm hearth without its cold surroundings; a light can shine only when it illuminates the darkness that surrounds it. . . . Along the same lines, a God deprived of the Ground of His existence is a mere lifeless abstraction, a 'divine principle', not an actual, living, personal God.

Incidentally, one often encounters the same platitudes in pseudo-Hegelian attempts to explain why the absolute Idea externalizes itself at all, why it renounces its immediate self-identity: so that, by overcoming this split, it can restore its unity at a higher level – disharmony is needed so that a new, higher, complex harmony can emerge; the greater the dissonance to be surmounted, the greater the harmony. . . . Hegel's effective position is far more disquieting: yes, in 'reconciliation', harmony is restored, but this 'new harmony' has nothing whatsoever to do with the restitution of the lost original harmony – in the new harmony, the loss of the original harmony is *consummated.* That is to say, the shift from utter 'perversion' to restored harmony concerns principally the notional standard by means of which we measure the 'perversion': it occurs when the subject abandons the (old) standard according to which the new state of things appeared to him 'perverted', and accepts a standard appropriate to the new constellation – as Hegel repeats again and again, when a state of things no longer fits its notion (its normative ground), the endeavour to bring this state of things back into harmony with its notion is vain: one has to change the notion itself.[16]

Schelling claims that the fact of freedom opens up the possibility of Evil as the reversal of the 'normal' relationship between *Logos* and its contractive Ground: Ground can prevail upon the Light of Reason and, instead of remaining in the (back)ground, directly posit itself as the dominant principle of the Whole. For Hegel, however, *this reversal is the very definition of subject*: 'subject' is the name for the principle of Selfhood which subordinates to itself the substantial Whole whose particular moment it originally was. The reversal is therefore always-already the *reversal of the reversal itself*: not in the sense that the subject has to abandon his 'egotistic pride', his central position, and again posit himself as the subordinate moment of a higher substantial Whole – what he has to abandon is the very standard of the substantial Whole which reduces him to a subordinated moment; instead, the subject has to raise a new, subjective Totality to the measure of 'normalcy'.

The ambiguous status of *lalangue*

In order to gain an apprehension of what is effectively at stake in this Hegelian 'reversal of the reversal', one should relate it to the key alternative of the contemporary 'poststructuralist' debate, epitomized by the couple Althusser–Foucault. The very proximity of the Althusserian notion of Ideological State Apparatuses to the Foucauldian notion of the 'micro-practices' of power renders visible the gap that separates them: in both cases, we are dealing with a 'drill' which compels the subject directly, bypassing the level of Meaning; the crucial difference resides in the fact that in Althusser the 'big Other' – the transferential relationship to the ideological Subject – is always-already here; whereas the whole point of the Foucauldian 'micro-physics of power' is to demonstrate that 'Power doesn't exist' (in strict analogy to Lacan's 'Woman doesn't exist') – there is no Power, only a dispersed, plural, 'non-all' network of local practices lacking reference to a central totalizing agency.

We must be careful here not to miss the elegant paradox of Foucault: when he asserts that 'Power doesn't exist' – that power relations form a 'feminine', non-all, non-totalizable collection – he thereby undertakes to apply to the domain of power relations the conceptual apparatus usually activated to account for the very *absence* of power in a network of relations – to put it succinctly, he *treats power as non-power* (within the traditional approach, at least, the imposition of the One as the exception which 'totalizes' the dispersed collection of relations is *the very definition of Power*). In short, Foucault strives to accomplish in the domain of power relations what the Lacanian notion of *lalangue* ('llanguage') accomplished in the domain of language: to delineate the contours of a 'non-all' complex network of contingent and inconsistent procedures not yet caught in the logic of totalization-through-castration, that is, through the exception of One – the One (the Lacanian 'big Other') is merely a secondary spectre which should be deduced from the immanent functioning of micro-practices. This is why – as a careful reading of *The Archaeology of Knowledge*, Foucault's 'discourse on method', makes clear – Foucault is not a 'structuralist': the Foucauldian 'episteme' is not a formal differential system, a structure whose terms are defined through their negative relationship to all other terms ('identity as a bundle of differences'), but a collection of contingent singularities, of the rules of their emergence and disappearance – in contrast to the structuralists' strict conceptual 'realism', Foucault is a radical conceptual 'nominalist'. In short, Foucault's problem is: how are we to conceive the *rule* of the emergence of singular events which is not yet a *law* (in the precise sense of the formal structure of differential mediations)?

Deleuze struggled with the same problem: for many years he felt confident that 'structuralism' itself was the theory of the rules of the emergence and disappearance of singular Sense-Events; only latterly did he fully apprehend the gap that separates structuralist 'differentialism' (in which the positive presence of every element is 'mediated' by negativity; even the consistency of the structure itself is maintained by the constant displacement of a central, constitutive lack) from Spinozean absolute positivity – Deleuze's reference to Spinoza is crucial in so far as he found in Spinoza an assertion of differences which remain absolutely positive, and thus avoid the pitfalls of negativity. Both Foucault and Deleuze thus endeavour to conceptualize a 'non-castrated' structure[17] – a structure which does not function as an externally imposed formal framework, with the positive elements merely filling their preordained places within it: the Foucauldian rules of the emergence and combination of events are to be taken as absolutely *immanent*, they are the inherent rules of these elements (events) themselves; there is no gap between an (empty) place in the structure and the element occupying this place.[18]

In the end, the alternative here is between idealism and materialism: is the 'big Other' (the ideal symbolic order) always-already here as a kind of insurmountable horizon, or is it possible to deploy its 'genesis' out of the dispersed 'non-all' network of contingent material singularities? This alternative accounts for the non-explicated tension in Jean-Jacques Lecercle's otherwise excellent *Violence of Language*:[19] the author clearly oscillates between two ultimately incompatible accounts of that which in language eludes the grasp of the synchronous formal order, the Lacanian one (elaborated by Jean-Claude Milner) and that of Deleuze and Guattari. On the one hand, Lecercle resorts to Lacanian *lalangue* to designate the 'remainder' of the symbolic order of language: all those features which bear witness to the fact that language 'ran amok' and started to speak by itself, bypassing the domination of meaning (wordplays, nonsense, etc.), as well as the violent inscriptions of 'pathological' power relations, of history in its utter contingency, which distort, displace, warp, language *qua* formal-neutral order. On the other hand, Lecercle follows Deleuze and Guattari's Nietzschean notion of language itself as the medium of violent intersubjective interventions, of 'metamorphoses' in contrast to benign 'metaphors': the formal-neutral system of language is nothing but the 'prolongation of violence by other means', a stratagem to impose one's perspective as the neutral universal framework, and thus to repress the life-force of other perspectives.

Although the line that separates these two accounts may seem almost indiscernible, they none the less differ radically: is *lalangue* – that is, all those features on account of which language cannot be reduced to a synchronous, formal-neutral, system for the transmission of Meaning – a secondary, albeit irreducible, 'remainder', or is the very system of language a secondary 'repressive' formation whose strategic aim is to keep in check the 'rhizomic' productivity of *lalangue*? The radical ambiguity of the *political* dimension of *lalangue* adds to the sense of urgency in this alternative. On the one hand *lalangue*, of course, stands for the emergence of the liberating plurality of inconsistent sprouts of enjoyment which thwart the formal system of language, and which the 'repressive' power of language endeavours to contain. . . . Does not *lalangue*, however, also stand for the emergence of social 'pathology' – say, for the obscene racist *jouissance* which, via a passing obscene innuendo or an aggressive joke, makes itself heard in the interstices of the 'civilized' democratic discourse governed by the notions of equality, tolerance and solidarity? Are not such disquieting moments, when the benign surface of official discourse is suddenly disturbed by gestures signalling disdain for women, cruel mockery of the weak and poor, the obscene display of power, ambiguous fascination with the superior sexual prowess of African-Americans, and so forth, exemplary cases of *lalangue*? Is not superego, then – in so far as the psychoanalytic term for this obscene aspect of the social Law is superego[20] – on the side of *lalangue*?

How does Lacan himself stand with regard to this alternative? The first impression, of course, is that he also oscillates: one of Lacan's leitmotivs is that the big Other is always-already here, so that the Real of the remainder has to be deduced, accounted for, from the inconsistencies of the Other; in apparent opposition to this status of *lalangue* as a secondary remainder, Lacan repeatedly asserted the *jouis-sense* of the letter as a kind of base out of which, via the operation of phallic exclusion ('symbolic castration'), the discursive order of the big Other emerges. Here, however, one should accomplish the ultimate Hegelian gesture of speculative identity: the (temporal as well as logical) precedence of *lalangue* over the big Other has to be conceived as *strictly correlative to idealism carried to extremes* – to the notion that the excess of the Real in its very material density results from a certain deadlock of symbolization. Let us elaborate this crucial point.

The great problem of Lacan's late teaching was – to put it in Maoist terms – how do we get from the One to the Other, how does the One split into Two? How does the order of pre-discursive 'letters' which materialize enjoyment transmute into the differential symbolic structure (the 'big Other'), into the order of communication and exchange – in short: into a discourse? How do we get from the 'acephalous', pre-subjective circulation of *letters* to the *signifier* which 'represents the subject for another signifier'? We can see now what Lacan is really after in his late ruminations on the enigma of how the big Other is intertwined with the remainder of *lalangue*: he endeavours to break out of the endless game of playing off language – the synchronous neutral-formal system – against *lalangue* – the inconsistent bric-à-brac of 'pathological' tics which signal the violent intrusion of the Real of history and drives into the symbolic order – by focusing on a *tertium datur*, a 'vanishing mediator' between these two poles. What the 'big Other' has to 'repress' in order to assert itself as a consistent neutral-formal order is *its own founding gesture*, the (endlessly repeated) violent cut by means of which language differs from *lalangue*, and at this point, of course, we again encounter the *Grundoperation* of German Idealism.

What is idealism?

What, then, are the variants of the relationship between the ideal order of the 'big Other' and the 'non-all', inconsistent collection of the fragments of the Real? The basic alternative, of course, is between the Deleuze–Foucauldian 'materialist' line and the traditional 'idealist' line: either we assert some kind of primordial pre-symbolic process – 'flux of desire', 'micro-practices of power', Kristeva's Semiotic, *lalangue*, and so on – which, through the meanderings of its self-limitation, 'splits into Two' and engenders the 'big Other' (the Oedipal symbolic order, the spectre of a centralized-totalized Power, etc.), or we deduce the very material density and opacity of the Real from the paradoxes of the negative self-relating of the Ideal ('reality' as the product of notional self-mediation).

Let us avoid a fatal misunderstanding: I definitely do not mention this 'idealist' solution solely as a negative example – in its most radical formulation, it is not foreign to Lacan himself. That is to say, what philosophical idealism, at its most subversive, effectively amounts to is *not* a kind of gradual emanation of material reality from the Absolute, *à la* Plotin, but the Hegelian notion of 'reality' as something which exists only in so far as Idea is not fully actualized, fulfilled: the very existence of (the 'hard', 'external') reality bears witness to the fact that Idea remains caught in a deadlock. Authentic idealism thus turns upside down the commonsensical (and also Kantian) intuition according to which reality infinitely exceeds what our finite reason is able to grasp, so that when we endeavour to comprehend the universe in its totality, we inevitably become entangled in a cobweb of antinomies and inconsistencies: the causal dependency effectively runs in the opposite direction – that is to say, far from being at the root of the antinomies of our comprehension, finite-temporal reality itself emerges *because* Reason, in its *inherent* movement, became involved in inconsistencies, and continues to exist only as long as Reason does not untangle them.

Eccentric as it may sound, this attitude is strictly analogous to the most 'concrete' logic of the symptom in psychoanalysis: the real of a symptom bears witness to some deadlock in the process of symbolization; the moment the traumatic kernel at its root is integrated into the symbolic order, the symptom dissolves by itself. . . . In this precise sense, the real emerges from the impasses of formalization (as Lacan puts it in his seminar *Encore*): the Real is not a hard external kernel which resists symbolization, but the *product* of a deadlock in the process of symbolization.

Perhaps the clearest example of what is effectively at stake in authentic idealism is provided by the Kantian distinction between constitutive and regulative notions. In our experience, we are confined to a spatially and temporally limited segment of reality; our apprehension of this segment as a tiny part of the 'universe', of the whole of reality which exists 'in itself', is a (necessary) transcendental illusion: in this apprehension, we totalize the segment given to us in our experience by relating it to the regulative Idea of the Universe (reality in its totality). That is Kant's idealist reversal: what we 'spontaneously' apprehend as the reality which exists 'out there', independently of our experience of it (the universe-in-itself as the whole of reality accessible to us only in tiny segments), is effectively the result of our (the perceiving subject's) contribution, it proceeds from the totalization of empirical fragments performed by the regulative Idea of reality in its totality (the 'universe').[21] The boundary between constitutive and regulative is thus not absolute: it is only the intervention of the regulative Idea which enables us to apprehend (the transcendentally constituted) reality as a consistent composite, not just a bric-à-brac of senseless fragments. In this way, Kant 'extraneates' (in the Brechtian sense) our most 'natural' experience of reality: what the subject, embedded in his 'natural' attitude, experiences as the unique and homogeneous reality whose part he is, is actually an 'artificial' composite, the fusion of two radically heterogeneous ingredients. This fusion does not concern only the transcendental synthesis of the multitude of sensible intuitions, that is, the network of a priori notions which confer upon the formless sensible multitude the form of consistent experiential reality; *the very emergence of this experiential reality hinges on the regulative Idea whose intervention enables the subject to experience reality as a consistent totality.*

Therein lies the properly ontological role of *imagination*: imagination in its radical (transcendental) sense is not merely an activity of imitating and recombining sensible perceptions, but an activity whose contribution is *constitutive* of our apprehension of reality itself as the consistent Whole of the 'universe'. *Imagination can perform this ontological function only in so far as reality is in itself 'incomplete', 'open'*, as in the well-known science-fiction idea of a universe whose creation is not yet completed, so that at its limits one can encounter strange half-constituted creatures: a table with a shape but no colour, a bird with a body but no voice, and so on, as if reality itself is not yet properly 'put together' and furnished with all its ingredients. . . .

Perhaps the best way to render palpable this basic paradox of idealism – it is our Reason which accounts for the very 'reality of reality' – is to recall a somewhat similar cinematic experience. Today, one often supplements a shot of 'real reality' with a computer-generated image (a 'live' picture of planes flying, of a waterfall . . .) which not only fits harmoniously into the framework of screen reality but is actually responsible for the shot's 'impression of reality': if one were to subtract this 'artificial', computer-generated element, the remainder would suddenly change into a puzzle with some crucial pieces still missing. . . . (At a more primitive level of cinematic technique, it was the painted detail in the background – the horizon, the buildings across the street – which brought about the 'impression of reality' and made us forget the studio setting.[22]) This is how authentic idealism overcomes the opposition between Idea and Reality: the Idea does not simply 'internalize', 'swallow', 'dissolve', 'generate', and so on, external reality – the point is, rather, that it is only the supplement of the Idea which makes consistent reality out of the chaos of empirical-sensible representations. Reality-in-itself, the 'universe' as the consistent totality of objects which exists independently of the apprehending subject, is an Idea of Reason, that is, a pure notional determination; owing to a kind of 'spontaneous' perspective illusion, the subject (mis)perceives this very contribution of his as the kernel of 'reality-in-itself'.

This is also what the Hegelian 'complete notional determination' is about: when an object is completely determined in its notion, it simply becomes part of 'reality'; it actually exists.[23] One of the standard criticisms of Hegel concerns his ambiguous use of the very notion of Notion [*Begriff*]: he sometimes resorts to the term *Begriff* to designate, in a commonsensical way, 'a mere Notion [*nur im Begriff*]' in opposition to external, 'true', actual existence; at other times, *Begriff* stands for the only true actuality (in opposition to the transient empirical reality). This ambiguity, however, is unavoidable, since it indexes the paradox of philosophical idealism: *it is the supplement of something whose status is that of a 'mere notion' (as opposed to reality, that is, in Kantian terms, an empty notion without positive content) which brings about the transformation of the confused multitude of empirical representations into fully existing actuality.*[24]

Let us, however, take a step further. The philosophical revolution of Schelling is best epitomized by the title *Real-Idealismus*: since it is not possible to generate the Real from the Ideal (or vice versa), one has to locate the Absolute in the 'and' itself ('the Real *and* the Ideal'), that is, to conceive it as the *indifference* of the two poles, as the neutral medium of their coexistence. Yet another possibility is to conceive this 'and' as the 'primordially repressed' *vanishing mediator* which generates the very *difference* between the Real and the Ideal. These four positions form a Greimasian semiotic square: the first axis in this 'mother of all squares' is that of materialism versus idealism (engendering the Ideal from the Real, or vice versa), while both the remaining two positions point towards a dimension beyond (or rather, beneath) the couple Ideal–Real – this dimension is then specified either in the 'idealist' way, as the neutral medium of the opposites, or in the 'materialist' way, as their vanishing mediator. The two 'idealist' positions thus correspond to what I have called the two 'formal envelopes of error', Hegel's and Schelling's; whereas the two 'materialist' positions are the engendering of the Ideal from the Real (what Deleuze, in *Logic of Sense*, called 'real genesis' as opposed to transcendental genesis) and the focusing on the vanishing mediator.[25]

Proof of the conceptual consistency of these four positions is provided by the fact that each of them involves a clearly defined notion of Evil. The Deleuzean 'materialist' perspective is, of course, Nietzschean: 'Evil' designates the subordination of the flux of desire to an Ideal which truncates its assertive life-power, its multiple productivity. In the 'idealist' perspective, on the contrary, Evil is the Fall of the finite, the severing of its ties with the Idea. In Schelling, as we have seen, the two poles (the Ideal and the Real, *Logos* and its Ground) are always united, so that Evil is not their split as such but, rather, their false unity (unity under the dominance of the egotistic ground). In the fourth version, Evil is Good itself 'in its becoming', that is, Good is Evil elevated to the Universal by means of its self-relating.

The 'repressed' genesis of modernity

We are thereby back to the *Grundoperation* of German Idealism. In order to delimit this *Grundoperation* in its contrast to the Hegelian 'formal envelope of error' as clearly as possible, it is necessary to tackle what is definitely the most boring and traditional question in Hegelian studies: the elementary matrix or model of the Hegelian dialectical process. Let us take as our starting point a rarely mentioned feature of the dialectical process: the fact that its dénouement always occurs in two stages. The State, for example, is first posited as the rational totality which sublates the contingency of individual destinies; then, however, in an additional 'turn of the screw', it becomes evident that the very actualization of the State hinges on the Monarch *qua* contingent bodily existence. One can thus give a proper answer to the standard criticism according to which the Hegelian dialectical process is caught in the closed loop of teleology, its end preordained by, contained in, its beginning: what undermines the smooth running of the teleological machine is the uncanny fact that there are *too many* of these ends – more precisely, *at least two.*

Among Erle Stanley Gardner's Perry Mason novels, *The Case of the Perjured Parrot* is famous for its double dénouement: after Perry performs his usual trick of pinpointing the murderer by means of a brilliant deduction, he is still bothered by a small detail which doesn't quite fit into his scheme of things; so he concocts a new interpretation which turns things upside down and finally accounts for everything. . . . One is tempted to claim that the Hegelian dialectical process provides the ultimate case of the perjured parrot, since the reversal of self-relating negativity into a new positivity follows the same rhythm of double dénouement. First, there is the 'negation of negation' *qua* absolute, self-relating loss, the 'loss of the loss'; in the dialectics of desire, this moment occurs when the frustrating experience of the inaccessibility of the object (of desire) turns into an awareness of how this object itself is a 'metonymy of lack': how it merely gives body to a certain inaccessibility/impossibility, that is, to the fundamental void which constitutes desire. Lacan's last word, however, is not the deadlock of desire: what follows is another 'turn of the screw', the reversal of *impasse* into *passe*, of the negativity of desire into the positivity of drive: we 'change gear', as it were, from desire to drive when we become aware of how our libido realizes its aim (finds satisfaction) in the very circular movement of its repeated failure to attain its goal. . . .

This logic of double dénouement brings us back to the question of the modern – Cartesian – subject *qua* \$, the empty point of self-reference: this subject is strictly correlative to the excremental remainder ('bone') which falls out at the end of the process. For that very reason it is, paradoxically, the *worker* who occupies the place of the subject in the antagonistic relationship between worker and capitalist: as Marx emphasized again and again, from *Grundrisse* to *Capital*, the worker is a subject, that is, he delivers himself from the last vestiges of substantiality the moment he offers himself – his productive force, the kernel of his being – on the market, and can be bought for money. This is why woman – in so far as she functions (also) as an object of exchange between men – is *more subject than man*: there is no subjectivity without the reduction of the substantial kernel of my being, of the *agalma* in me, the secret treasure which accounts for my worth and dignity, to a freely circulating and available excrement. . . .

This paradoxical constellation belies the 'official' story of the genesis of subjectivity, which runs as follows: the traditional individual is embedded in the framework of Destiny, his place is preordained by the power of Tradition, and his tragedy resides in the obligation to repay the debt he contracted with no active participation on his part, but by his mere place of inscription in the network of family relations – he is guilty because of what he is (in his symbolic place), not because of what he effectively did or desired. The modern subject, on the contrary, gets rid of this burden of Tradition, he asserts himself as a self-responsible and autonomous master of his fate; Tradition counts for him only in so far as it has been tested by the independent tribunal of Reason. The conjecture of Hegel, Marx and Lacan, however, is that the passage from the pre-modern individual embedded in the framework of Tradition to the modern autonomous subject cannot occur directly –

there is something in between the two, a kind of 'vanishing mediator' – and in order to designate the gesture of horrifying, senseless renunciation which plays the role of this 'vanishing mediator' – which accounts for the repressed 'genesis of modernity' – Lacan resorts to the Freudian concept of *Versagung*. In what, then, does this *Versagung* consist?

Die Versagung: from Paul Claudel . . .

Lacan deploys the contours of this concept in his detailed commentary on Paul Claudel's Coufontaine trilogy, which he elevates into a contemporary counterpart to *Antigone*. The reference to Lacan's Antigone as the exemplary case of the ethics of desire has become a commonplace in recent years, in significant contrast to the non-reactions to Lacan's commentary on Claudel's play. This absence of reactions, however, is not really·surprising, since here things are far more disquieting: no flashes of beauty generated by the sublime pathos of the tragic events on stage, merely a repulsive tic. . . .

We shall limit ourselves to the first part of the trilogy, *The Hostage* [*L'otage*]. The play takes place towards the end of Napoleonic rule, on the estate of the impoverished noble family of Coufontaine in the French countryside. After many years of assiduous endeavour, Sygne de Coufontaine, a somewhat faded beauty in her late twenties and the last member of the family to remain there, has succeeded in bringing together what was left of the estate after the revolutionary turmoil. One stormy night she receives an unexpected secret visit from her cousin Georges, heir of the family and a fervent Royalist, who emigrated to England; caught in a mystical trance comparable to Wagner's *Tristan*, Sygne and Georges take a vow of eternal love which simultaneously expresses their profound attachment to the family land and title. The two lovers are united in the prospect of marrying and continuing the family tradition: they have dedicated and sacrificed ·everything, their youth and happiness, to it; the family title and a small piece of land are all they have. However, new troubles are already looming on the horizon: Georges has returned to France on a very sensitive secret political mission – he has brought into their manor the Pope, who is on the run from Napoleon.

The next morning Sygne is visited by Toussaint Turelure, Prefect of the region and a *nouveau riche*, a person she thoroughly despises: Turelure, son of her servant and wet nurse, has used the Revolution to promote his career – as a local Jacobin potentate, he ordered the execution of Sygne's parents in the presence of their children. This same Turelure, the arch-enemy of the family, now approaches Sygne with the following proposal: his spies have informed him of the presence of Georges and the Pope, and of course he has strict orders from Paris to arrest the two immediately; however, he is ready to let them slip away if only Sygne will marry him and thus transfer to him the Coufontaine family title.... Although Sygne proudly rejects the offer and dismisses Turelure, a long ensuing conversation with the local priest, confidant of the family, makes her change her mind. In his paradigmatically modern strategy of inducing her to accept Turelure's offer of marriage, and thus save the Pope, the priest renounces any direct appeal to her duty and obligation: he repeats again and again that nobody, not even God Himself, has the right to ask of her such a horrifying sacrifice – the decision is entirely hers, she has the right to say no without any reproach....

A year later, Turelure, now Sygne's husband and Prefect of Seine, conducts the negotiations for the surrender of Paris to the advancing Royalists; by means of his negotiating skills, he ensures for himself one of the most powerful positions in post-Napoleonic France. The chief negotiator for the returning King is none other than Georges; moreover, negotiations take place on the very day when a son is born to Sygne and Turelure. Unable to bear the fact that the corrupt and opportunistic Turelure has usurped the family title, Georges gets involved in a violent fight with him. There is a shoot-out between the two men in the presence of Sygne; Georges is mortally wounded, while Sygne shields Turelure with her own body, intercepting Georges's bullet. In an alternative version of the scene which follows this shoot-out, Turelure, standing by the bed of the fatally wounded Sygne, desperately asks her to give a sign which would confer some meaning on her unexpected suicidal gesture of saving the life of her loathed husband – anything, even if she didn't do it for love of him but merely to save the family name from disgrace. The dying Sygne utters not a sound: she merely signals her rejection of a final reconciliation with her husband by means of a compulsive tic, a kind of convulsed twitching which repeatedly distorts her gentle face. Here Lacan is fully justified in reading the very name 'Sygne' as a distorted 'signe' (French for 'sign'): what Sygne refuses to do is to provide a sign which would integrate her absurd act of sacrificing herself for her loathed husband into the symbolic universe of honour and duty, thereby softening its traumatic impact. The last scene of the play: while Sygne is dying of her wound, Turelure bids a pathetic welcome to the King on behalf of a faithful France....

The Pope is portrayed as a powerless, sentimental, half-senile old man, definitely out of touch with his time, personifying the hollow ritual and lifeless wisdom of an institution in decay; the restoration of the *ancien régime* after Napoleon's fall is an obscene parody in which the most corrupt parvenus of the Revolution, dressed up as Royalists, run the show. Claudel thus clearly signals that the order for which Sygne accomplishes the ultimate sacrifice is not the authentic old order but its shallow and impotent semblance, a mask under the guise of which the new forces of corruption and degeneration fortify their rule. In spite of this, however, her word obliges her – or, as Lacan puts it, she is the hostage of her Word – so she goes through the empty motions of sacrificing herself for her husband, whom she is supposed not only to obey but also to respect and love wholeheartedly. . . . Therein resides the horrifying senselessness of her suicidal gesture: this gesture is empty, there is no substantial Destiny which predetermines the symbolic co-ordinates of the hero's existence, no guilt he has to assume in a pathetically heroic gesture of self-sacrifice. 'God is dead' – the substantial Universal for which the subject is ready to sacrifice the kernel of his being is but an empty form, a ridiculous ritual devoid of any substantial content, which none the less holds the subject as its hostage.

The modern subject constitutes himself by means of such a gesture of redoubled renunciation, that is, of sacrificing the very kernel of his being, his particular substance for which he is otherwise ready to sacrifice everything. In other words, he sacrifices the substantial kernel of his being on behalf of the universal order which, however, since 'God is dead', reveals itself as an impotent empty shell. The subject thus finds himself in the void of absolute alienation, deprived even of the beauty of tragic pathos – reduced to a state of radical humiliation, turned into the empty shell of himself, he is compelled to obey the ritual and to feign enthusiastic allegiance to a Cause he no longer believes in, or even utterly despises. The more than obvious fact that *The Hostage* often approaches ridiculous and excessive melodrama is, therefore, not a weakness; rather, it functions as the index of a subjective deadlock which can no longer express itself in tragic pathos – the subject is bereft of even the minimum of tragic dignity.

The gap that separates Claudel's piece from *Antigone* is clearly perceptible here: if one were to rewrite *Antigone* as a modern tragedy, one would have to change the story so as to deprive Antigone's suicidal gesture of its sublime dignity and turn it into a case of ridiculously stubborn perseverance which is utterly out of place, and is in all probability masterminded by the very state power it pretends to call into question. . . . Lacan's precise formulation of this key point fits like a glove the position of the accused in the Stalinist show trials: in the modern tragedy, the subject 'is asked to assume with enjoyment the very injustice at which he is horrified [*il est demandé d'assumer comme une jouissance l'injustice même qui lui fait horreur*]'.[26] Is not this a perfect description of the impasse of a Stalinist subject? Not only is he forced to sacrifice everything that really matters to him – tradition, loyalty to his friends, etc. – to the Party; in addition, he is requested to do it with enthusiastic allegiance.... One is therefore tempted to risk the hypothesis that the Stalinist show trials, with their absolute (self-relating) humiliation of the accused (who is compelled to request the death penalty for himself, etc.) provide the clearest actualization in social reality itself of the fundamental structure of the modern tragedy articulated by Lacan apropos of Claudel.[27]

In so far as the subject betrays the kernel of his being, he as it were cuts off the possibility of a dignified retreat into tragic authenticity – what, then, remains for him but a 'No!', a gesture of denial which, in Claudel, appears in the guise of the dying Sygne's convulsive twitches. Such a grimace, a tic that distorts the harmony of a beautiful feminine face, registers the dimension of the Real, of the subject *qua* 'answer of the real'. This tiny, barely perceptible tic – 'a refusal, a *no*, a *non*, this tic, this grimace, in short, this flexion of the body, this psychosomatics'[28] – incomparably more horrifying than the Cyclopean vortex of the Real celebrated by Schelling, is the elementary gesture of hysteria: by means of her symptoms, the hysterical woman says 'No' to the demand of the (social) big Other to 'assume with enjoyment the very injustice at which she is horrified' – say, to pretend to find personal fulfilment and satisfaction in carrying out her 'calling' as it is defined by the ruling patriarchal order.

One should recall here Lacan's reversal of Dostoevsky's famous proposition from *The Brothers Karamazov*: *If God doesn't exist*, the father says, *then everything is permitted.* Quite evidently, a naive notion, for we analysts know full well that if God doesn't exist, then nothing at all is permitted any longer. Neurotics prove that to us every day.'[29] In other words, the fact that there is no longer a Destiny preordaining the contours of my guilt in no way allows me to enjoy the innocence of the autonomous subject delivered from any externally imposed standard of guilt: rather, this absence of Destiny makes me *absolutely guilty* – I feel guilty without knowing what I am effectively guilty of, and this ignorance makes me even more guilty. It is this 'abstract guilt' that renders the subject vulnerable to the 'totalitarian' trap. So there is a glimmer of truth in the conservative claim that the freedom of the modern subject is 'false': a hysterical disquiet pertains to his very existence because he lacks any firm social identity, which can come only from a substantial sense of Tradition. This abstract, indefinite, and for that very reason absolute guilt, which weighs down on the subject delivered from the rule of Destiny, is the ultimate object of psychoanalysis, since it lies at the root of all forms of 'psychopathology'. In this precise sense, Lacan maintains that the subject of psychoanalysis is the Cartesian subject of modern science – the subject characterized by permanent nervous strain and discontent, which come from lack of support in the big Other of Destiny.

Is not the ultimate proof of the pertinence of Lacan's reversal of Dostoevsky the shift from the Law *qua* Prohibition to the rule of 'norms' or 'ideals' we are witnessing today: in all domains of our everyday lives, from eating habits to sexual behaviour and professional success, there are fewer and fewer prohibitions, and more and more norms–ideals to follow. The suspended Law–Prohibition re-emerges in the guise of the ferocious superego that fills the subject with guilt the moment his performance is found lacking with respect to the norm or ideal. Therein resides the lesson of Catholicism much appreciated by Lacan: the function of a clear and explicit external Prohibition is not to make us guilty but, on the contrary, to relieve the unbearable pressure of the guilt which weighs upon us when the Prohibition fails to intervene. In our late-capitalist universe, the subject is not guilty when he infringes a prohibition; it is far more likely that he feels guilty when (or, rather, because) he is not happy – the command to be happy is perhaps the ultimate superego injunction. . . .[30]

. . . to France Prešeren

Slovene literature offers an example of *Versagung* which is in no way inferior to Claudel's: France Prešeren's *Baptism at Savica*, a long epic poem from the 1840s about the violent ninth-century Christianization of the Slovenes. According to the mythical narrative of origins, this poem 'founded' the Slovene nation; the truth is that – up till now, at least – every Slovene schoolboy has had to learn it by heart. A Prologue describes the heroic struggle of the last pagan Slovenes: the site of their last stand is a mountain castle surrounded by Christians. In a sanguinary night battle they are all slaughtered, with the sole exception of Črtomir, their young leader; after taking advantage of the confusion of the night to slip away, he takes refuge in an isolated pagan sanctuary run by the beautiful priestess Bogomila, his great love. Here, however, a nasty surprise awaits Črtomir: in the meantime, while he was fighting his battles, Bogomila has been converted to Christianity; she now tries passionately to persuade him to be baptized himself – the two of them can be united only in Christ. His love for her is so strong that he is ready to renounce everything for it – that is to say, the old pagan mores which form the very substance of his being. After Črtomir nods his agreement, however, expecting that in this way he will win Bogomila, he discovers another turn of the screw to the affair: Bogomila now asks him also to renounce herself, his carnal love for her – if he truly loves her, he must accept what matters to her most: a chaste life in the service of Christ.

How does Črtomir break down for the second time and renounce Bogomila herself – that is, in Lacanese, how does he fully assume symbolic castration? What intervenes at this precise point is the fascinating image: Črtomir looks at Bogomila and is struck by the beatitude of her heavenly image – the moment this image casts its spell over him, he is lost. This image is the lure *par excellence*, the place-holder of lack, or, in Lacanese, the *objet petit a* (object-cause of desire) standing over minus phi (castration) – 'castration' is generally presented in the guise of a fascinating image. The final scene: Črtomir, totally broken, undergoes the ceremony of baptism at the waterfall of Savica, in what are now the Slovene Alps. The last lines of the poem only tersely report that immediately after his baptism Črtomir went to Aquilea (a city in what is now northern Italy), was trained as a missionary and devoted his remaining days to converting pagans to Christianity; he and Bogomila never saw each other again in this world. . . .[31]

In Slovene literary theory and criticism, this poem has given rise to two opposed series of interpretations: 'Leftist' readings focus on the Prologue and assert the heroic resistance to the violent imposition of a foreign religion – Črtomir as a forerunner of contemporary struggles for national independence . . .; 'Rightist' readings take Christianization at face value and claim that the ultimate message of the poem is hope, not despair – at the end, Črtomir finds inner peace in Christ. Both series miss the subjective position of Črtomir at the end, which, of course, is precisely that of *Versagung*: after renouncing everything that matters to him – his ethnic roots, the very substance of his social being – for the sake of his love, Črtomir is led to renounce the fulfilment of this love itself, so that he finds himself 'beyond the second death', reduced to a shell of his former self and forced to promulgate a faith he himself does not believe in. . . .

One pop-psychological cliché about the so-called 'Slovene national character' is that this subjective position of Črtomir epitomizes the proverbial compromising, irresolute, self-defeating, character structure of the typical Slovene: instead of making a clear choice and assuming all its consequences (which means, in this case, either sticking to our particular ethnic roots whatever the cost, or wholeheartedly embracing the new universal Christian order), a typical Slovene prefers the undecided intermediate state – Christianity, yes, but not quite; let us keep our fingers crossed and maintain an inner distance; better a finger crossed than a finger burnt. . . .[32] The problem, however, is that the intersection of the two sets, the particular (one's ethnic roots) and the universal (Christianity), is empty, so that if one chooses the intersection, one loses everything – and the name of this radical loss, of course, is 'subject'.

In other words, the modern subject is strictly correlative with the dimension 'beyond the second death': the first death is the sacrifice of our particular, 'pathological' substance for the universal Cause; the second death is the sacrifice, the 'betrayal', of this Cause itself, so that all that remains is the void which is $, the 'barred' subject – the subject emerges only via this double, self-relating sacrifice of the very Cause for which he was ready to sacrifice everything.[33] Perhaps the fundamental fantasy of Modernity concerns the possibility of a 'synthesis' of the Particular and the Universal – the dream of a (universal) language permeated by (particular) passions, of universal-formal Reason permeated by the substance of a concrete life-world, an so on – in short, fantasy *fills out the empty set of the intersection*; its premiss is that this set is *not* empty.[34] One of the ironies of our intellectual life is that in the eyes of philosophical *doxa*, Hegel – the very philosopher who articulated the logic of the 'sacrifice of the sacrifice' – is considered the paradigmatic representative of this fantasy. Kierkegaard, Prešeren's contemporary and Hegel's great opponent, is uncannily close to Hegel in this respect: does not the Kierkegaardian notion of the Religious involve a strictly analogous gesture of double, self-relating sacrifice? First, we have to renounce the particular 'aesthetic' content for the sake of the universal ethical Law; then, Faith compels us to suspend this Law itself. . . .

We can now provide a precise definition of the trap in which Claudel's Sygne and Prešeren's Črtomir become ensnared: they both abstractly oppose the Thing itself (for Sygne, the Christian religion; for Črtomir, his love for Bogomila) to the particular life-context within which only this Thing can thrive (Sygne's attachment to the family estate and feudal tradition; Črtomir's roots in the old pagan life-world) – that is to say, they both fail to note how their renunciation of the particular content on behalf of the Thing itself effectively amounts to renunciation of the Thing.[35] In Hegelian terms: they both cling to the illusory belief that the Thing (the true Universal) can somehow persist, retain its consistency, outside its concrete conditions of existence (that the Christian religion can retain its meaning outside the *ancien régime*, in new, post-revolutionary conditions . . .). Therein resides the 'existential' kernel of the Hegelian 'negation of negation': the subject has to experience how the negation (sacrifice) of a particular content on behalf of the Thing is already the negation-sacrifice of the Thing, of that on behalf of which we sacrifice the particular content. In Claudel, Christianity – the Thing – survives, but as a mere lifeless shell of itself, bereft of its life-substance; in Prešeren, Črtomir survives as a shell of his former self, bereft of his substantial content – in short, as a *subject*.[36] That is to say, only through such a double movement of the 'sacrifice of the sacrifice' which deprives the subject of its entire substantial content can the pure subject *qua* $ emerge – can we pass from Substance to Subject.[37] (What one should bear in mind here, of course, is the way sexual difference accounts for the different attitudes of the two heroes after the experience of *Versagung*: the *man* Črtomir continues to participate in the social game – he himself becomes the agent of the very Christianization which brought about his downfall – whereas the *woman* Sygne persists in her 'No!' to the social ritual . . .)

The dialectical transubstantiation

The director's masterly deceptive manipulation of the point of view in Fritz Lang's *Secret Beyond the Door*, a variation on the Bluebeard theme, provides a disturbing case of such a loss of substantial content. Celia (Joan Bennett) is more and more convinced that her husband Mark (Michael Redgrave) is a psychopath intending to kill her; late one evening, she succumbs to panic and runs wildly out of the house into the mist-filled garden, where she confronts a male figure – the fade-out follows so quickly that the spectator is not able to ascertain its identity. This confrontation, of course, follows the classic rules of Gothic horror: when the prospective victim decides to run away, she runs into the murderer who already awaits her, as if he was aware of her attempt to escape and included it in his plan. At this point, the film cuts to Mark's voice-over and his imagined trial for Celia's murder: we are led to believe that she has been murdered by her husband. However, as Mark wanders through her room, Celia suddenly appears at the door – her unexpected appearance surprises not so much Mark (since he knows he has not killed her) but, rather, the spectator; we soon learn that the figure in the mist was not Mark but Bob, her protective brother-like ex-fiancé who had answered her call and come to save her. . . .

The surprise here is double. First, the spectator, accustomed to the standard rules of the genre, is led to expect that after the victim's *aphanisis* which follows the confrontation with the horrifying figure in the mist, the film will pass from the subjective (point-of-view) narrative to the 'objective' (impersonal) narrative; however, contrary to the spectator's expectations, the scene that follows the heroine's *aphanisis* is also told in the mode of the point-of-view narrative (of the alleged murderer). In addition, it soon becomes clear that the alleged murderer is not a murderer at all – that the crime was merely fantasized: *her (the victim's) anxiety 'overlapped' with his (the murderer's) fantasy.*[38] The reversal is thus double: first from her point of view to his; then her sudden (re)appearance which 'fictionalizes' both her narrative and his.

The libidinal economy of such a reversal from one subject's to another subject's point of view, after the first subject confronts the figure of ultimate horror and fades out, involves a kind of 'transubstantiation': it is as if the very reality of the second subject materializes, gives body to, the dream of the first – that is, as if *in the second subject, the first survives his death.* And this is what the Hegelian 'return of the Spirit to itself' is about: in the 'negation of negation', the Spirit does 'return to itself'; however, it is absolutely crucial to bear in mind the 'performative' dimension of this return – the Spirit changes in its very substance through this return-to-itself. *The Spirit to whom we return, the Spirit that returns to itself, is not the same as the Spirit that was previously lost in alienation* – what occurs in between is a kind of transubstantiation, so that this very return-to-itself marks the point at which the initial substantial Spirit is definitely lost.[39]

Suffice it to recall the loss, the self-alienation, of the Spirit of a substantial community that takes place when its organic links dissolve with the rise of abstract individualism: at the level of 'negation', this dissolution is still measured by the standard of organic unity, and therefore experienced as a loss; the 'negation of negation' occurs when the Spirit 'returns to itself' – not by way of the restitution of the lost organic community (this immediate organic unity is lost for ever), but by the full consummation of this loss, that is, by the emergence of the new determination of society's unity: no longer the immediate organic unity but the formal legal order that sustains the civil society of free individuals. This new unity is *substantially* different from the lost immediate organic unity. To put it another way: 'castration' designates the fact that the 'full' subject immediately identical with the 'pathological' substance of drives (S) has to sacrifice the unimpeded satisfaction of drives, to subordinate this substance of drives to the injunctions of an alien ethico-symbolic network – how does this subject 'return to himself'? By fully consummating this loss of substance, that is, by shifting the 'centre of gravity' of his being from S to $, from the substance of drives to the void of negativity: the subject 'returns to himself' when he no longer recognizes the kernel of his being in the substance of drives, but identifies with the void of negative self-relating. From this new standpoint, drives appear as something external and contingent, as something that is not 'truly himself'.[40]

We are now in a position to elucidate the misunderstanding at work in the usual (mis)perception of Hegel's critique of Kant. That is to say, when we are dealing with Hegel's repudiation of Kant's thesis on the unknowable character of the transcendental subject, we must be very careful to avoid the usual trap that runs as follows: according to Kant, the subject is unknowable, inaccessible to himself in his noumenal dimension, *qua* Thing, since self-consciousness is confined to the categorial opposition of subject and object (i.e. in the act of self-consciousness, the subject becomes its own object: self-consciousness is a consciousness of oneself as object). Consequently, the subject (which, precisely, is a non-object) cannot be adequately comprehended by means of the categories that define and constitute the phenomenal objective reality; for that reason, Kant is compelled to conceive of it as an unknowable X. However, the categories of objective reality (Kant's table of twelve categories) are categories of Understanding, they are fit only for the comprehension of isolated ('abstract') positive entities; in clear contrast, Hegel develops a dialectical logic of Reason that enables us to comprehend the specific dimension of subjectivity without reducing the subject to another empirical, positive object (for that reason, the second part of Hegel's *Logic*, the 'logic of Essence' which remains within the domain of 'objective logic', is followed by a third part, the 'logic of Notion', which belongs to the higher domain of 'subjective logic' and reaches beyond Kant). . . .

This argumentation, self-evident as it may appear, misses the very gist of Hegel's critique of Kant: Hegel does *not* supplement Kant's logic of abstract Understanding, which gets stuck on the threshold of the Unknowable, with *another* logic, the logic of Reason capable of penetrating Things-in-themselves; what Hegel effectively accomplishes is merely a kind of reflective inversion by means of which the very feature (mis)perceived by Kant as an epistemological obstacle turns into a positive ontological determination. The 'unknowableness' of the subject *qua* Thing is simply the way Understanding (mis)perceives the fact that the subject 'is' a non-substantial void – when Kant asserts that the transcendental subject is an unknowable, empty X, all one has to do is confer an ontological status on this epistemological determination: the subject *is* the empty Nothingness of pure self-relating. . . .

This notion of the modern, Cartesian subject *qua* the radical negativity of the double (self-relating) sacrifice also enables us to demarcate the paradoxical place of the theories of Georges Bataille, that is, of Bataille's fascination with the 'real', material sacrifice, with the different forms of holocaust and of the excessive destruction of (economic, social, etc.) reality.[41] On the one hand, of course, Bataille's topic is modern subjectivity, the radical negativity implied in the position of the pure transcendental subject. On the other hand, Bataille's universe remains the pre-Newtonian universe of balanced circular movement, or – to put it in a different way – his notion of subjectivity is definitely pre-Kantian: Bataille's 'subject' is not yet the pure void (the transcendental point of self-relating negativity), but remains an *inner-worldly, positive force*. Within these co-ordinates, the negativity which characterizes the modern subject can express itself only in the guise of a violent destruction which throws the entire circuit of nature off the rails. It is as if, in a kind of unique short circuit, *Bataille projects the negativity of the modern subject backwards, into the 'closed', pre-modern Aristotelian universe of balanced circular movement, within which this negativity can materialize itself only as an 'irrational', excessive, non-economical expenditure*. In short, what Bataille fails to take note of is that the modern (Cartesian) subject no longer needs to sacrifice goat's intestines, his children, and so on, since *his very existence already entails the most radical (redoubled, self-relating) sacrifice, the sacrifice of the very kernel of his being*. Incidentally, this failure of Bataille also throws a new light on the sacrificial violence, the obsession with the ultimate twilight of the universe, at work in Nazism: in it, we also encounter the reinscription of the radical negativity characteristic of the modern subject into the closed 'pagan' universe in which the stability of the social order is guaranteed by some kind of repeated sacrificial gesture – what we encounter in the libidinal economy of Nazism is *the modern subjectivity perceived from the standpoint of the pre-modern 'pagan' universe.*[42]

How does the Spirit return to itself?

A postmodern commonplace against Hegel is the criticism of 'restrained economy': in the dialectical process, loss and negativity are contained in advance, accounted for – what gets lost is merely the inessential aspect (and the very fact that a feature has been lost counts as the ultimate proof of its inessential status), whereas one can rest assured that the essential dimension will not only survive, but even be strengthened by the ordeal of negativity. The whole (teleological) point of the process of loss and recuperation is to enable the Absolute to purify itself, to render its essential dimension manifest by getting rid of the inessential, like a snake which, from time to time, has to cast off its skin in order to rejuvenate itself. . . .

We can see now where this reproach, which imputes to Hegel the obsessional economy of 'I can give you everything *but that*', goes wrong and misses its target: Hegel's basic premiss is that every attempt to distinguish the Essential from the Inessential always proves itself false –

whenever I resort to the strategy of renouncing the Inessential in order to save the Essential, sooner or later (but always when it's already too late) I am bound to discover that I made a fatal mistake when I decided what is essential, and the essential dimension has already slipped through my fingers. The crucial aspect of a proper dialectical reversal is this shift in the very relationship between the Essential and the Inessential – when, for example, I defend my unprincipled flattery of my superiors by claiming that it amounts to mere external accommodation, whereas deep in my heart I stick to my true convictions and despise them, I blind myself to the reality of the situation: I have already given way on what really matters, since it is my inner conviction, sincere as it may be, which is effectively 'inessential'. . . .

The 'negation of negation' is not a kind of existential sleight of hand by means of which the subject pretends to put everything at stake, but effectively sacrifices only the inessential; rather, it stands for the horrifying experience which occurs when, after sacrificing everything I considered 'inessential', I suddenly realize that the very essential dimension for the sake of which I sacrificed the inessential is already lost. The subject does save his skin, he survives the ordeal, but the price he has to pay is the loss of his very substance, of the most precious kernel of his individuality. More precisely: prior to this 'transubstantiation' the subject is not a subject at all, since *'subject' is ultimately the name for this very 'transubstantiation' of substance* which, after its dissemination, 'returns to itself', but not as 'the same'.

It is all too easy, therefore, to be misled by Hegel's notorious propositions concerning Spirit as the power of 'tarrying with the negative', that is, of resurrecting after its own death: in the ordeal of absolute negativity, the Spirit in its particular selfhood *effectively dies*, is over and done with, so that the Spirit which 'resurrects' *is not the Spirit which previously expired.* The same goes for the Resurrection: Hegel emphasizes again and again that Christ dies on the Cross for real – he returns as the Spirit of the community of believers, not in person. So, again, when, in what is perhaps the most famous single passage from his *Phenomenology*, Hegel asserts that the Spirit is capable of 'tarrying with the negative', of enduring the power of the negative, this does not mean that in the ordeal of negativity the subject has merely to clench his teeth and hold out – true, he will lose a few feathers, but, magically, everything will somehow turn out OK. . . . Hegel's whole point is that the subject *does NOT survive* the ordeal of negativity: he *effectively* loses his very essence, and passes over into his Other. One is tempted to evoke here the science-fiction theme of changed identity, when a subject biologically survives, but is no longer the same person – this is what the Hegelian transubstantiation is about, and of course, it is this very transubstantiation which distinguishes Subject from Substance: 'subject' designates that X which is able to survive the loss of its very substantial identity, and to continue to live as the 'empty shell of its former self'.

An analogous transubstantiation is at work in the Hegelian 'cunning of reason': in the triad of Ends, Means and Object, the effective unity, the mediating agency, is not the End but the *Means*: the means effectively dominate the entire process by mediating between the End and the external Object in which the End is to be realized-actualized. The End is thus far from dominating the means and the Object: the End and the external Object are the two objectivizations of means *qua* the movable medium of negativity. In short, Hegel's result is that the End is ultimately a 'means of means themselves', a means self-posited by means to set in motion its mediating activity. (It is similar with the *means* of production in Marx: the production of material goods is, of course, a means whose aim is to satisfy human needs; at a deeper level, however, this very satisfaction of human needs is a means self-posited by the means of production to set in motion its own development – the true End of the entire process is the development of the means of production as the assertion of man's domination over nature, or, as Hegel puts it, as the 'self-objectivization of the Spirit.') The point of the 'cunning of reason' is thus not that the End realizes itself via a detour: the End the subject has been pursuing throughout the process is effectively lost, since the actual End is precisely what agents caught up in the process experience as mere Means. In the end, the End is realized, but not the End which was posited at the outset, as with the subject who returns to himself, but is no longer the same 'self' as the subject who got lost at the outset. . . .

This is also how one should reformulate the different status of reflection in the 'objective' logic of essence and the 'subjective' logic of notion: the logic of essence still involves the 'objective', substantial, notion of Essence as a kind of substratum which reflects itself in its Other, that is, which posits Otherness as its inessential double (its effect, form, appearance . . .), but is unable to effectuate its full mediation with it – it endeavours to preserve the kernel of its self-identity 'undamaged', exempted from the reflective mediation, which is why it becomes entangled in a mass of aporias. It is only at the level of the notion that 'substance' effectively 'becomes subject', since in it reflection is 'absolute'; that is to say, the process of 'transubstantiation' gets under way through which substance itself becomes the predicate of (what was) its own predicate. The standard criticism of Hegel – according to which the Hegelian absolute Subject does not really expose itself to Otherness, but merely plays a narcissistic game of self-alienation and reappropriation with itself – fails to take into account the fact that in Hegelian 'alienation', the substance is *lost for good.*

Against this background, it is also possible to decipher the enigmatic ambiguity of Althusser's reference to Hegel: although Hegel is Althusser's *bête noire*, the paradigmatic case of dialectics *with* a Subject (the absolute Idea which, as it were, pulls the strings of the entire process), he is nevertheless compelled to identify the very same Hegelian dialectics as the main source of the materialist concept of a 'process without a subject [*procès sans sujet*]'. To cut a long story short, Althusser's 'process without a subject' should be rephrased as 'process without a substance', as a process not constrained by any underlying substantial unity, since what takes place in it is the very displacement of this unity from one 'centre of gravity' to another. Precisely as such, however, this process has a 'subject' – its subject is the very 'vanishing mediator' between these multiple figures of substantial unity which displace one another, the *non-lieu*, the empty set, the 'constitutive lack', which sets this process of permanent displacement in motion.

There is no subject without an empty signifier

One can also make the same point by focusing on the dialectics of In-itself and For-itself. In today's ecological struggles, the position of the 'mute In-itself' of the abstract Universal is best epitomized by an external observer who apprehends 'ecology' as the neutral universality of a genus which then subdivides itself into a multitude of species (feminist ecology, socialist ecology, New Age ecology, conservative ecology, etc.); however, for a subject who is 'within', engaged in the ecological fight, there is no such neutral universality. For a feminist ecologist, say, the impending threat of ecological catastrophe *results from* the male attitude of domination and exploitation, so that she is not a feminist *and* an ecologist – feminism provides her with the specific content of her ecological identity, that is, for her a 'non-feminist ecologist' is not another kind of ecologist, but simply somebody who *is not a true ecologist.* The – properly Hegelian – problem of the 'For-itself' of a Universal is therefore: how, under what concrete conditions, can the universal dimension become 'for itself', how can it be posited 'as such', in explicit contrast to its particular qualifications, so that I experience the specific feminist (or conservative or socialist or . . .) qualification of my ecological attitude as something contingent with respect to the universal notion of ecology?

And, back to the relationship between Derrida and Lacan – therein resides the gap which separates them: for Derrida, the subject always remains substance, whereas for Lacan (as well as for Hegel) subject is precisely that which is *not* substance. The following passage from *Grammatology* is typical:

> . . . however it [the category of the subject] is modified, however it is endowed with consciousness or unconsciousness, it will refer, by the entire thread of its history, to the substantiality of a presence unperturbed by accidents, or to the identity of the proper/selfsame in the presence of self-relationship.[44]

For Derrida, then, the notion of subject involves a minimum of substantial self-identity, a kernel of self-presence which remains the same beneath the flux of accidental changes; for Hegel, on the contrary, the term 'subject' designates the very fact that the substance, in the kernel of its identity, *is* perturbed by accidents. The 'becoming-subject of substance' stands for the gesture of *hubris* by means of which a mere accident or predicate of the substance, a subordinated moment of its totality, installs itself as the new totalizing principle and subordinates the previous Substance to itself, turning it into its own particular moment. In the passage from feudalism to capitalism, for example, money – in medieval times a clearly subordinated moment of the totality of economic relations – asserts itself as the very principle of totality (since the aim of capitalist production is profit). The 'becoming-subject' of the Substance involves such a continuous displacement of the Centre: again and again, the old Centre turns into a subordinate moment of the new totality dominated by a different structuring principle – far from being a 'deeper' underlying agency which 'pulls the strings' of this displacement of the Centre (i.e. of the structuring principle of totality), 'subject' designates the void which serves as the medium and/or operator of this process of displacement.

We are now in a position to specify the difference between the three parts of Hegel's logic: 'Being', 'Essence', and 'Notion'. In the sphere of Being, we are dealing with immediate, fixed determinations unable to endure any kind of internal dynamics – any contact with their Otherness entails their decomposition, that is to say, each of the determinations of Being simply *passes over* into another determination. In the sphere of Essence, the dynamics is already located *within* each determination: the self-identical Essence expresses-reflects itself in the plurality of its appearances. Each essential determination thus already contains its Otherness (there is no Essence which does not appear, no Cause without an effect, etc.); the problem, however, is that this Otherness is reduced to an 'inessential' attribute of a fixed, self-identical Essence unaffected by change – the process of change concerns only the 'inessential' appearances. For that very reason, each essential determination turns into its opposite: the Ground reveals itself as something which depends on what it grounds; substantial Honesty reveals itself as more vile than the superficial unprincipled opportunism it despises so much; the entire content of Essence comes from its 'inessential' appearing; and so on – therein, in these sudden turnabouts, resides the 'vertiginous' character of the logic of Essence.

In other words, dialectics takes its revenge for the assertion of the Essence as the substantial Ground exempted from the process of mediation: the very Otherness which Essence is trying to mediate-internalize as its 'inessential' appearance 'reifies' itself into a kind of counter-image to the immediate self-identity of the Essence, turns into an impenetrable Substance impervious to reflective mediation. (For example, in the eyes of the 'totalitarian' State which endeavours to establish itself as the absolute Centre of social life, society itself sooner or later appears as an impenetrable substantial Other which eludes its grasp. . . .) We pass into the sphere of Notion the moment we drop this residual self-identical Ground of the process, so that the process effectively becomes a 'process without a substance', the process of the very permanent displacement of every totalizing principle, every 'centre of gravity' – *therein* resides the notorious 'fluidity' of the Notion.

The trap to be avoided here, therefore, is to conceive Notion as a reflection of Essence which has succeeded: as if the movement of reflection which, within the 'logic of Essence', fails to internalize its other, and therefore remains caught in the external duality of the couples of opposites (Essence–Appearance, etc.), in the 'logic of Notion' finally *succeeds* in sublating–mediating its Otherness, in turning it into a transparent medium of its own self-identity. What such a reading of Hegel fails to take into account is the price which has to be paid for this 'transparency': the process becomes 'transparent' at the price of 'transubstantiation' – there is no longer a unique Centre, a central agent which can be said to remain substantially 'the same' in the process of 'externalizing' itself and then reappropriating its Otherness, since in the movement of the 'return-to-itself' the very identity of this 'self' is irreversibly displaced.[45]

We should therefore renounce the usual formulas of the Hegelian 'concrete Universal' as the Universal which is the unity of itself and its Other (the Particular) – that is, not abstractly opposed to the wealth of the particular content, but the very movement of self-mediation and self-sublating of the Particular: the problem with this standard 'organic' image of 'concrete Universal' as a living substantial Totality which reproduces itself through the very movement of its particular content is that in it, the Universal is not yet 'for itself', that is, posited as such. In this precise sense, the emergence of the subject is correlative to the positing of the Universal 'as such', in its opposition to the particular content.

Let us return to our example of ecology: every attempt to define a substantial core of ecology, the minimal content with which every ecologist has to agree, is necessarily doomed to fail, since this very core shifts in the struggle for ideological hegemony. For a socialist, the ultimate cause of the ecological crisis is to be found in the profit-orientated capitalist mode of production, which is why anti-capitalism is for him the very core of a true ecological attitude; for a conservative, the ecological crisis is rooted in man's false pride and will to dominate the universe, so that humble respect for tradition forms the very core of a true ecological attitude; for a feminist, the ecological crisis results from male domination; and so forth. What is at stake in the ideologico-political struggle, of course, is the very positive content which will fill out the 'empty' signifier 'ecology': *what will it mean* to be an 'ecologist' (or a 'democrat', or to belong to a 'nation' . . .)? And our point is that *the emergence of 'subject' is strictly correlative to the positing of this central signifier as 'empty'*: I become a 'subject' when the universal signifier to which I refer ('ecology', in our case) is no longer connected by an umbilical cord to some particular content, but is experienced as an empty space to be filled out by the particular (feminist, conservative, state, pro-market, socialist . . .) content. This 'empty' signifier whose positive content is the 'stake' of the ideologico-political struggle 'represents the subject for the other signifiers', for the signifiers which stand for its positive content.

Derrida often draws attention to the 'Yes!' of a response demanded by even the most self-inclusive dialectical totality of the accomplished System: even such a totality, in order to assert itself, has to address itself to an Other with a request to say 'Yes!' to it, and is what it is only by this redoubling 'Yes!', by being 're-marked' by it – only through this act of re-marking is a System performatively constituted, and acquires the actuality of an event. What if, however, at this very point where he seems to open up a crack in the edifice of Absolute Knowing, Derrida is much closer to Hegel than he seems? That is to say, what if this performative necessity of a minimal address to the Other provides the properly Hegelian answer to one of the standard criticisms of Hegel: why does the dialectical process 'move forward' at all? What necessity urges a 'figure' to dissolve itself and to pass into a 'higher' one? The answer resides in the fact that a 'figure' is never directly 'itself': it *becomes itself* via a minimal referral to an Other, via a re-mark which introduces a minimum of inconsistency into it, and it is this irreducible externality of the re-mark inscribed into the very self-identity of a figure which prevents it from resigning itself to a complacent paralysis. . . .

The precipitate identification

This step from Hegel's and Schelling's 'formal envelope of error' to their common *Grundoperation* also enables us to dispel another temptation, perhaps no less dangerous than the 'philosophical' reading of Lacan which focuses on the notions of symbolic castration and lack: the obverse, almost complementary, temptation of identifying the *pure positivity of drive* as the hidden centre of gravity upon which Lacan was slowly converging. As with the other temptation, the possibility of this (mis)reading is also contained in Lacan's own texts: Lacan's unmistakable nostalgia for Spinoza in the last pages of his *Seminar XI* acquires prime importance when, following Deleuze's path-breaking interpretations, Spinoza is put alongside Nietzsche as the philosopher who asserted a pure, positive difference delivered from the vestiges of negativity, lack and mediation.

Paraphrasing the best-known Sherlock Holmes lines, one should draw attention to the curious accident with Nietzsche in Lacan's texts and seminars: for all practical purposes, Nietzsche is never mentioned – and therein resides the curious accident. That is to say, is not the pure drive, its repetitive circular movement, as that which remains of desire after *la traversée du fantasme*,[46] another name for the Nietzschean 'eternal return of the same', for an assertive movement which wills to happen forever, again and again, what it wills once? It is tempting, therefore, to interpret the deeply symptomatic fact that Nietzsche is the 'big Absent' of Lacan – apart from a couple of cursory mentions,[47] one looks in vain for Nietzsche's name in Lacan's texts and seminars – as the negative proof that the 'eternal return of the same' already provides the definitive philosophical formulation of the enigmatic subjective position of drive beyond the framework of fantasy, the position Lacan was approaching hesitantly towards the end of his teaching. In this way we arrive at the unconstrained 'lightness of being': the circular movement of repetition loses its inert weight; no longer anchored to a traumatic kernel which it tries (and repeatedly fails) to recuperate, it turns into a free-floating dance of *jouissance* which wants to enjoy itself for all eternity. . . . [48] Our premiss, however, is the exact opposite to this 'Nietzscheanization' of Lacan: what gets lost in it is precisely the *Grundoperation* of German Idealism, the logic of 'vanishing mediator' we have endeavoured to articulate. . . .

At stake here is probably the most radical of all philosophical questions: is the alternative of *desire* and *drive*, of *lack* and *positivity* – the alternative between, on the one hand, remaining within the constraints of the negative ontology of lack, of man's constitutive 'out-of-jointedness', and so on, and, on the other, yielding to the pure positivity of drive *qua* the eternal return of the will which wills its object for ever – truly the ultimate, unavoidable alternative of our lives?[49] Our premiss, of course, is that the *Grundoperation* of German Idealism points towards a *tertium datur*; and, furthermore, that it is only this third position which enables us to confront the key problem of 'the morning after': what happens – not at the end of the psychoanalytic cure, but *afterwards*, once the cure is over? That is to say: it is easy to suspend the big Other by means of the act *qua* real, to experience the 'nonexistence of the big Other' in a momentary flash – however, what do we do *after* we have traversed the fantasy? Is it not necessary to resort again to some kind of big Other? How are we to avoid the painful conclusion that the experience of the nonexistence of the big Other, of the act *qua* real, is merely a fleeting 'vanishing mediator' between two Orders, an enthusiastic intermediate moment necessarily followed by a sobering relapse into the reign of the big Other? What corresponds to it in the domain of politics is the resigned conservative notion of revolution as a transitory moment of liberation, the suspension of social authority, which unavoidably gives rise to the backlash of an even more oppressive power.

Is the battle for freedom worth fighting, then? What are the modalities of the big Other which emerges after the experience of its nonexistence? Is there enough difference between the 'old' and the 'new' big Other? The obvious solution, of course, is *cynicism* as the post-revolutionary attitude *par excellence*: fully aware of the nullity of the big Other, we feign allegiance to it and play its game, as it were, 'with our fingers crossed' – in this way, however, one merely ducks the issue, since cynical distance, by definition, covers the true dimension of our actual involvement.[50] Are we then condemned to the resigned conclusion that the founding gesture is necessarily eclipsed by the very state of things to which it gives birth?

The way out of this deadlock is none the less already indicated in Lacan's early writing on logical time;[51] here is a somewhat simplified and abbreviated version of the logical puzzle of the three prisoners apropos of which Lacan develops the three modalities of logical time. The govenor of a prison can, on the basis of an amnesty, release one of three prisoners. In order to decide which one, he sets them a test of logic. The prisoners know that there are five hats, three white and two black. Three of these hats are distributed to the prisoners, who then sit in a triangle, so that each of them can see the colour of the hats of the other two, but not the colour of the hat on his own head. The winner is the first to guess the colour of his own hat, which he signifies by standing up and leaving the room. We have three possible situations:

- If one prisoner has a white hat and the other two have black hats, the one with the white hat can immediately 'see' that his is white by a simple process of deduction: 'There are only two black hats; I can see them on the others' heads, so mine is white.' So there is no time involved here, only an 'instant of the gaze'.

- The second possibility is that there are two white hats and one black hat. If mine is white, I will reason like this: 'I can see one black hat and one white, so mine is either white or black. However, if mine is black, then the prisoner with the white hat would see two black hats and immediately conclude that his is white – since he has not done so, mine is white too.' Here, some time had to elapse – that is to say, we already need a certain 'time for understanding': I, as it were, 'transpose' myself into the reasoning of the other; I arrive at my conclusion on the basis of the fact that the other does not act.

- The third possibility – three white hats – is the most complex. Here the reasoning goes like this: 'I can see two white hats, so mine is either white or black. If mine is black, then either of the two remaining prisoners would reason in the following way: "I can see a black hat and a white hat. So if mine is black, the prisoner with the white hat would see two black hats, and would stand up and leave immediately. However, he has not done so. So mine is white – I shall stand up and leave." But since none of the other two prisoners is standing up, mine is white too.'

Here, however, Lacan points out how this solution requires a double delay and a hindered, interrupted gesture. That is to say: if all three prisoners are of equal intelligence, then after the first delay, that is, upon noticing that none of the others is making any move, they will all get up at the same moment – then stiffen, exchanging perplexed glances: the problem is that they will not know the meaning of the other's gesture (each of them will ask himself: 'Did the others get up for the same reason as me, or did they do it because they saw a *black* hat on my head?'). Only now, upon noticing that they all share the same hesitation, will they be able to jump to the final conclusion: the very fact of the shared hesitation is proof that they are all in the same boat – they all have white hats on their heads. At this precise moment, delay shifts into haste, with each of the prisoners saying to himself 'I must rush to the door before the others overtake me!'

It is easy to recognize how a specific mode of subjectivity corresponds to each of the three moments of logical time: the 'instant of gaze' implies the impersonal 'one' ('one sees'), the neutral subject of logical reasoning without any intersubjective dialectic; the 'time for understanding' already involves intersubjectivity – that is to say, in order to arrive at the conclusion that my hat is white, I have to 'transpose' myself into the other's reasoning (if the other prisoner with the white hat were to see a black hat on my head, he would immediately know that his must be black and stand up – since he has not done so, mine is white too). However, this intersubjectivity remains that of the 'indefinite reciprocal subject', as Lacan puts it: a simple reciprocal capability to take the other's reasoning into account. It is only the third moment, the 'moment of conclusion', which provides the true 'genesis of the I': what takes place in it is the shift from $ to S_1, from the void of the subject epitomized by the radical uncertainty as to what I am – that is, by the utter undecidability of my status – to the conclusion that I am white, to the assumption of symbolic identity – 'That's me!'.

We must bear in mind here the anti-Lévi-Straussian thrust of these Lacan's ruminations. Claude Lévi-Strauss conceived the symbolic order as an asubjective structure, an objective field in which every individual occupies, fills in, his or her preordained place; what Lacan invokes is the 'genesis' of this objective socio-symbolic identity: if we simply wait for a symbolic place to be allotted to us, we will never live to see it – that is to say, in the case of a symbolic mandate, we never simply ascertain what we are, we 'become what we are' by means of a precipitate subjective gesture. This precipitate identification involves the shift from object to signifier: the (white or black) hat is the object I am, and its invisibility to me expresses the fact that I can never get an insight into 'what I am as an object' (i.e. $ and *a* are topologically incompatible) – when I say 'I am white', I assume a symbolic identity which fills out the void of the uncertainty as to my being. What accounts for this anticipatory overtaking is the *inconclusive* character of the causal chain: the symbolic order is ruled by the 'principle of insufficient reason': within the space of symbolic intersubjectivity, I can never simply ascertain what I am; this is why my 'objective' social identity is established by means of 'subjective' anticipation. The significant detail usually passed over in silence is that Lacan quotes as the exemplary political case of such collective identification the Stalinist Communist's affirmation of orthodoxy: I hasten to promulgate my true Communist credentials out of fear that others will expel me as a revisionist traitor. . . .

So – back to our problem of the emergence of the big Other – what strikes the eye when one reads Lacan's text on logical time 'backwards', applying to it concepts which were elaborated later, is how *the big Other (intersubjectivity in its proper dimension) emerges only in the third time (the 'moment for concluding')*. The first time (the 'instant of looking') involves a solitary subject who immediately 'sees' the state of things; in the second time (the 'time for understanding'), the subject transposes himself into the reasoning of the other – we are dealing here with the mirror-relationship to the other, not yet with the big Other. It is only with the third time – when, by means of the gesture of precipitate identification, of an act *not covered by the big Other's guarantee*, I recognize myself in my symbolic identity-mandate (as a Communist, an American, a democrat …) – that the dimension of the big Other becomes operative. The big Other is not 'always-already here', ready to provide a cover for my decision: I do not merely fill in, occupy, a preordained place which awaits me in the symbolic structure – on the contrary, it is the very subjective act of recognition which, by means of its precipitate character, *establishes* the big Other *qua* atemporal–synchronous structural order.

The semblance of the 'objective Spirit'

It is against this background that one should consider the shift in Lacan's teaching from his radical anti-nominalism – from his 'realism' of the symbolic structure (the big Other which predetermines the subject's acts) – of the 1950s to his 'fictionalism' (rather than nominalism) of the 1970s ('the big Other doesn't exist', the symbolic order is an order of fictions): in the last years of his teaching, Lacan increasingly emphasizes that the symbolic order is a *semblant*, a fiction with no guarantee of validity. The identity of A and *a*, of the big Other and the act *qua objet petit a*, is comprehensible only if one conceives the big Other as the 'virtual' order of symbolic fictions. When Lacan passes from the 'realism' of the big Other to the notion of its fictional nature, this shift is thus strictly correlative to the assertion that there is no Other of the Other, no meta-guarantee of the validity of the symbolic order within which the subject dwells; the most succinct formulation of this lack of the ultimate guarantee was provided by Wittgenstein's sceptical paradox which renders visible the uncanny fact that I can never be absolutely certain – not only about the rule my partner in communication is following, but even about the rule I myself obey in what I do.

The crucial point not to be missed here is that this undecidability, this radical uncertainty, this lack of guarantee concerning the meaning of my partner's words or the rules which regulate his/her use of well-known words ('How can I ever be sure that he means the same thing as me by his word?') is not a deficiency but a positive feature, the ultimate proof of my inclusion in the big Other: the big Other 'functions' as the substance of our being, we are 'within', effectively embedded in it, precisely and only in so far as its status is irreducibly undecidable, lacking any guarantee – any proof of its validity would presuppose a kind of external distance of the subject towards the symbolic order. It was Hegel who pointed out that the spiritual substance is always marked by such a tautological abyss – 'it is because it is'.

This notion of the 'virtual' big Other also enables us to approach anew the traditional sociological alternative of methodological individualism, whose basic premiss is the primacy of individuals and which, consequently, insists on the need to derive trans-individual collective entities from the interaction of individuals, from the mutual recognition of their intentions ('common knowledge'), and so on; and, on the other hand, of the Durkheimian presupposition of Society as the substantial Order which is 'always-already here', that is, which precedes individuals and serves as the spiritual foundation of their being, somewhat like the Hegelian 'objective Spirit'. The 'realist' Lacan of the 1950s continues to conceive, in a Durkheimian mode, the big Other as the substantial order which is 'always-already here', providing the unsurpassable horizon of the subjective experience; whereas the late 'fictionalist' Lacan derives the social substance (the 'big Other') from the interaction of individuals, but with a paradoxical twist which turns upside down the individualist-nominalist reduction of the social Substance to 'common knowledge', to the space of mutually recognized subjective intentions. At stake here is nothing less than the enigma of the emergence of the big Other: how is it possible for an individual to perceive his intersubjective environs not as the multitude of *others*, fellow-creatures like himself, but as a radically asymmetrical field of the 'big Other'? How does he pass from the mirror-like mutual reflection of other individuals ('I think about what he thinks that I think that he thinks', etc.) to 'objective Spirit', to the order of Mores *qua* impersonal 'reified' Order which cannot be reduced to the simple collection of 'all others'? When, for example, does the social injunction change from '(I'm saying that) you should do this!' to the impersonal 'This is how *it is done*!'?

What we encounter here is the key Hegelian problem of how we are to think Substance simultaneously as posited by subjects and as an In-itself: how is it possible for individuals to *posit* their social Substance by means of their social activity, but to posit it precisely as an *In-itself*, as an independent, presupposed foundation of their activity? From the individualist-nominalist point of view, the big Other emerges as the outcome of the process in the course of which individuals gradually recognize some shared content: when, again and again, I experience the fact that most of the people around me react in a similar way to the same signal or situation, this mode of reaction 'reifies' into an impersonal 'rule'. The individualist nominalist, of course, is quick to add that a margin of uncertainty always remains: this shared content is never fully guaranteed, it is always possible that some new experience will belie it – however, notwithstanding such extreme cases, we are all engaged in the gradual formation of the universe of shared values and rules. . . .

Lacan's Hegelian solution to this impasse is paradoxical and very refined. He accepts the communitarian critique of nominalist individualism, according to which it is illegitimate to reduce social Substance to the interaction of individuals: the spiritual Substance of a community is *always-already here* as the foundation of the individuals' interaction, as its ultimate frame of reference, so it can never be generated from this interaction. The passage from individuals' interaction to social Substance involves a leap, a kind of leap of faith, which can never be accounted for by the individual's strategic reasoning about the intentions of other individuals: no matter how intricate and reflective this reasoning, the gap of a fundamental impossibility forever separates the interaction of individuals from the In-itself of the spiritual substance. However, the conclusion Lacan draws from this impossibility is not the obvious one: his point is not that since one cannot derive spiritual Substance from the interaction of individuals, one has to presuppose it as an In-itself which precedes this interaction. In an (unacknowledged) Hegelian way, Lacan asserts that *it is this very impossibility which links an individual to his spiritual substance*: the collective substance emerges *because* individuals can never fully co-ordinate their intentions, become transparent to each other.

This impossibility of co-ordinating intentions, of course, points towards the 'materialist notion of subject': the primordial experience of the other subject as an opaque Thing. The very surplus of the 'objective Spirit' over (other) individuals, of the *collective* over the mere *collection* of others, thus bears witness to the fact that others forever remain an impenetrable enigma. In short, *impossibility is primordial, and the spiritual substance is the virtual supplement to this impossibility*: if individuals were able to co-ordinate their intentions via shared knowledge, there would be no need for the big Other, for the spiritual Substance as a spectral entity experienced by every individual as an external In-itself – the Habermasian intersubjectivity, the interaction of subjects grounded in the rules of rational argumentation, would suffice. The problem is that our everyday intersubjective experience of belonging to a spiritual Substance always relies on an In-itself beyond direct intersubjective interaction – a 'Nation', for example, is 'effectively' nothing more than the collection of the individuals who form it; it acquires effective existence only in the deeds of these individuals; however, it is part of the very structure of a Nation, of national identification, that each of these individuals experiences it as his spiritual–social Substance which exists independently of him and provides the foundation of his being.

One should bear in mind the Hegelian nature of this reversal – its strict anaology with Hegel's critique of the Kantian Thing-in-itself (the barrier of impossibility comes first; the Thing is ultimately nothing but the spectre which fills out the void of this impossibility): the big Other is a fiction, a pure presupposition, an *unsubstantiated* (in all the connotations of the term) hypothesis which fills out the void of the radical uncertainty as to the other's intentions (*'Che vuoi?'*). Derrida seems to follow the same logic when, in *The Gift of Death*, he reverses the relationship between the notion of an innermost secret in the heart of the subject, hidden even from himself (the mystery of the unaccountable act of decision, for example) and God (the gaze of the Other who sees this innermost secret hidden even from ourselves): 'God is the name of the possibility I have of keeping a secret that is visible from the interior but not from the exterior.'[52] Therein consists what one is tempted to call, without even the minimum of irony, the *materialist notion of God*: 'God' is nothing but a name for the possibility of this unaccountable secret of 'pure gift' beyond all accountancy, beyond all economy of exchange. For that reason, the criticism that the notion of God (the gaze which sees it all) 'reinscribes' the pure secret into the economy of presence (there is the One-God who sees it all, who takes the unaccountable into account, who economizes the pure expenditure . . .) somehow misses the point: 'God' merely keeps open, as it were, the possibility of the pure expenditure beyond the 'restrained economy' of exchange. In our everyday language, 'God only knows' means that *nobody* (no actual subject) knows; along the same lines, 'God only sees the secret of our decision' means that the secret is impenetrable.

The transcendence of the big Other *qua* substantial In-itself – that is, the order of 'objective spirit' which exists independently of the subject's activity – is therefore a kind of necessary perspective illusion; it is the form in the guise of which the subject (mis)perceives his very incapacity to attain the In-itself of the real other whose true intentions remain impenetrable. In this precise sense, the status of the spiritual Substance is virtual: what is virtual about the big Other is its very In-itself, that on account of which the big Other cannot be reduced to the intentions, meanings, psychical states, and so on, of effectively existing individuals.

An individual experiences his society not as a mere collection of individuals but as an order which transcends these individuals and forms the substance of their lives – and it is this very substantial In-itself which is purely virtual, a symbolic fiction, since it exists merely as the *presupposition*, by each of the individuals, of the already-existing co-ordination of all other individuals. In other words, far from depending on a kind of minimal co-ordination individuals were able to reach *in spite of* the opacity of their true intentions, the spiritual Substance emerges as the way to avoid the impasse of this opacity by *presupposing the co-ordination-of-intentions as already given* in the purely virtual Third Order of impersonal rules, so that now the problem is no longer 'Do individuals truly understand *each other*?', but 'Does every individual follow the *common rules*?'. In this precise sense, every human community is 'virtual': founded upon rules, values, and so on, whose validity is by definition *presupposed*, never conclusively *proven* – the status of the big Other is forever that of a *semblance*.

The symbolic sleight of hand

Hegel's answer to the perennial question of the Enlightenment – 'Is it possible to deceive the majority of the people?' – is a decisive 'No!'. However, the reasoning behind it has nothing whatsoever to do with confidence in the substantial good sense and prudence of the majority; rather, it relies on a circular-performative definition of what is 'true' in the social domain: even if some notion was first imposed as a purely instrumental means of ideological deception, the moment the majority of the people fully accept this notion as the foundation of their social existence, we are no longer dealing with a lie but with the substantial truth of a community.

In the domain of contemporary pragmatics and theory of actions, Pierre Livet reached the same conclusion: crucial for the functioning of a symbolic community is the *undecidable status of error*.[53] Livet's starting point is the strategic reasoning of an individual in a situation epitomized by the well-known prisoner's dilemma: as long as the individual remains within the 'rational' pursuit of his egotistic interest, caught in the mirror-game of what he knows others know that he knows, and so on, true co-operation can never take place; the only solution, the only way out of the impasse, is for him to make a move which, from the standpoint of pure rational strategic reasoning, is an 'error', an 'irrational' move – everything then depends on how his partners react to this 'error'. If they, as it were, pick it up and answer it with a corresponding 'error' of their own, we shift from strategic interplay to genuine co-operation. However, we can never be sure of how our 'irrational' first move will function: will it be received as a mere error, or will it set genuine co-operation in motion, that is, will it function as what Derrida, in his reading of Hegel in *Glas*, called the primordial Yes!, the gesture of 'irrational' gift which sets in motion the process of exchange. This 'magic' reversal of an 'error' into the founding gesture of co-operation can also occur in the opposite direction, 'backwards': in the course of the disintegration of an 'organic' community into egotistic individualism, it can well happen that a gesture which has hitherto been part of the standard procedures of co-operation (the code of honour, solidarity with those in distress, etc.) is suddenly perceived as a stupid error to be taken advantage of. . . .

And again, the crucial point is that this structural impossibility of verifying the rules or intentions which underlie our socio-symbolic activity, this undecidability between error and co-operation, is the positive condition of genuine co-operation: the moment we invest another subject with the capacity to possess and determine the rules which control the true meaning of our speech, we no longer participate in genuine symbolic co-operation, since we conceive ourselves as a pure instrument manipulated by those who control the rules of the game. In this case, *the symbolic order loses its virtual status* – that is the most succinct definition of *paranoia*. Let us recall the reference to Nation: Nation is an 'open' notion; no subject controls its 'true meaning'; *and, for that very reason, it can serve as the frame for genuine co-operation*, that is, as the substance of our social being, not a mere deceptive ploy manipulated by the rulers in order to control and exploit their subordinates.

We are effectively dealing with 'spiritual Substance' when a notion which was originally imposed as a means of ideological deception and manipulation unexpectedly escapes the control of its creator and starts to lead a life of its own. The Christian religion, violently imposed on a colonized population by the colonizing power, was often appropriated by the colonized and used as a means of articulating their genuine aspirations. The exemplary case of such a 'reinscription' is the 'Virgin of Guadeloupe', the dark-skinned Virgin Mary who appeared in 1531 in a vision to an Indian called Juan Diego, on a hill near Mexico City where Tonatzin, mother of the Aztec gods, had long been worshipped – this apparition marks the moment of the reappropriation of Christianity by the aboriginal Indian population.

A genuine community thus emerges by means of such a paradoxical reversal: instead of endlessly pursuing the hopeless search for some positive common denominator, I *presuppose this denominator as already present* – and the price to be paid is the *virtualization* of this denominator. What we are dealing with here is a kind of short circuit, a deceptive substitution: future is confused with past, what is to come is confused with – referred to, presented as – what is already here. The gesture of 'declaration' – of declaring oneself a free subject, for example – is always performed 'on trust': it refers to, relies on, something which, perhaps, will emerge as the outcome of this very act of declaration. In other words, such a gesture sets in motion a process which, retroactively, will ground it – and if this process is to take off, the deception is necessary: that is to say, its (possible) consequence *must* be presupposed as already present. One can see how the very basic structure of the symbolic order involves the illusion of predestination – or, to use the psychoanalytic term, the loop of 'transference': for Meaning to emerge, it must be presupposed as already given. This *futur antérieur* of Meaning bears witness to the virtual character of the big Other: the big Other is a hypothesis which never directly 'is', it merely 'will have been'.

Therein resides the fundamental enigma of the symbolic community: how is it possible to perform this sleight of hand constitutive of the symbolic order, this deceitful presentation of what is yet to come as already given? Lacan provides a precise answer: the presupposed co-ordination concerns not the level of the signified (of some shared positive content) but the level of the *signifier*. The undecidability with regard to the signified (do others really intend the same as me?) converts into an exceptional signifier, the empty Master-Signifier, the signifier-without-signified. 'Nation', 'Democracy', 'Socialism' and other Causes stand for that 'something' about which we are never sure what, exactly, it is – the point is, rather, that by identifying with Nation we signal our acceptance of *what others accept*, with a Master-Signifier which serves as the rallying point for all the others. In other words, identification with such an empty Master-Signifier is, in its most basic dimension, *identification with the very gesture of identification*. We can now see in what precise sense the status of the signifier as such is virtual: virtuality is the virtuality of the signified, that is, the signifier relies on a 'meaning-to-come' which, although it is never fully actualized, functions as if it is already effective. When the signifier 'our Nation' starts to function as the rallying point for a group of people, it *effectively* co-ordinates their activity, although each of them may have a different notion of what 'our Nation' means.[54]

The ending of Michael Curtiz's *Casablanca* (Humphrey Bogart staying in Casablanca and letting Ingrid Bergman go with her heroic husband) is so deeply satisfactory because it condenses, in one and the same gesture, three attitudes which correspond to the triad of Aesthetic–Imaginary, Ethical–Symbolic and Religious–Real. The first, 'aesthetic', way to read Bogart's gesture is to discern in it an awareness that although they are passionately in love, the fulfilment of their relationship (the two of them staying together) would necessarily turn sour – so it's better to maintain the dream of possible happiness. . . . The second reading is ethical: Bogart gives preference to the universal political Cause over the idiosyncrasy of private pleasure (thereby proving worthy of Bergman's love). There is, however, a third possible reading which portrays Bogart's final renunciation as a cruel narcissistic act of vengeance on Bergman – as a punishment for her letting him down in Paris: now that he has made her confess that she truly loves him, it is now his turn to reject her in a gesture whose cynical message is 'You wanted your husband – now you're stuck with him, even if you prefer me!'. This very logic of vengeful, humiliating and cruel 'settling of accounts' makes Bogart's final gesture 'religious', not merely 'aesthetic'.

Of course, our point is that Bogart's gesture of renunciation is the symbolic gesture at its purest, which is why it is wrong to ask 'Which of these three readings is true?' – the impact of Bogart's final gesture relies precisely on the fact that it serves as a kind of neutral 'container' for all three libidinal attitudes, so that one and the same gesture satisfies a multitude of inconsistent, even contradictory, desires (to avoid the disappointment of realizing one's desire; to fascinate the woman by assuming a moral stance of self-sacrifice; to take vengeance for a narcissistic wound). Therein resides the paradoxical achievement of symbolization: the vain quest for the 'true meaning' (the ultimate signified) is supplanted by a unique signifying gesture.

'A is a'

Our first result, therefore, is that the act and the big Other, far from being simply opposed, are intertwined in a constitutive way: the symbolic order *qua* 'atemporal' transsubjective structure which predetermines the subject's place *hinges on a temporal act (of precipitate recognition) not 'covered' by the big Other* (in the banking-financial meaning of the term). When I recognize myself as a 'Socialist', I thereby posit the very 'objective' frame of reference which allows for my 'subjective' identification. Or – to put it in a slightly different way – the 'objectivity' of the big Other implies a redoubled 'subjective' reflection: I am what (I think that others think that I think that) I am. . . . This precise formulation also places an obstacle in the path of the 'humanist' misreading of the interdependence of the subject and the big Other: the point is *not* that the big Other (the symbolic structure) is 'always-already here', but incomplete, 'non-all', and that the subject somehow finds a niche of his own, a margin of freedom, in the inconsistencies and lacks of the big Other. When Lacan asserts that there is a subject only in so far as there is a lack in the Other, only in so far as the structure is 'non-all', inconsistent, he has something quite different in mind: it is the very supplement of my 'subjective' act of decision (of precipitate identification) which changes the dispersed, 'non-all' collection of signifiers into the 'objective' order of the big Other.[55]

From a strictly Hegelian standpoint, the alternative between persisting in the solitude of the act which suspends the big Other and 'compromising one's desire' by accepting one's place in the big Other (the socio-symbolic order) is a false one, the last trap laid by abstract Understanding in order to prevent us from attaining true philosophical speculation. The ultimate speculative identity is the identity of the act and the Other: an authentic act momentarily suspends the big Other, but it is simultaneously *the 'vanishing mediator' which grounds, brings into existence, the big Other*. In other words, the proposition 'A is *a*' displays the precise structure of *speculative judgement* in which the identity of the two elements is mediated by a central impossibility: A, the big Other, the symbolic order, is inherently 'barred', hindered, structured around the void of a central impossibility; it always falls short of its notion; this central impossibility is its condition of possibility, and the *objet a* is precisely the paradoxical object which gives body to this impossibility, which is nothing but the materialization of this impossibility.[56] In this precise sense, *a* is the object-cause of desire: *it does not effectively pre-exist desire as that which arouses it, it merely gives body to its inherent deadlock, to the fact that desire is never satisfied by any positive object*; that is to say, apropos of every positive object, the subject's experience will always be a 'this is not *that*'.[57]

Or – to put it in a slightly different way – one should draw all the consequences from the fact that the big Other is the field of *supposed* knowledge, that is, that it is strictly correlative to the effect of *transference* (in exactly the sense in which Kant claims that the moral Law acquires actual existence only in the subject's *respect* for it). 'Transference' designates the subject's trust in the meaning-to-come: in the psycho-analytic cure, for example, the transferential relationship with the analyst bears witness to the patient's confidence that the analyst 'is in the know' – the analyst's presence is the guarantee that the patient's symptoms possess some secret meaning yet to be discovered. Consequently, in so far as the big Other functions as the guarantee of the meaning-to-come, the very fact of the big Other involves the subjective gesture of precipitation. In other words: how do we pass from the 'non-all', dispersed, inconsistent collection of signifiers to the big Other *qua* consistent order? By supplementing the inconsistent series of signifiers with a Master-Signifier, S_1, a signifier of the pure potentiality of meaning-to-come; by this precipitation (the intervention of an 'empty' signifier which stands in for the meaning-to-come) the symbolic field is completed, changed into a closed order.[58] Since, however, the transferential relationship is by definition dependent on a subject which is in itself divided/split, a subject which stands under the sign of lack and negativity (only such a dislocated subject has the urge to establish a support for itself in the big Other via the gesture of precipitate identification), this means that the big Other hinges on a divided/split subject. For that reason, the dissolution of transference (at the end of the psychoanalytic cure), the experience that 'the big Other doesn't exist', and 'subjective destitution' are strictly equivalent.

In so far as, according to Lacan, the status of the act is ultimately that of the object (*objet petit a*), it would be expedient to mention here Dieter Hombach's recent attempt to account for the status of strange objects like quarks or gluons in quantum physics: although theory itself defines these objects as entities which can never be empirically isolated and verified, one has to presuppose them if the theoretical edifice is to maintain its consistency. According to Hombach, these objects are a kind of pseudo-object brought about by the self-referential generative movement of the theory itself: they merely materialize, give body to, a statistic fictional entity.[59] Our point, of course, is that the status of the Lacanian *objet petit a* is exactly homologous: is not *language*, the symbolic order, the crucial example of a 'self-organized' system, a system which itself brings about the otherness to which it refers, a system which always self-referentially intervenes in ('disturbs') its object, so that it ultimately speaks only about itself? And *objet petit a* is precisely the paradoxical object generated by language itself as its 'fall-off', as the material left-over of the purely self-referential movement of signifiers: *objet a* is a pure semblance of an object which gives body to the self-referential movement of the symbolic order.

One can also put it in the following way: the symbolic order (the big Other) is organized around a hole in its very heart, around the traumatic Thing which makes it 'non-all'; it is defined by the impossibility of attaining the Thing; however, it is this very reference to the void of the Thing that opens up the space for symbolization, since without it the symbolic order would immediately 'collapse' into the designated reality – that is to say, the distance that separates 'words' from 'things' would disappear. The void of the Thing is therefore *both things at the same time*: the inaccessible 'hard kernel' around which the symbolization turns, which eludes it, the cause of its failure, *and the very space of symbolization*, its condition of possibility. That is the 'loop' of symbolization: the very failure of symbolization opens up the void within which the process of symbolization takes place.

This ultimate identity of opposites, the identity of the Thing and the

Other, perhaps the hardest speculative nut to crack, also enables us to provide an answer to a criticism of Lacan which – on a first approach, at least – cannot but strike us as convincing: is not Lacanian theory confined to a very limited aspect of subjectivity – to what keeps us, human subjects, caught in the vicious cycle of compulsion-to-repeat, constrained by the phantasmatic frame, overdetermined by the symbolic network, captivated by the mirror-image, and so on? Does not Lacan's fundamental triad of Imaginary–Symbolic–Real effectively amount to a matrix of the three modes of a subject's captivity, of its being at the mercy of some external mechanism or cause: imaginary captivation, overdetermination by the symbolic structure, the attraction exerted by some traumatic encounter of the real? But is this the whole truth? Is there not also another side to human experience, the dimension of invention and creativity, the subject's capacity to define his/her own space of realization, to concoct his/her own existential project, to 'define' him- or herself? Is there a place in Lacan's theoretical edifice for this dimension?

The answer is a definite 'yes' – it is contained in Lacan's unexpected vindication of the notion of creativity at its most radical, that is, as *creatio ex nihilo*: by means of reference to the void of the Thing in the midst of the symbolic structure, the subject is able to 'bend' the symbolic space she inhabits, and thus to define his/her desire in its idiosyncrasy. The paradox, again, is that there is by definition no 'proper measure' here: there is simultaneously not enough and too much creativity. Not enough, since the symbolic structure which is always-already here overdetermines my acts; too much, since I am none the less fully responsible for the way I relate to the structure. I am never 'caught in the structure without remainder'; there is always a remainder, a void around which the structure is articulated, and by locating myself at this void I can assume a minimal distance towards the structure, 'separate' myself from it.

Although one has to be careful here not to confound the act *qua* real with the performative gesture of the Master-Signifier, the two are none the less closely connected: the ultimate paradox of the process of symbolization, its 'highest mystery', is the fact that the act *qua* real (i.e. the gesture which, once the symbolic order is established, functions as its suspension, as *excessive* with regard to it) is simultaneously the 'vanishing mediator' that *founds* the symbolic order. An act, in its most fundamental dimension, is the 'vanishing mediator' between the In-itself and the For-itself: between the pre-symbolic, 'virtual', not yet fully actualized reality, and the reality which is already re-marked, symbolized. A symbolic order involves the structure of the hermeneutic circle: it is by definition 'auto-poetic' and all-encompassing; as such, it has no externality, so that the human subject who dwells in language can never step out of it and assume a distance towards it – the very 'external' reality always appears as such from within the horizon of language. The act, however, is precisely the 'impossible' gesture which opens up the unfathomable line of separation between 'things' and 'words' (*der Unter-Schied*, as Heidegger put it), the gesture which is 'repressed' once we are 'within' (the domain of Meaning). And the Master-Signifier is the act itself, perceived only 'from within', from the already-established symbolic horizon. In short, the act *qua* real and the Master-Signifier are not 'substantially' different, they are one and the same entity, conceived either in the mode of 'becoming' or in the mode of 'being'.

Voice as a supplement

How, at a closer glance, are we to conceive of this coincidence – tautology, even – of the act *qua* real and the signifier? Have we not already encountered something similar in the tautology of voice, that is, apropos of the coincidence of the voice *qua* medium of the subject's transparent self-presence with the voice *qua* opaque stain which undermines this self-presence? Perhaps, then, the key will be provided by the status of the excessive voice which stands for the eclipse of meaning. In order to give expression to this uncanny voice, it is sufficient to cast a cursory glance at the history of music – it reads as a kind of counter-history to the Derridean history of Western metaphysics as the domination of voice over writing. What we encounter in it again and again is a voice which threatens the established Order and which, for that reason, has to be brought under control, subordinated to the rational articulation of spoken and written word, fixed into writing.

In order to designate the danger that lurks here, Lacan coined the neologism *jouis-sense*, enjoyment-in-meaning – the moment at which the singing voice 'runs amok', cuts loose from its anchoring in meaning and accelerates into a consuming self-enjoyment. The two exemplary cases of this eclipse of meaning in consuming self-enjoyment are, of course, the climax of the (feminine) operatic aria and the mystical experience. The effort to dominate and regulate this excess runs from Ancient China, where the Emperor himself legislated music, to the fear of Elvis Presley that brought together the conservative moral majority in the USA and Communist hardliners in the Soviet Union. In his *Republic*, Plato tolerates music only in so far as it is strictly subordinated to the order of Word. Music is located at the very crossroads of Nature and Culture; it seizes us, as it were, 'in the real', far more directly than the meaning of words; for that reason, it can serve as the mightiest weapon of education and discipline, yet the moment it loses its footing and gets caught in the self-propelling vicious circle of enjoyment, it can undermine the very foundations not only of the State, but of the social order as such. In medieval times, Church power confronted the same dilemma: it is amazing to observe how much energy and care the highest ecclesiastical authority (the popes) put into the seemingly trifling question of the regulation of music (the problem of polyphony, the 'devil's fourth', etc.).

The figure who personifies the ambiguous attitude of Power towards excess of the Voice is, of course, Hildegard von Bingen, who put mystical enjoyment into music and was thus constantly on the verge of excommunication, although she was integrated into the highest level of the hierarchy of power, counselling the Emperor, and so on. The same matrix is at work again in the French Revolution, whose ideologues endeavoured to assert 'normal' sexual difference under the domination of the male spoken word against decadent aristocratic indulgence in the pleasures of listening to castrati. One of the last episodes in this everlasting struggle is the notorious Soviet campaign instigated by Stalin himself against Shostakovich's *Katarina Ismailova*: rather curiously, one of the main accusations was that the opera is a mass of unarticulated screams. . . . So the problem is always the same: how are we to prevent the voice from sliding into a consuming self-enjoyment that 'effeminates' the reliable masculine Word?[60]

The voice functions here as a 'supplement' in the Derridean sense: one endeavours to restrain it, to regulate it, to subordinate it to the articulated Word, yet one cannot dispense with it altogether, since a proper dose is vital for the exercise of power (suffice it to recall the role of patriotic-military songs in the building up of a totalitarian community, or – an even more flagrant obscenity – the US Marine Corps's mesmeric 'marching chants': are not their debilitating rhythm and sadistic-nonsensical content an exemplary case of consuming self-enjoyment in the service of Power?).

The sexual status of this self-enjoying voice is extremely interesting: it is as if, in it, opposites coincide. On the one hand, the excess, the 'surplus-enjoyment', that pertains to this voice is experienced as distinctly feminine, it is a voice that *seduces par excellence* (in a consuming coloratura, for example);[61] as such, it stands for the moment of divinization of the woman (*Diva*); on the other hand, it is asexual, the voice of an angel personified in the figure of the singing castrato. It thus designates the paradoxical overlapping of the most passionate sensuality with asexual purity. And is not the case of the castrato exemplary of Lacan's formula of the fetishist object *qua* disavowal of castration: $-\frac{a}{phi}$? The castrato reaches the sublime height of the asexual voice-object by means of a radical renunciation, a literal cut into his body, its mutilation. (The feminine counterpart to this mutilation is the widespread legends about the physical sufferings and renunciations to which a true *diva* has to expose herself in order to attain the divine Voice.)

What strikes the eye in Gérard Corbeau's *Farinelli*, the film biography of the famous eighteenth-century castrato-singer, is the way the hero *prides himself on his lack*: he shamelessly exhibits his voice, which bears witness to his mutilation – that is to say, while he is singing, he defiantly meets the gaze of his public; it is the members of the public who are ashamed of this display sooner of later, and lower their gaze. In what resides the privilege which gives the castrato the right to show off his lack? To evoke the virtuosity of his voice clearly does not suffice, since this voice is the monument to his loss: its virtuosity is a supplement which fills out and thereby exhibits his lack. Rather, the true question is: what *prerogative* is attested by the castrato's mutilation? The key feature of the castrato's voice is that it functions as a Freudian 'partial object': a spectral remainder, place-holder, of what is lost with the sexualization of a human being. In other words, *'real' castration can have this effect of producing a voice-object only in so far as it is preceded by a loss which marks 'full', 'normal' sexuality* – the Lacanian name for this loss, of course, is symbolic castration. 'Real' castration (of the singer) is thus in a sense *the loss of the loss itself* – an attempt to undo the symbolic castration, to regain what is lost with the entry into the domain of sexual difference. This also accounts for the paradoxical conjunction of a plus and a minus in the figure of woman: precisely in so far as she 'has no phallus', in so far as she is effectively underprivileged *within* the phallic sexual economy, woman has an advantage over man with respect to what is lost with the prevalence of the phallic economy of sexual difference. At a more radical level, one can say that – in so far as the dimension of voice *qua* object inhabits speech as such – *every speaking subject is in the position of a castrato*, of the disavowal of sexual difference which gives access to the asexual voice-object: this disavowal is the only way to maintain the neutral-asexual surface of Sense.

The shofar

There is, however, another voice which cannot be reduced to this excess of *jouis-sense*, although it also functions as the remainder of the Real. In a classical essay from the 1920s, Theodor Reik drew attention to the painfully low and uninterrupted trumpeting of the 'shofar', a horn used in the Yom Kippur evening ritual which marks the end of the day of meditations. Reik links the sound of the shofar to the Freudian problematic of the primordial crime of parricide (from *Totem and Taboo*): he interprets the horrifyingly turgid and leaden drone of the shofar, which evokes an uncanny mixture of pain and enjoyment, as the last vestige of the primordial father's life-substance, as the endlessly prolonged scream of the suffering-dying-impotent-humiliated father. In other words, the shofar is the trace of 'primordial repression', a kind of vocal monument to the killing of the pre-symbolic substance of enjoyment: the father whose dying scream reverberates within is the 'non-castrated' Father-Enjoyment. As further proof of his thesis, Reik also calls attention to the similarity of the shofar to another primitive instrument, the 'bullroarer', which imitates the roaring of the stabbed bull dying in the arena: the bullfight as the re-enactment of the murder of the primordial Father-*Jouissance*.[62]

On the other hand, the Jewish tradition conceives the sound of the shofar as an echo of the thunder that accompanied the solemn moment of God's handing over to Moses the tablets inscribed with the Ten Commandments; as such, it also stands for the Covenant between the Jewish people and their God, that is, for the founding gesture of Law. The sound of the shofar is therefore a kind of 'vanishing mediator' between the mythical direct vocal expression of the pre-symbolic life-substance and articulated speech: it stands for the gesture by means of which the life-substance, via its retreat, its self-erasure, opens up the space for symbolic Law. Here, apropos of the shofar *qua* 'vanishing mediator', we again encounter the *Grundoperation* of German Idealism at work in the depths of Schelling's and Hegel's thought: the shofar, this strange sound which stands for the self-sublation of the vocal substance in the articulated Word, is strictly analogous to the unconscious act of establishing the difference between the unconscious vortex of drives and the field of *Logos* in Schelling. This is how psychoanalysis enables us to break the vicious cycle of oscillating between the 'disciplining' Word and the 'transgressive' consuming Voice: by focusing on an excessive voice which serves as the founding gesture of the articulated speech itself.

That is to say: what, properly speaking, is articulation? A structure that is 'artificial'. Suffice it to recall a perspicacious detail of Umberto Eco's analysis of *Casablanca*: Victor Laszlo (Paul Henreid), Resistance hero and Ingrid Bergman's husband, orders a different drink on every occasion (whisky, vermouth, liqueur ...). At first sight, this feature cannot but strike a discordant note in the 'official' character of this person (the ascetic fighter for freedom who sacrifices everything for the Cause, and clearly has no time for small private pleasures) – if we were to maintain Laszlo's psychological unity and consistency, we would be compelled to indulge in speculation about the dark, decadent-hedonistic underside of this hero of the Resistance. As Eco points out, however, one should approach the problem in a *non-psychological* way – the screenwriters simply heaped up discursive fragments of different conducts in different situations, they were not concerned with the problem of the psychological consistency of the person to whom all these conducts are attributed. What we have to do here is to accomplish a step further and to assert that *the same also goes for 'real-life' people*: our conduct is not held together by some coherent psychological attitude, it consists of a *bricolage* of heterogeneous fragments.

A reference to Bach might help to clarify this point. The outstanding feature of the second movement (Fugue) of Bach's Sonatas for solo violin – especially his Sonata No. 1, BWV 1001 – is its melodic polyphony: several 'voices' are implied in a single melodic line. The extraordinary effect of this movement (which is lost in the transcriptions for organ) hinges on the 'condensation' of the multitude of voices in one sound-line: the listener is aware all the time that only one instrument (the violin) is actually playing. One is tempted to claim that Bach's melodic polyphony dialectically sublates the opposition between 'horizontal' melody and 'vertical' polyphony – a vertical multitude is somehow 'projected' on to a single horizontal axis, like the analogous procedure of projecting the paradigmatic on to the syntagmatic axis in poetic speech. Oswald Ducrot aims at something similar with his concept of the 'polyphonous' structure of speech:[63] a single line of enunciation always contains a multiplicity of 'voices' which relate to each other in the mode of questioning, ironic overtones and so on – what we have here again is *articulation*, a subject whose voice condenses an articulated *bricolage*.

The shofar, however, reminds us of the impossibility of passing directly from immediate pre-symbolic life-experience to articulated speech: the 'vanishing mediator' between the two is the Voice of death itself, epitomized by the cry of the dying animal:

> Every animal finds a voice in its violent death, it expresses itself as sublated Self. (Birds have song, which other animals làck, because they belong to the element of air – articulating voice, a more diffused self.)
>   In the voice, meaning turns back into itself; it is negative self, desire [*Begierde*]. It is lack, absence of substance in itself.[64]

The intimate link between language and death is, of course, a philosophical commonplace with a long and venerable pedigree: as a rule, one quotes here Hegel's assertion that a word is the death of a thing, that the thing is 'murdered' in its name – when I say 'This is an elephant', I thereby suspend the animal's massive presence, reducing it to the ethereal sound of its name. Here, however, the distance – the gap that forever separates 'words' from 'things' – is already instituted; what the death song confronts us with, on the contrary, is this institution 'in its becoming', as Kierkegaard would have put it. That is to say: in order for this distance to be instituted, the *speaker himself* has to 'die', to 'sublate' himself, to relate to himself as dead. The death song designates this unique intermediate phase when the life-substance is not yet fully 'sublated [*aufgehoben*]', when the process of dying is still going on: it is the trace, the leftover, of the passing-away of its 'enunciator', of the passage from S to $, from the full 'pathological' subject to the empty 'barred' subject.

What we encounter here is the crucial difference between the two modalities of Spirit first elaborated by Schelling: on the one hand the pure, ideal Spirit *qua* medium of self-transparency of the rational thought; on the other, spirit *qua* ghost, spectral apparition. The voice of the shofar and/or of the death song, although already detached from its bearer and provided with a spectral autonomy, is not yet the voice *qua* transparent medium of spiritual meaning: it confronts us with the paradox of 'spiritual corporeality' (Schelling) which, like the living dead, or vampires, undermines the duality of bodily density and spiritual transparency.[65] In this precise sense, the difference Spirit/ spectre overlaps with the Freudian difference between the two fathers, the Oedipal dead father who rules as a symbolic agency of prohibition and the obscene primordial father-*jouissance*: the shofar is the spectral voice of the obscene primordial father who is dying in order to begin to reign as his Name, as the agent of symbolic authority.[66]

Apropos of the shofar – this vocal leftover from parricide – Lacan accomplishes one of his unique *tours de force* by asking a simple question: to whom is the uncanny sound of the shofar addressed? The standard answer, of course, would have been: the addressees are the Jewish believers themselves, that is, the sound of the shofar is meant to remind them of their pact with God, of the divine Law they are obliged to obey. Lacan, however, turns things round: the true addressee of the shofar is not the community of believers but *God himself*.[67] When Jewish believers sound a shofar, they intend to remind him – of what? *That he is dead.* At this point, to be sure, horror shifts into divine comedy – that is to say, we enter the logic of the famous Freudian dream (reported in *The Interpretation of Dreams*) of a father who 'didn't know he was dead'. The God-Father doesn't know he is dead, which is why he acts as if he is still alive and continues to pester us in the guise of a superego spectre; for that reason, one has simply to remind him that he is dead, and he will collapse like the proverbial cat in the cartoons, who plummets the moment he becomes aware of the lack of ground beneath his feet. From this perspective the function of the shofar is profoundly *pacifying*: its roaring, horrible as it may sound, is actually meant to pacify and neutralize the 'pagan' superego dimension of God, that is, to ensure that He will act as a pure agency of Name, of a symbolic Pact. In so far as the shofar is associated with the pact between man and God, its sound therefore serves as a reminder to God to live up to his status of the bearer of the symbolic Pact, and not to harass us too much with outbursts of traumatic sacrificial *jouissance*. In other words, the condensation of two features in the sound of the shofar (the roaring of the dying primordial Father-Enjoyment and the scene of proclaiming the Ten Commandments) calls God's attention to the fact that He can legitimately rule only as dead.[68]

This voice *qua* reminder/remainder of the dying father, of course, is not something that can be erased once the reign of Law is established: it is constantly needed as the ineradicable support of the Law. For that reason its reverberation was heard when Moses was receiving the Commandments from God – that is to say, at the very moment when the reign of (symbolic) Law was being instituted (in what Moses was able to discern as the articulated Commandments, the crowd waiting below Mount Sinai apprehended only the continuous, non-articulated sound of the shofar): the voice of the shofar is an irreducible *supplement* of the (written) Law. It is only the *voice* that confers on the Law its performative dimension, that is, makes it operative: without this support in the senseless voice (voice *qua* object), Law would be a piece of powerless writing obliging no one. By means of the shofar *qua* voice, the Law acquires its *enunciator*, 'subjectivizes' itself, thereby becoming an effective agency which *obliges*. In other words, it is the intervention of a voice which transmutes the signifying chain into an act of creation.

What is crucial apropos of the shofar, therefore, is the association of its sound with the traumatic, shattering moment of the *institution of the Law*: in so far as we remain *within* the Law, its 'origin' is *stricto sensu* unthinkable – that is to say, the rule of Law presupposes the 'foreclosure' of its ('illegal') origins; its performative efficiency relies on our accepting it as always-already given. Within the domain of the Law, its impossible 'origins' can thus be present only in the guise of a void, as a constitutive absence; and the role of the fantasy, of the phantasmic narrative of origins, is precisely to fill in this void.[69] The (written) Law necessitates this phantasmic supplement – in its absence, the void in the midst of the legal edifice would become visible, thus rendering the Law inoperative. Voice thus relates to the (written) Law as fantasy relates to the synchronous symbolic structure: as the stand-in for its unthinkable 'origins', it fills in (and, at the same time, holds the place of) its constitutive lack.

For that reason, presence and absence are indiscernibly intertwined in the shofar. This voice is the 'little piece of the real' which remains of the pre-symbolic Father-Enjoyment; as such, it stands for the *presence* of the traumatic origins of the Law. On the other hand, the voice of the shofar bears witness to the *absence* of the origins of Law – that is to say, its dull sound is the phantasmic object *par excellence*: a pure semblance, an object whose fascinating presence renders the subject blind to the radical inconsistency of the symbolic order, a stand-in for (a place-holder of) the missing ultimate signifier which would guarantee the consistency and authority of the symbolic order (the 'big Other'). Therein resides the ultimate paradox signalled by the voice of the shofar: symbolic authority is by definition the authority of the *dead* father, the Name-of-the-Father; but if this very authority is to become effective, it has to rely on a (phantasmic) remainder of the living father, on a piece of the father which survived the primordial murder.

We can now see the precise structural place of the strange sound of the shofar: it enables us to break out of the oscillation between the disciplining Word and the consuming self-enjoyment of the Voice by rendering the remainder of the traumatic founding gesture of the Word. So, on a first approach, it may seem that the lesson of the shofar is simply this: *logos*, the articulated speech carrying over symbolic authority, can dominate-overcome the substance of enjoy-meant – that is, the voice still permeated by *jouissance*, only by enlisting the services of another, even more traumatic voice – the battle between *logos* and the excessive *jouissance* can be won by *logos* only when it is transformed into the immanent battle of the two voices. However, the question still remains: what is the precise relationship between these two voices, which of the two has primacy? The sound of the shofar, the equivalent of the dying father's roaring, is not simply a different kind of voice from the self-consuming enjoyment of a feminine song, but the same voice in a different modality: the two are 'identical' in the precise sense of Hegelian speculative identity. We are dealing here with the two modalities of the leftover: *remainder* and *excess*. Both are 'on the same side', on the side of enjoyment against *Logos*. The remainder points towards its homonymic reminder.

In arithmetic, a remainder is the amount left over when one number cannot be exactly divided by another – when the substance of enjoyment cannot be exactly divided (structured, articulated, counted) by the signifying network. In a somewhat analogous way, the sound of the shofar is the objectal remainder-reminder of the dying Father-*Jouissance*: the leftover of the founding gesture of the Law, its *indivisible remainder*. The relationship of *Logos* to feminine self-consuming voice is, on the contrary, the relationship of the *already-established* symbolic Order to its transgression: feminine voice is *excessive* with regard to the Law. Or – to put it in a slightly different way – the shift from the excessive-consuming Voice to the reverberation of the shofar transposes the tension between Law and its transgression into the inner splitting of the domain of Law itself – the Law's *external* relationship to its transgression is *internalized* into the Law's relationship to its own traumatic founding gesture – as we have already pointed out, the reverberation of the shofar serves as a kind of phantasmic screen which points towards the mystery of the 'impossible' origins of Law.

How not to read Lacan's 'formulas of sexuation'

This identity also offers a clue to how we are to conceive Lacan's deeply Hegelian paradoxical assertion that 'Woman is one of the names of the father': femininity is a masquerade, and what we encounter when we tear down this mask is the obscene figure of the pre-Oedipal Father-Enjoyment. Is not an indirect proof of this provided by the unique figure of the Lady in courtly love, this capricious implacable *dominatrix*? Does not this Lady, like the 'primordial father', stand for Enjoyment unbridled by any Law? The phantasmic figure of Woman is thus a kind of 'return of the repressed', of the Father-Enjoyment removed by means of the primordial crime of parricide – that is to say, what returns in her seductive voice is the roar of the dying father. . . . We thus find ourselves at the exact opposite of the New Age approach, with its standard reference to the allegedly 'archetypal' figure of a primordial Woman: according to New Age ideology, Father is a derivative, a symbolic sublimation, a pale reflection, of the primordial Woman, so that if one scratches a little of the polish off the face of paternal symbolic authority, one soon comes upon the contours of the Mother-Thing. In short, if, for New Age obscurantism, 'Father' is one of the names of the primordial Woman, of the Mother-Thing, for Lacan, on the contrary, it is Woman who is one of the names of the father. . . .

The usual way of misreading Lacan's formulas of sexuation[70] is to reduce the difference between the 'masculine' and the 'feminine' side to the two formulas that define the masculine position, as if 'masculine' were the universal phallic function and 'feminine' the exception, the excess, the surplus that eludes the grasp of the phallic function. Such a reading completely misses Lacan's point, which is that this very position of the Woman as Exception (say, in the guise of the Lady in courtly love) is a masculine fantasy *par excellence*. As the exemplary case of the exception constitutive of the phallic function, one usually mentions the phantasmic obscene figure of the primordial father-*jouisseur* who was not encumbered by any Prohibition and as such was able fully to enjoy all women – however, does not the figure of the Lady in courtly love fully fit this description of the primordial father? Is she not, as we have just seen, in a strictly analogous way, also a capricious Master who 'wants it all' – who, herself not bound by any Law, charges her knight-servant with arbitrary and outrageous ordeals? In this precise sense, Woman is 'one of the names of the father'. The crucial detail not to be missed here is the use of the plural and the lack of capital letters: not 'Name-of-the-Father', but 'one of the names of the father' – one of the nominations of the excess called 'primordial father'.[71] In the case of Woman – the mythical 'She', the Queen from Rider Haggard's novel of the same name, for example – as well as in the case of the primordial father, we are dealing with an agency of Power which is pre-symbolic, unbridled by the Law of castration; in both cases, the role of this phantasmic agency is to fill out the vicious cycle of the symbolic order, the void of its 'origins': what the notion of 'Woman' (or of the primordial father) provides is the mythical starting point of unbridled fullness whose 'primordial repression' constitutes the symbolic order.[72]

A second misreading consists in rendering the 'sting' of the formulas of sexuation obtuse by introducing a semantic distinction between the two meanings of the quantifier 'all [*tout*]': according to this (mis)-reading, in the case of the universal function, 'all' (or 'non-all') refers to a singular subject (x), it signals whether 'all of it' is caught in the phallic function; whereas the particular exception ('there is one ... ') refers to the set of subjects and signals whether, within this set, 'there is one' who is (or is not) entirely exempt from the phallic function. The feminine side of the formulas of sexuation thus allegedly bears witness to a cut that splits every woman from within: no woman is entirely exempt from the phallic function, and for that very reason no woman is entirely submitted to it – that is to say, there is something in every woman that resists the phallic function. In a symmetrical way, on the masculine side, the asserted universality refers to a singular subject (every male subject is entirely submitted to the phallic function) and the exception to the set of male subjects ('there is one' who is *entirely* exempt from the phallic function). In short, since one man is entirely exempt from the phallic function, all the others are wholly submitted to it; and since no woman is entirely exempt from the phallic function, no woman, similarly, is wholly submitted to it. In the one case the splitting is 'externalized' (it stands for the line of separation which, within the set of 'all men', distinguishes those who are caught in the phallic function from the 'one' who is exempt from it); in the other it is 'internalized' (every single woman is split from within: part of her is submitted to the phallic function and part of her is exempt from it).

If we are fully to assume the true paradox of Lacan's formulas of sexuation, however, we have to read them far more 'literally': woman undermines the universality of the phallic function by the very fact that there is no exception in her, nothing that resists it. In other words, the paradox of the phallic function resides in a kind of short circuit between the function and its meta-function: the phallic function coincides with its own self-limitation, with the setting up of a non-phallic Exception. Such a reading is prefigured by the somewhat enigmatic mathemes that Lacan wrote under the formulas of sexuation, where woman (designated by the crossed-out 'La') is split between the big Phi (of the phallus) and S($\cancel{A}$), the signifier of the crossed-out big Other that stands for the nonexistence/inconsistency of the Other, of the symbolic order. What one should not fail to notice here is the deep affinity between the Phi and S($\cancel{A}$), the signifier of the lack in the Other – the crucial fact that the Phi, the signifier of phallic power, phallus in its fascinating *presence*, merely 'gives body' to the impotence/ inconsistency of the big Other. Suffice to recall a political Leader: what is the ultimate support of his charisma? The domain of politics is by definition incalculable, unpredictable; a person stirs up passionate reactions without knowing why; the logic of transference cannot be mastered, so one usually refers to the 'magic touch', to an unfathomable *je ne sais quoi* which cannot be reduced to any of the Leader's 'actual' features – it seems as if the charismatic Leader dominates this 'x', as if he pulls the strings where the big Other of the symbolic order is incapacitated.

This situation is analogous to the common notion of God as a person criticized by Spinoza: in their endeavour to understand the world around them by formulating the network of causal connections between events and objects, people sooner or later reach the point at which their understanding fails, encounters a limit, and 'God' (conceived as an old bearded wise man, etc.) merely 'gives body' to this limit – we project into the personalized notion of 'God' the hidden, unfathomable cause of all that cannot be understood and explained via a clear causal connection. The first operation of the critique of ideology is therefore to recognize in the fascinating presence of God the 'filler' of the gaps in the structure of our knowledge – that is, the element in the guise of which the lack in our positive knowledge acquires positive presence. And my point is that it is somewhat analogous to the feminine 'non-all': this 'non-all' does not mean that woman is not entirely submitted to the Phallus; rather, it signals that she 'sees through' the fascinating presence of the Phallus, that she is able to discern in it the 'filler' of the inconsistency of the big Other. Yet another way to put it would be to say that the passage from S(Ⱥ) to the big Phi is the passage from impossibility to prohibition: S(Ⱥ) stands for the impossibility of the signifier of the big Other, for the fact that there is no 'Other of Other', that the field of the Other is inherently inconsistent; and the big Phi 'reifies' this impossibility into the Exception, into a 'sacred', prohibited/unattainable agent who avoids castration and is thus able 'really to enjoy' (the primordial Father, the Lady in courtly love).[73]

Femininity as masquerade

We can now see how the logic of the formulas of sexuation ultimately coincides with that of public power and its inherent transgression:[74] in both cases, the crucial feature is that *the subject is effectively 'in' (caught in the phallic function, in the web of Power) only and precisely in so far as he does not fully identify with it but maintains a kind of distance towards it* (posits an exception to the universal phallic function; indulges in inherent transgression of the public Law); and, on the other side, the system (of public Law, of phallic economy) is effectively undermined by identification with it without reservation.[75]

Stephen King's *Rita Hayworth and the Shawshank Redemption* tackles this problem with great stringency apropos of the paradoxes of prison life. The commonplace about prison life is that I am effectively integrated into it, ruined by it, when my accommodation to it is so overwhelming that I can no longer stand or even imagine freedom, life outside prison, so that my release brings about a total psychical breakdown, or at least gives rise to a longing for the lost safety of prison life. The actual dialectic of prison life, however, is somewhat more refined. Prison effectively destroys me, attains a total hold over me, precisely when I do *not* fully consent to the fact that I am in prison but maintain a kind of inner distance towards it, stick to the illusion that 'real life is elsewhere' and indulge all the time in daydreaming about life outside, about nice things that are waiting for me after my release or escape. I thereby get caught in the vicious cycle of fantasy, so that when eventually I am released, the grotesque discord between fantasy and reality breaks me down. The only true solution, therefore, is fully to accept the rules of prison life and then, within the universe governed by these rules, to work on a way to beat them. In short, inner distance and daydreaming about Life Elsewhere effectively enchain me to prison, whereas full acceptance of the fact that I am really there, bound by prison rules, opens up a space for true hope.[76]

The paradox of the phallic function (which symmetrically inverts the paradox of the feminine non-all) is therefore that the phallic function acts as its own self-limitation, that it posits its own exception.[77] And in so far as the phallic function – that is, the phallic signifier – is the quasi-transcendental signifier, the signifier of the symbolic order as such, one can say that this paradox of the phallic function merely reveals the fundamental feature of the symbolic order at its purest, a certain short circuit of different levels that pertains to the domain of modal logic.

In order to illustrate this a priori possibility of the short circuit between different levels that pertains to the symbolic order *qua* order of symbolic mandates-titles, let us recall the opposition father/uncle: 'father' *qua* severe authority versus 'uncle' *qua* good fellow who spoils us. The seemingly meaningless, contradictory title 'father uncle' can none the less be justified as the designation of a father who is not ready fully to exert his paternal authority but, instead, spoils his offspring. (To avoid misunderstanding: far from being a kind of eccentric exception, 'father uncle' is simply the 'normal' everyday father who maintains a distance towards his symbolic mandate – who, *fully taking advantage of his authority*, at the same time affects camaraderie and gives an occasional wink to his son, letting him know that, after all, he is also only human. . . .) We are dealing here with the same short circuit as that found in *The History of VKP(B)*, the holy text of Stalinism, where – among other numerous flashes of the logic of the signifier – one can read that at a Party congress 'the resolution was *unanimously* adopted *by a large majority*' – if the resolution was adopted unanimously, where is the (however tiny) minority opposed to the 'large majority'? The way to solve the riddle of this 'something that counts as nothing' is, perhaps, to read the quoted statement as the condensation of two levels: the delegates resolved by a large majority that their resolution is to count as unanimous. . . .

The link with the Lacanian logic of the signifier here is unmistakable: the 'minority' which mysteriously disappears in this enigmatic/absurd overlapping between 'majority' and 'unanimity' is none other than the exception which constitutes the universal order of unanimity.[78] The feminine position, on the contrary, is defined by the *rejection* of this short circuit – how? Let us take as our starting point the properly Hegelian paradox of *coincidentia oppositorum* that characterizes the standard notion of woman: woman is simultaneously a representation, a spectacle *par excellence*, an image intended to fascinate, to attract the gaze, *and* an enigma, the unrepresentable, that which a priori eludes the gaze.[79] She is all surface, lacking any depth, *and* the unfathomable abyss.

In order to elucidate this paradox, suffice it to reflect on the implications of a discontent that pertains to a certain kind of feminist critique which persistently denounces every description of 'femininity' as a male cliché, as something violently imposed on women. The question that instantly crops up is: what, then, is the feminine 'in itself' obfuscated by male clichés? The problem is that all answers (from the traditional 'eternally feminine' to Julia Kristeva and Luce Irigaray) can again be discredited as male clichés. Carol Gilligan, for example,[80] opposes to the male values of autonomy, competitiveness, and so on, the feminine values of intimacy, attachment, interdependence, care and concern, responsibility and self-sacrifice, and so forth – are these 'authentic' feminine features or male 'clichés' about women, features imposed on women in patriarchal society? The point is undecidable, so that the only possible answer is 'both at once'.[81]

The issue thus has to be reformulated in purely topological terms: with regard to the positive content, the male representation of woman is *the same* as woman in herself; the difference concerns only the place, the purely formal modality of the comprehension of the same content (in the first case, this content is conceived as it is 'for-the-other'; in the second, as it is 'in-itself') – this purely formal shift in modality, however, is crucial. In other words, the fact that every positive determination of what woman is 'in herself' brings us back to what she is 'for the other' (for man) in no way forces us to the 'male-chauvinist' conclusion that woman is what she is only for the other, for man: what remains is the topological cut, the purely formal difference between 'for-the-other' and 'for-herself'.

Here, one should recall the passage from consciousness to self-consciousness in Hegel's *Phenomenology of Spirit*: what one encounters in the suprasensible Beyond is, in its positive content, the same as our terrestrial everyday world; this same content is merely transposed to a different modality. Hegel's point, however, is that it would be false to conclude from this identity of content that there is no difference between the terrestrial reality and its Beyond: in its original dimension, 'Beyond' is not some positive content but an empty place, a kind of screen on to which one can project any positive content whatsoever – and this empty place 'is' the subject. Once we become aware of this, we pass from Substance to Subject, that is, from consciousness to self-consciousness.[82] In this precise sense, woman is the subject *par excellence*. The same point could also be made in Schelling's terms – in terms, that is, of the difference between the subject *qua* original void, deprived of any further positive qualifications (in Lacan's mathemes: $), and the features that this subject assumes, 'puts on', which are ultimately always artificial, contingent:[83] it is precisely in so far as woman is characterized by an original 'masquerade', in so far as all her features are artificially 'put on', that she is more subject than man, since according to Schelling, what ultimately characterizes the subject is this very radical contingency and artificiality of her every positive feature, that is, the fact that 'she' in herself is a pure void that cannot be identified with any of these features.

We are thus dealing with a kind of convoluted, curved space, as in the story of Achilles and the tortoise: the male representations (which articulate what woman is 'for the other') endlessly approach the woman-tortoise, yet the moment the man leaps over, overtakes, the woman-tortoise, he finds himself back where he already was: within the male representations about what woman is 'in herself' – woman's 'in itself' is always-already 'for the other'. Woman can never be caught, one can never catch up with her; one can either endlessly approach her or overtake her, for the very reason that 'woman-in-herself' designates no substantial content but just a purely formal cut, a limit that is always missed – this purely formal cut 'is' the subject *qua* $.

One is thus tempted to paraphrase Hegel again: everything hinges on our conceiving woman not merely as Substance but also as Subject – that is to say, on accomplishing a shift from the notion of woman as a substantial content beyond male representations to the notion of woman *qua* pure topological cut that forever separates the 'for-the-other' from the 'in-itself'. The asymmetry of the sexual difference resides in the fact that in the case of man we are not dealing with the same cut, we do not distinguish in the same way between what he is 'in himself' and what he is 'for the other', *qua* masquerade. True, so-called 'modern man' is also caught in the split between what (it seems to him that) the other (woman or social environment in general) expects of him (to be a strong macho type, etc.) and what he effectively is in himself (weak, uncertain of himself, etc.). This split, however, is of a fundamentally different nature: the macho image is experienced not as a delusive masquerade but as the ideal ego one is striving to become. Behind the macho image of a man there is no 'secret', just a weak ordinary person who can never live up to his ideal, whereas the 'trick' of the feminine masquerade is to present itself as a mask that conceals the 'feminine secret'. In other words, in opposition to man, who simply tries to live up to his image – to give the impression that he really is what he pretends to be – woman deceives by means of deception itself; she offers the mask *as mask*, as false pretence, in order to provoke the search for the secret behind the mask.[84]

In praise of hysteria

This problematic of femininity *qua* masquerade also enables us to approach in a new way Lacan's earlier attempt (from the late 1950s, in

'The Signification of the Phallus') to conceptualize sexual difference as internal to the phallic economy, as the difference between 'having' and 'being' (man *has* the phallus, woman *is* the phallus). A criticism that immediately arises here concerns the reliance of this difference on Freud's naive anthropologist evolutionism whose premiss is that the primitive 'savage' does not *have* an unconscious, since he *is* (our, civilized man's) unconscious: does not the attempt to conceptualize sexual difference by means of the opposition of 'being' and 'having' imply woman's subordination to man: the notion of woman as a lower, less 'reflected', more 'immediate' stage, somewhat in the sense of Schelling's notion of progression as the passage from 'being' to 'having'? That is to say, in Schelling's philosophy, (what previously was) a Being becomes a predicate of a higher Being, (what previously was) a Subject becomes an object of a higher Subject: an animal, for example, is immediately its own Subject, it 'is' its living body, whereas man cannot be said to 'be' his body, he merely 'has' a body which is thus degraded to his predicate. . . .

However, as a close reading of Lacan's text instantly attests, the opposition we are dealing with is not that of 'being' versus 'having' but, rather, the opposition *to have/ to appear*: woman 'is' not the phallus, she merely 'appears' to be the phallus, and this appearing (which, of course, is identical with femininity *qua* masquerade) points towards a logic of lure and deception. The phallus can perform its function only as veiled – the moment it is unveiled, it is no longer the phallus; what the mask of femininity conceals, therefore, is not directly the phallus but, rather, the fact that there is nothing behind the mask. In a word: the phallus is a pure semblance, a mystery which resides in the mask as such. On that account, Lacan can claim that a woman wants to be loved *for what she is not*, not for what she 'truly is': she offers herself to man not as herself, but in the guise of a mask.[85] Or – to put it in Hegelian terms – the phallus stands not for an immediate Being but for a Being which is only in so far as it is for-the-other, that is, for a pure appearing. On that account, the Freudian primitive 'is' not immediately the Unconscious, he is merely the unconscious *for us*, for our external gaze: the spectacle of his Unconscious (primitive passions, exotic rituals) is his masquerade by means of which, like the woman with her masquerade, he fascinates the other's (our) desire.

The unfortunate millionaire's complaint from one of Claude Chabrol's films ('If only I could find a woman who would love me only for my millions, not for myself!') is therefore so unsettling in so far as it is professed by a man, whereas it should be professed by a woman. Man wants to be loved for what he truly is; this is why the archetypal male scenario of the trial of woman's love is that of the prince from a fairy-tale who first approaches his beloved in the guise of a poor servant in order to ensure that the woman will fall in love with him for himself, not for his princely title. This, however, is precisely what a woman does not want – and is this not yet another confirmation of the fact that woman is more subject than man? A man stupidly believes that, beyond his symbolic title, there is deep in himself some substantial content, some hidden treasure which makes him worthy of love; whereas a woman knows that there is nothing beneath the mask – her strategy is precisely to preserve this 'nothing' of her freedom out of reach of man's possessive love. . . .

A recent English television advertisement for a beer encapsulated perfectly this asymmetry in the relationship between the sexes. The first part stages the well-known fairy-tale anecdote: a girl walks along a stream, sees a frog, takes it gently into her lap, kisses it, and, of course, the ugly frog miraculously turns into a beautiful young man. However, the story isn't over yet: the young man casts a covetous glance at the girl, draws her towards himself, kisses her – and she turns into a bottle of beer the man triumphantly holds in his hand. . . . For the woman, the point is that her love and affection (signalled by the kiss) turn a frog into a beautiful man, a full phallic presence (in Lacan's mathemes, the big Phi); for the man, it is to reduce the woman to a partial object, the cause of his desire (in Lacan's mathemes, the *objet petit a*). On account of this asymmetry, 'there is no sexual relationship': we have either a woman with a frog or a man with a bottle of beer – what we can never obtain is the 'natural' couple of the beautiful woman and the beautiful man. . . . So, to conclude: two clichés are to be avoided apropos of the hysterical nature of feminine subjectivity:

- on the one hand, the dismissive treatment of the (feminine) hysterical subject as a confused babbler unable to confront reality and therefore taking refugee in impotent theatrical gestures (an example from the domain of political discourse: from Lenin onwards, Bolsheviks regularly stigmatized their 'liberal' political opponents as 'hysterics' who 'do not know what they really want');

- on the other hand, the false elevation of hysteria to a protest of woman's 'body language' against male domination: by means of hysterical symptoms, the (feminine) subject signals her refusal to act as the empty screen or medium for the male monologue.

Hysteria has to be comprehended in the complexity of its strategy, as a radically ambiguous protest against the Master's interpellation which simultaneously bears witness to the fact that the hysterical subject needs a Master, cannot do without a Master, so that there is no simple and direct way out. For that reason, one should also avoid the historicist pitfall of rejecting the notion of hysteria as belonging to a bygone era: the notion that today, borderline disturbances, not hysteria, are the predominant form of 'discontent' in our civilization. 'Borderline' *is* the contemporary form of hysteria, that is, of the subject's refusal to accept the predominant mode of interpellation whose agent is no longer the traditional Master but the 'expert knowledge' of the discourse of Science. In short, the shift from the classic form of hysteria to borderline disturbances is strictly correlative with the shift from the traditional Master to the form of Power legitimized by Knowledge.

A more than sufficient reason for maintaining the notion of hysteria is that *the status of the subject as such is ultimately hysterical.* That is to say, when Lacan asserts that the most succcinct definition of the subject is 'that which is not an object', the apparent banality of this claim should not deceive us: the subject – in the precise psychoanalytic sense of the subject of desire – exists only in so far as the question remains open of *what she is for the Other as an object,* that is, I am a subject in so far as the radical perplexity persists as to *the Other's desire,* as to what the Other sees (and finds worthy of desire) in me. In other words, when Lacan claims that there is no desire without an object-cause, this does not amount to the banality according to which every desire is attached to its objective correlative: the 'lost object' which sets the subject's desire in motion is ultimately *the subject herself,* and the lack in question concerns her uncertainty as to her status for the Other's desire. In this precise sense, desire is always desire of the Other: the subject's desire is the desire to ascertain her status as object of the Other's desire.

The status of the Lacanian '*Che vuoi?*', 'What do you want?', is thus radically ambiguous. On the one hand, it emanates from the Other – that is to say, it stands for the question the big Other (the analyst) addresses to the (hysterical) subject whose desire is inconsistent and, as such, self-impeding: 'What do you actually want? Do you really want what you are saying you want?' On the other hand, '*Che vuoi?*' articulates the perplexity of the subject himself confronted with an impenetrable Other who wants something from him, although the subject is never able to ascertain what this something actually is (the basic constellation of the great Kafka's novels) – what does the Other want from me? And the fact that 'the desire of the subject is the desire of the other' means precisely that these two forms are co-dependent: I, the subject, never know what I really want, since the Other's desire remains forever an enigma to me. . . .

That is the vicious circle of hysteria: on the one hand hysteria is secondary, a reaction against interpellation, a failed interpellation, a rejection of the identity imposed on the subject by the predominant form of interpellation, a questioning of this identity ('Am I really what you're saying I am?'); at another, more fundamental level, however, hysteria is primary, it articulates the radical, constitutive uncertainty as to what, as an object, I am for the other; and the symbolic identity conferred on me via interpellation is a response, a way out of the deadlock of hysteria. In other words, one could say that hysteria expresses the feminine subject's refusal of the predominant patriarchal symbolic order, the questioning of the authority of the Name-of-the-Father; however, one should simultaneously assert that this symbolic paternal authority itself emerges in order to render invisible, to 'gentrify', the impasse of hysteria. Or – to put it even more pointedly – it is not that 'Woman doesn't exist' because, on account of patriarchal 'repression', she is not allowed to express herself freely and constitute her full symbolic identity, but, rather, the other way round – patriarchal symbolic authority emerges in order to 'gentrify' the scandal of 'Woman doesn't exist', to constrain the feminine subject to a determinate place in the symbolic structure.

Lacan's 'Woman doesn't exist' is therefore thoroughly different from the Foucauldian constructionist anti-essentialism according to which there is no Woman *qua* eternal essence, since feminine sexual identity is the result of multiple historical discursive and power practices: there is no Sex, there is only sexuality as the heterogeneous field of practices which produces the mirage of Sex. . . . In clear contrast to this assertion of the 'constructed' character of feminine sexual identity, Lacan's 'Woman doesn't exist' means that, precisely, *'woman' cannot be constructed*: 'woman' is an entity whose symbolic construction necessarily fails, in opposition to 'man', who *does* exist – that is, who can be constructed (in the logical sense of the term, since there is a limit, an exception, which allows for this construction). Lacan's point, of course, is that this 'less' is 'more': the claim that 'woman' cannot be constructed equals the claim that the status of the subject is feminine – that which eludes logical construction, the reef of impossibility at which symbolic construction fails, is precisely the subject *qua* $, the lack in the signifying chain.

From the Althusserian point of view (whose theoretical rigour is not to be underestimated), it is possible to construct a coherent counter-argument to the Lacanian thesis that interpellation ultimately always fails, that is to say, that the subject never fully recognizes itself in the interpellative call; and that this resistance to interpellation (to the symbolic identity provided by interpellation) *is* the subject. The status of the subject as such *is* hysterical; the subject *does* always maintain a minimal of 'inner distance' towards the apparatuses and rituals in which ideology acquires material existence – his attitude towards this externality is always an 'I am not that' (my true self does not hinge on this stupid mechanism); ideological identification is always, as it were, an identification with fingers crossed. . . .

Is not this hysterical distance towards interpellation, however, the very form of ideological misrecognition? Is not this apparent failure of interpellation, its self-relating disavowal – the fact that I, the subject, experience the innermost kernel of my being as something which is not 'merely that' (the materiality of rituals and apparatuses) – *the ultimate proof of its success*, that is to say, of the fact that the 'effect-of-subject' really took place? And in so far as the Lacanian term for this innermost kernel of my being is *objet petit a*, is it not justifiable to claim that this *objet petit a*, the secret treasure, *agalma*, is the *sublime object of ideology* – the feeling that there is 'something in me more than myself' which cannot be reduced to any of my external symbolic determinations, that is, to what I am for others? Is not this feeling of an unfathomable and inexpressible 'depth' of my personality, this 'inner distance' towards what I am for others, the exemplary form of the *imaginary* distance towards the symbolic apparatus? Therein resides the crucial dimension of the ideological *effet-sujet*: not in my direct identification with the symbolic mandate (such a direct identification is potentially psychotic, it makes me into a 'depthless mechanical doll', not into a 'living person') but in my experience of the kernel of my Self as something which pre-exists the process of interpellation, as subjectivity *prior* to interpellation. The anti-ideological gesture *par excellence* is therefore the act of 'subjective destitution' by means of which I *renounce* the treasure in myself and fully admit my dependence on the externality of symbolic apparatuses – fully assume the fact that my very self-experience of a subject who was already here prior to the external process of interpellation is a retroactive misrecognition brought about by that very process of interpellation. . . .[86]

In order to provide a Lacanian answer to this criticism, it is necessary to introduce the distinction between subject *qua* pure void of self-relating negativity ($) and the phantasmic content which fills out this void (the 'stuff of the I', as Lacan puts it). That is to say: the very aim of the psychoanalytic process is, of course, to induce the subject to renounce the 'secret treasure' which forms the kernel of his phantasmic identity; this renunciation of *agalma*, the 'going-through the fantasy [*traversée du fantasme*]', is strictly equivalent to the act of 'subjective destitution'. However, the subject prior to interpellation–subjectivization is not this imaginary phantasmic depth which allegedly precedes the process of interpellation, but the very void which remains once the phantasmic space is emptied of its content – when, that is, to paraphrase Mallarmé's *Un coup de dés*, nothing takes place but the place itself. The process of interpellation fills out an empty place which must already be here if this process is to take place.

'Desire is the desire of the Other'

Today, everyone in the world, even those who otherwise excel in the art of deriding Lacan, repeats after him in one way or another that 'man's desire is the desire of the Other'. What this common reference fails to take note of is not only the precise place in Lacan's work at which this statement occurs (in the midst of discussing the *hysteric's* desire, which means that, for Lacan, the hysterical 'desire to desire', far from being a defective mode of desire, is, rather, its paradigmatic case, desire *tout court*), but also the fact that it has to be read in three ways, in accordance with the triad I–S–R:

• *Imaginary* is the imitation of my fellow-man, who serves as my ideal ego: 'I want what he wants', that is, I desire an object only in so far as it is the object of the other's desire. Here desire is founded in envy, in the rivalry between me and my double-competitor: in what Lacan refers to as 'the identification with the *imago* of the counterpart and the drama of primordial jealousy'.[87]

• At the *symbolic* level, 'the desire of the Other' is to be read both as *genitivus subjectivus* and as *genitivus objectivus*. First, there is the dialectic of recognition in which the other's desire is the object of my desire: what I desire is to be desired–recognized by the other ('the first object of desire is to be recognized by the other'[88]). Secondly, 'it is *qua* Other that he [the subject] desires'[89] – that is, what I desire is predetermined and decided at the Other Place of the anonymous-transsubjective symbolic order, it is 'mediated' by the symbolic network of the cultural tradition to which I belong. The 'big Other' prescribes to the subject the matrix of his or her desiring, inclusive of the possible forms of 'transgression': 'desire is an effect in the subject of the condition that is imposed on him by the existence of the discourse, to make his need pass through the defiles of the signifier'; and the Other – the transsubjective symbolic order – is precisely 'the locus of the deployment of speech'.[90] What we encounter here, in this duality of *genitivus subjectivus* and *genitivus objectivus*, is, of course, the antagonistic solidarity between the Lacan of Hegelian intersubjectivity and the 'structuralist' Lacan.

167

• However, when Lacan asserts that 'the question *of* the Other, which comes back to the subject from the place from which he expects an oracular reply in some such form as "*Che vuoi?*", "What do you want?", is the one that best leads him to the path of his own desire',[91] he aims at something even more fundamental: the enigma of the Other's desire in its impenetrability, in so far as it eludes symbolization – in short, the Other's desire confronts me with the opacity of the impossible *Real* that resists symbolization. Lacan's point is that I can fully assume the gap that constitutes my desire only via the confrontation with the enigma of the Other's desire. When, in the last years of his teaching, Lacan granted such a pivotal role to the desire of the analyst, the analyst was here no longer conceived as the privileged representative of the big Other (the symbolic order); what Lacan refers to as the 'presence of the analyst', rather, stands for the enigma of desire as such: the analyst's desire is not the desire for something determinate (say, a successful interpretation) but a kind of 'white' desire that emerges when I encounter an Other whose actual wants are not clear, although he does seem to want something from me, like the mysterious agency that addresses the subject in Kafka's novels (the Court, the Castle).

What immediately follows from this triad are the three possible foundations of ethics:

• The ethics of the Imaginary is founded upon the reference to some supreme Good in its entire span, from the most 'vulgar' utilitarian pleasure to contemplative immersion in the divine substance – in rejecting this ethics, Lacan is behaving like a good Leninist. That is to say, one of the unmistakable features of Lenin's style was that when he was confronted by a 'formal' bourgeois category, he always countered it with a malicious question about its concrete content and the context of its subject of enunciation: 'Freedom – *for whom? To do what?*' Lacan addresses the same question to the philosophers who advocate an ethics of the good: 'For the good of whom?'[92] There is no neutral Good; every positive determination of the 'Good' involves us in an inescapable deadlock.

• The minimal criterion of the ethics of the Symbolic is the priority of justice over any form of Good: one's duty is defined by the moral Law which prescribes what one should do. What we are dealing with here is the ethics of the Word: I have to obey the moral law, to follow its word, irrespective of my 'pathological' inclinations, even if it goes against my (or anybody else's) Good or well-being.

• The ethics of the Real, finally, brings into play the moral Law in its impenetrable aspect, as an agency that arouses anxiety by addressing me with the empty, tautological and, for that very reason, enigmatic injunction 'Do your duty!', leaving it to me to translate this injunction into a determinate moral obligation – I, the moral subject, remain forever plagued by uncertainty, since the moral Law provides no guarantee that I 'got it right'. . . .

One can thus 'save' Kant from the traditional Hegelian criticism concerning the purely formal nature of the categorical imperative: according to this criticism, the abstract form of the imperative is the obverse of the effective enslavement of the Kantian moral subject to the empirical, contingent content – the only way for him to pass from the abstract obligation to do his duty to some concrete, effective duty is to look around into the contingent 'pathological' content of his concrete life-situation. It is this very apparent weakness of the categorical imperative, however, that accounts for its compelling impact: the injunction of the categorical imperative is unconditional in that it is empty–tautological. This void signals that the moral subject is fully responsible for the translation of the categorical imperative into a concrete moral obligation. In this precise sense, one is tempted to risk a parallel with Kant's *Critique of Judgement*: the concrete formulation of a determinate ethical obligation has the structure of an aesthetic judgement, that is, of a judgement by means of which, instead of simply applying a universal category to a particular object or subsuming this object under an already-given universal determination, I as it were *invent* its universal-necessary-obligatory dimension, and thereby elevate this particular-contingent object (act) to the dignity of the ethical Thing. On that account, there is always something sublime about pronouncing a judgement that defines our duty – in it, I 'elevate an object to the dignity of the Thing' (Lacan's definition of sublimation).

What we encounter here is the unexpected reverse – usually passed over in silence – of Kant's prohibition on our invoking external circumstances or human weakness as an excuse for *not accomplishing* our duty ('I know I should do it, but what can I do? I'm simply too weak, such is my nature . . .'): we are also prohibited from invoking circumstances (say, the pressure of the voice of conscience) as a pretext for *accomplishing* our duty – that is to say, in this case I also bear full responsibility for what I promulgate as my ethical-obligation duty, so that I am not permitted to say: 'Sorry, I know it was unpleasant, but I couldn't help it, the moral law imposed that act on me as my unconditional duty!'. According to Lacan, the analyst authorizes himself, by means of his act, without any guarantee in the big Other (of the psychoanalytic community, of the theoretical knowledge he possesses . . .) – the same goes for the Kantian ethical subject, who also 'authorizes himself' in the sense of being fully responsible for what he refers to as his duty. In short, to go to extremes – that is, to tautology: duty cannot serve as an excuse for doing our duty. Kant is thus effectively not a pervert: what is thoroughly foreign to him is, say, the perverse attitude of a Stalinist Communist who justifies his terror by claiming that he is simply fulfilling historical necessity – a pervert's conduct is unethical in so far as he shifts the responsibility for it to the big Other ('laws of history', etc.) and claims to act merely as its instrument.[93]

It is therefore wrong to conceive the Kantian categorical imperative as a kind of formal mould whose application to a concrete case relieves the moral subject of the responsibility for a decision: I am not sure if to accomplish the act X is my duty or not. No problem – I test it by submitting it to the double formal criterion implied by the categorical imperative (Can this act be universalized? Does it treat other human beings also as ends in themselves, not only as means?), and if the act X stands the test, I know where my duty lies. . . . The whole point of Kantian argumentation is the exact opposite of this automatic procedure of verification: the fact that the categorical imperative is an empty form means precisely that it can deliver no guarantee against misjudging our duty (in this precise sense, the empty form of the imperative coincides with its opposite, pure formlessness). The structure of the categorical imperative is tautological in the Hegelian sense of the repetition of the same that fills up and simultaneously announces an abyss that gives rise to unbearable anxiety: 'Your duty is . . . [to do your duty]!' It is easy to play the game of trying to provide a minimal positive definition of the ethical act; in the case of a man, for example, the best candidate is probably 'Dress up as a woman and commit suicide in public'.[94] But whatever we do, we always do it in order to fill up the abyss of tautology that resonates in 'Do your duty!'[95]

Here, however, we seem to stumble again upon the old reproach of Lacanian ethics: is the ethical Law not thereby reduced to a superego agency that makes us a priori guilty? Is it not the case that whatever positive content we put forward as our concrete ethical obligation, we never fully succeed in appeasing the anxiety that announces itself in the void that gapes in the very heart of 'Do your duty!'? Does not the fact that I can never be sure what my duty is brand me with an indelible mark of guilt? In short, does not the categorical imperative's double-bind message irradiate the malevolent neutrality of a superego sadist: I am bombarded with an unconditional injunction to accomplish my duty, yet the moment I translate this injunction into a concrete obligation, the ethical Other assumes the attitude of a malevolent neutral observer, whose message to me changes all of a sudden into 'I certainly don't want anything from you! It was you who defined your duty, so you have to bear the consequences as well as the responsibility for it! Now let's take a seat and watch how you handle the mess you've got yourself into!' . . . It is crucial here, however, to take into account the fact that 'the big Other doesn't exist' (Lacan): we are guilty in so far as we accept that the big Other exists in the guise of a transcendent agency which plays a perverse game of cat and mouse with us, knowing very well what our duty is yet concealing it from us, letting us grope around and make blind guesses. We leave the domain of superego guilt behind the moment we become aware that the Other itself does not know what my duty is.

To put it differently: it is essential, in our reading of Kant, to distinguish the true from the false transcendence of Law: this distinction coincides with the one between 'pure' symbolic Law and superego. In false transcendence, the moral Law appears as an external 'terrorizing' agency which threatens me in the guise of two objects, voice and gaze (the *voice* of conscience that haunts me; the all-penetrating *gaze* that unerringly detects my guilt). However, this very notion of the moral Law as an external terrorizing agency already gentrifies/softens its true transcendence by transforming it into an external agent with whom a relationship of exchange, sacrifice, 'haggling', is possible – in short, the moral Law is implicitly reduced to the level of 'representation [*Vorstellung*]'; it turns into an object that stands opposite ourselves, not the absolute Other. The pure Law, on the contrary, stands for the Otherness of an Imperative that has nothing whatsoever to do with the field of vocal or visual representations, for the empty Otherness of absolute transcendence – and the implicitely Hegelian point of Kant, of course, is that this absolute transcendence coincides with pure immanence. Let us recall Antigone: she was driven by an imperative untainted by any superego coercion, that is to say, she acted as she did not out of any pressure exerted on her by the 'voice of her conscience' but for the simple reason that she could not act otherwise.

On a first approach, we are dealing here with the distinction between the moral Law 'in itself' and the way this Law affects us, its subjects. The Law 'in itself' is a pure imperative; the problem is that we, human beings, are always tainted with 'pathology', prone to tangible impressions; so, in order to become effective, this pure agency of the categorical imperative has to assume, in its relationship to us, the tangible form of a voice and/or a gaze (like God, the unfathomable and unrepresentable Absolute, whom we, ordinary humans, depict as a wise bearded old man). . . . A deeper approach, however, compels us exactly to invert the terms. In so far as we 'reify' the moral law into an agency that exists 'in itself' and exerts its pressure upon us from without, we reduce its status to that of a representation (of a voice and/or gaze) – voice and/or gaze designate precisely the way the Law 'in itself' exists *for us*. In clear contrast, the moral Law *qua* pure transcendence is no longer an entity that exists independently of its relationship to us; it is *nothing but* its relationship to us (to the moral subject).

Here, in his determination of the relationship between the subject and the moral Law, Kant comes unexpectedly close to the Hegelian speculative reflective inversion. That is to say: when Kant defines the relationship between the subject and the moral Law as that of 'respect' or 'reverence [*Achtung*]', he adds a crucial qualification: 'reverence' does not simply designate the way the subject relates to the Law, his or her 'subjective experience' of the Law; rather, it stands for *the Law itself in its subjective existence, that is, in its actuality* (since the moral Law is actual only in so far as it is disclosed in the subject's experience). The 'Hegelian' feature here is the inversion of the 'normal' relationship between subject and predicate: that which, on a first approach, should possess the status of a mere predicate (the effect, the mode of existence of the Law), is the Law itself in its actuality; and vice versa, that which appears as the Law 'in itself', existing independently of the subject, is effectively a subjective phantasmagoria, a spectral non-entity that merely materializes, gives body to, the non-purity of the subject's ethical stance.[96]

And our point, of course, is that Lacan's '*ne pas céder sur son désir*' ('do not compromise your desire') involves exactly the same tautological injunction (a new corroboration of the fact that, as Lacan put it, Kant's moral law is simply desire in its pure state): it provides no positive guarantee or support of our desire, that is, the subject is not allowed to say: 'I know this is reprehensible, but what can I do? This is what I desire, and I cannot give it up . . .' – the subject is fully responsible for what she or he desires. For that reason, the injunction 'do not compromise your desire' is empty, impossible to comply with fully, that is to say, it touches the real.

So: to conclude, it would be appropriate to return to the theme which, perhaps, provides the key to the entire Lacanian theoretical edifice: 'Kant avec Sade'. How are we to conceive this paradoxical thesis on Sade as the truth of Kantian ethics? The first answer offers itself with delusive self-evidence: of course, everybody knows that superego sadism is the hidden truth of the Kantian ethics! That is to say, is not Kant's rigorist ethics patently 'sadistic'; is not the agency which pronounces the ethical imperative a sublime version of the sadistic torturer who demands the impossible and finds enjoyment in humiliating the subject, that is, in the subject's failure to comply with his demand? If, as Lacan put it, Hegel is the most sublime of all hysterics, is not therefore Kant the most sublime of all sadists? However, although it may appear that at least some of Lacan's statements effectively point in this direction (does not Lacan emphasize that Sade put Kant's cards on the table by rendering visible the sadistic agent who is the true subject of enunciation of the categorical imperative?), a careful reading soon makes it clear that what Lacan has in mind is the exact opposite of this thesis on the 'sadistic' character of Kantian ethics: Lacan's aim is not to 'besmirch' the purity of the Kantian imperative – that is, to discern beneath it the 'pathological' sadistic enjoyment – but, on the contrary, to demonstrate that *the Sadeian Will-to-Enjoy ['Volonté de Jouissance'] is thoroughly 'pure', ethical in the strictest Kantian sense*. The imperative which sustains the Sadeian subject's endless search for enjoyment fulfils all the criteria of the categorical imperative. Far from 'besmirching' Kant, Lacan 'purifies' Sade: the sadist Will-to-Enjoy is the exemplary case of a pure, non-pathological desire. Perhaps therein resides the ultimate cause of all the troubles with so-called modern subjectivity.

Notes

1. Leaving aside the two traditional, pre-Lacanian readings, of course: the ego-psychological 'the Ego has to occupy the territory of the Id', as well as the irrationalist 'the Ego has to give way to the Id, to drives which form the core of man's personality beneath the rational Ego'.

2. Jacques Lacan, *Écrits: A Selection*, New York: Norton 1977, p. 319.

3. See Rudolf Bernet, 'Subjekt und Gesetz in der Ethik von Kant und Lacan', in *Ethik und Psychoanalyse*, ed. Hans-Dieter Gondek and Peter Widmer, Frankfurt: Fischer 1994.

4. See Bernard Baas, 'Das öffentliche Ding', in *Ethik und Psychoanalyse*.

5. This crucial distinction is elaborated by Peter Widmer in his 'Ethik und Psychoanalyse', in *Ethik und Psychoanalyse*, p. 16.

6. On this Lacanian myth of lamella, see Chapter 3 of Slavoj Žižek, *Tarrying with the Negative*, Durham, NC: Duke University Press 1993. Incidentally, what we have just said in no way implies that the Real of drives is, in its ontological status, a kind of full substantiality, the positive 'stuff' of formal–symbolic structurations. What Lacan did with the notion of drive is strangely similar to what Einstein, in his general theory of relativity, did with the notion of gravity. Einstein 'desubstantialized' gravity by reducing it to geometry: gravity is not a substantial force which 'bends' space but the name for the curvature of space itself; in an analogous way, Lacan 'desubstantialized' drives: a drive is not a primordial positive force but a purely geometrical, topological phenomenon, the name for the curvature of the space of desire – for the paradox that, within this space, the way to attain the object (*a*) is not to go straight for it (the surest way to miss it) but to encircle it, to 'go round in circles'. Drive is this purely topological 'distortion' of the

natural instinct which finds satisfaction in a direct consumption of its object.

7. Mikkel Borch-Jakobsen's otherwise very consistent critique of Lacan, according to which Lacan remains confined to the Cartesian subject of (symbolic) representations, and is therefore able to comprehend the pre-symbolic Real only in a purely negative way, as a lack, void, or absence, is justified only in so far as we reduce Lacan to this 'philosophical' aspect and see in him a theoretician of 'constitutive lack', 'symbolic castration', etc. (See Mikkel Borch-Jakobsen, *Lacan: The Absolute Master*, Stanford, CA: Stanford University Press 1991.)

There is yet another problem with Borch-Jakobsen: when he makes the critical claim that Lacan's notion of the unconscious ('structured like a language') remains all too rational-Cartesian, since it conceives the unconscious as composed of symbolic representations, and thereby stops short of the 'true' unconscious which is not merely a shadowy, incompletely actualized representation but beyond (or rather, beneath) the very domain of representations, he – as it were – knocks at an open door, and thoroughly misses Lacan's point. The notion of an unconscious beyond *cogito* (beyond discourse, beyond representations . . .) never posed a problem for modern philosophy: the whole of *Lebensphilosophie* hinges on just such a purely 'irrational' instinctual unconscious; the traumatic aspect of the Freudian unconscious, rather, resides in the fact that it possesses precisely those qualities which are usually conceived as the privilege of rational-discursive consciousness: far from being composed of blind, 'irrational' drives, it is, on the contrary, a network of signifying representations, a discourse with a 'rationality' of its own – *this* is what makes it so traumatic for the ordinary philosophical attitude. . . .

8. Raymond Chandler, *The High Window*, New York: Vintage 1992, p. 45.

9. From time to time, Derrida also evokes the possibility that the voice might function as a 'supplement' whose free floating has to be anchored to the firm contours of writing; for him, however, this is merely a subordinate, secondary reversal of the more primordial conjunction of writing being subverted by the self-presence of the voice.

10. This difference between Derrida and Lacan also involves a different strategy of 'deconstruction' (if, of course, one accepts as pertinent the claim that Lacan also practises a kind of 'deconstruction'). In Derrida, the subordinated term of some traditional metaphysical dyad is first asserted as decisive, and gains the upper hand over its counterpart; then, subsequently, one endeavours to delineate the elusive contours of a more 'original' movement which generates the very dyad in question and can be grasped only *sous rature*, never 'as such': from writing (which gains predominance over speech) to arche-writing, for example. In Lacan (and Hegel), on the contrary, the very privileged term of metaphysics is asserted as the form of appearance of its Other: 'voice' itself is simultaneously the medium of self-transparency and the opaque foreign body which undermines the subject's self-presence; 'centre' is supplement itself; etc.

11. What we encounter here, of course, is another variant of the vicious cycle of symbolization: on the one hand, the universe of symbols is a cobweb of retreats from the Thing, of its copies, imitations, simulacra; on the other, this Thing itself does not pre-exist its simulacra, but is their retroactive effect – the central point of reference, the ultimate Cause, is an effect of its effects.

12. An excellent example of such a Third which acts as the neutral medium of the polar extremes is provided by Schelling's reading of speculative identity: when I claim that 'A is B', I thereby assert the existence of an X which is (in one respect) A and (in another respect) B. The identity of the Ideal and the Real, for example, does not entail that the Real is merely a predicate of the Ideal (or vice versa); it points towards the Absolute *qua* the absolute indifference which contains the Ideal and the Real as its two modes.

13. Here, it is again crucial to bear in mind the difference between the three stages of Schelling's thought: in his 'identity-philosophy' the two poles, the Ideal and the Real, meet in the neutral medium of absolute indifference; in the highly problematic and unstable 'monism of freedom' of his middle stage Schelling is at his most subversive, and heralds the problematic of materialist genesis; finally, in his late 'positive philosophy', the unbearable tension of the second stage is resolved via 'regression' to the traditional ontological oppositions of essence and existence, etc.

14. This point was developed by Robert Pfaller in his intervention 'Zum Althusserianischen Nominalismus' at the colloquium *Der Althusser-Effekt*, Vienna, 17–20 March 1994.

15. F.W.J. Schelling, *Sämtliche Werke*, ed. K.F.A. Schelling, Stuttgart: Cotta 1856–61, vol. VII, p. 470.

16. This, of course, has nothing whatsoever to do with the empiricist assertion of the 'infinite wealth of real life' beyond the reach of abstract notions: the point is not that our theoretical preconceptions have to accommodate to 'real life'. For Hegel, as a radical idealist, the surplus of 'life' over its notional determinations always signals an inherent insufficiency of these determinations themselves: when we experience 'reality' as something infinitely more complex and rich than our abstract conceptual network, this does not mean that we have dwelt too much in theory and should deal more with 'life itself' – it means, on the contrary, that *we did not think enough*, that our thought remained too 'abstract'.

17. For a more detailed account of this notion of 'castration', see 'The Parerga of hainamoration', in Renata Salecl and Slavoj Žižek, eds, *Gaze and Voice as Love Objects* (SIC Series 1), Durham, NC: Duke University Press 1996.

18. What corresponds to this shift in the history of music is perhaps the crucial shift, formulated and practised by Webern, from the *Klangstruktur* to the *Strukturklang*: from the sound which follows the (imposed) tonal structure, the 'structure of sounds', to an unheard-of sound which is directly the 'sound of the structure itself' – that is, to a structure which is directly the structure of the sound itself in its positive materiality. This is what 'modern music' is really about: the suspension of tonality renders palpable the presence of sounds in the real of their material density.

19. See Jean-Jacques Lecercle, *Violence of Language*, London and New York: Routledge 1990.

20. See Chapter 3 of Slavoj Žižek, *The Metastases of Enjoyment*, London: Verso 1994.

21. Leibniz provides one of the most pregnant formulations of this fundamental feature of philosophical idealism. Common sense seems to tell us that ideas are mental ('subjective') representations locked within our mind, whereas the true reality which exists independently of our mind is the actual material universe; according to Leibniz, however, it is the impenetrable material world which is merely a blurred, 'subjective' representation of the lower monads: for God, the perfect monad able to perceive things *sub specie aeternitatis*, the way they effectively are, there is no matter, only spiritual entities.

22. Two further examples. A close examination of the text of Wagner's *Ring* reveals that precisely those elements which are 'spontaneously' apprehended as the most archaic-mythical (the beginning of *Rheingold*, with Alberich's theft of the gold guarded by the Rhine maidens, for example) have no basis whatsoever in old Nordic or German mythology, and are Wagner's own invention. It is similar with Brecht's *Jasager*: a detailed comparison with the old Japanese *No*-play which Brecht used as his base shows that all the elements which were perceived as the extreme expression of the 'Oriental spirit' of unconditional obedience to Authority and 'irrational' sacrifice were provided by Brecht himself. . . .

23. The usual (in this case Kantian) idea of the complete notional determination of intuition, which would abolish the gap that separates (the universal) notion from intuition – that is, would bring the specification of universal notional determinations to its conclusion, thereby enabling us to conceptualize the uniqueness of a singular entity – is therefore the very opposite of Hegel's 'concrete universal': a nonsensical excess of Understanding.

24. Today's 'postmodern' decomposition of the self-identical Subject, who is more and more reduced to an inconsistent *bric-à-brac* of fragmentary 'experiences', confirms *per negationem* this dependency of 'objective reality' on the gesture of subjective positing, in that it does not, as one would expect, make the pre-subjective 'objective reality' any closer or more directly accessible: as the result of the subject's dissolution it is, on the contrary, this very 'objective reality' which loses its ontological consistency and changes into a multitude of simulacra.

25. And are we not dealing with something strictly analogous in the domain of politics?

Is not the entire dialectic of overdetermination generated from the fact that the basic opposition between the classes ('class struggle') is necessarily supplemented by the couple of Power and the populist opposition to it, with no guarantee that the two terms will be superposed in a 'proper', 'natural' unity (the exploited class's populist opposition to the ruling class's Power) – class struggle is never 'pure', it is always displaced through the couple of Power and populism, so that the possibility is always open for the emergence of an 'unnatural', 'perverted' link between the ruling class and populism: the origin of all troubles is 'right-wing populism'.

26. Jacques Lacan, *Le Séminaire, livre VIII: Le transfert*, Paris: Éditions du Seuil 1991, p. 355.

27. In Chapter 5 of Slavoj Žižek, *Enjoy Your Symptom!*, New York: Routledge 1993, I endeavoured to demonstrate that Brecht's 'learning plays' – especially *The Measure Taken*, which directly alludes to Stalinist trials – exhibit the structure of *Versagung* even more exemplarily than Claudel's trilogy. The very passage from Leninism to Stalinism, reminiscent of the Hegelian reversal of the warlord nobleman who silently serves the State into the corrupted courtier who flatters the Monarch (see the chapter on 'Alienation' in his *Phenomenology of Spirit*), provides an exemplary case of *Versagung*. In its ruthless devotion and fidelity to the Communist Cause, Leninism is definitely not without a kind of ethical sublimity: constrained neither by the norms of bourgeois morality nor by consideration for his personal happiness, a true Leninist is ready to stake everything for his Cause. In Stalinism, this devotion turns into the unprincipled flattery of the Master who personifies the Cause, conditioned by the struggle for personal survival and the striving to maintain privileges.

The crucial point, of course, is to comprehend this reversal of pure revolutionary devotion into its opposite (conformist flattery) in its necessity, which consists precisely in the logic of *Versagung*: first, we renounce everything for the Cause (Communism); subsequently, the Cause itself loses its substance, it turns into the empty shell of its true content, whose sole *raison d'être* is to legitimate the brutal exercise of power and towards which both executioners and their victims entertain a cynical distance. In other words, Stalinism is the 'truth' of Leninism precisely in so far as it involves Leninism's radical perversion: it is the very sincere and authentic devotion of a Leninist Communist to his Cause, his very readiness to suspend 'external' ethical, etc., considerations in ruthless pursuit of the Cause, which brings about the conversion to purely external flattery. . . .

28. Jacques Lacan, *Le Séminaire, livre VIII: Le transfert*, p. 355.

29. *The Seminar of Jacques Lacan. Book II: The Ego in Freud's Theory and in the Technique of Psychoanalysis*, New York: Norton 1988, p. 128. A somewhat pathetic corroboration of Lacan's reversal of Dostoevsky is the plight of ex-dissident intellectuals in post-Communist East European countries: while Communist censorship was still operative, it was possible to pass the subversive message between the lines – the very fact of censorship attuned readers' attentiveness to the hidden message, so that everybody understood what a text was about. Now that there is no censorship and that everything is permitted, the prohibition is universalized: it is impossible to pass on the subversive message, readers simply miss it, the critical intellectuals' speech finds no echo. . . .

30. This story about happiness begins with the French Revolution. To what, precisely, does Saint-Just's statement that happiness is a political factor amount? The point is not simply that now that people have escaped the yoke of tyranny they have the right to be happy, and the new State is obliged to work for the happiness of its subjects; what lurks behind is a potential 'totalitarian' inversion: it is your *duty* to be happy – that is to say, if, in the midst of the Revolution, when such unheard-of events are taking place, you are unhappy, it means that you are a counterrevolutionary traitor.

Robespierre was the unsurpassed expert at manipulating this guilt about feeling unhappy and ill at ease: in one of his great speeches, after scaring the life out of the members of the National Assembly by claiming that there were numerous traitors among them (nobody could be sure that he was not on the list), Robespierre continued: 'If, at this very moment, anyone in this hall feels frightened, this is irrefutable proof that he is a traitor!' What we are dealing with here is not merely the variation on the well-known theme 'If you're not guilty, you have nothing to fear!', but also a masterful manipulation of the audience's *desire*: the guilt Robespierre refers to is ultimately the guilt of nourishing a perverse desire which makes us resist our own true happiness – in short, the guilt of having a desire *tout court*.

Robespierre's implicit reasoning could also be formulated as follows: the subject who reacts with fear to his accusation that there are traitors in the room thereby gives preference to his individual safety and well-being over the well-being and freedom of the French people, that is, over the revolutionary Cause – and this attitude in itself is already treacherous, it is treason at its purest, a form of treason prior to any determinate treacherous act. The same logic is at work in the Stalinist's insistence that the accused at a political trial who claims that he is innocent is guilty even if his protestations of innocence are true at the level of facts: he thereby focuses on his individual destiny and displays total indifference to the proletarian Cause, to the fact that his protestations of innocence seriously undermine the authority of the Party, and thereby weaken its unity – and in this bourgeois-individualist attitude resides his true guilt. . . .

31. And perhaps such a gesture also defines the birth of a poet, who first has to sacrifice all for his Lady, and then has to sacrifice the Lady herself.

32. The mythical narrative of the Slovene past is the narrative of a series of choices in which the authentic ethical decision would have led to extinction: in the Slovene collective memory, the eighth-century Christianization is inscribed as a painful compromise – those who yielded survived, while those who remained faithful to their pre-Christian tradition were massacred. The violent suppression of Protestantism followed the same logic – those who persisted in the Protestant faith were either killed or emigrated to German Protestant countries, and the scum with no backbone were the ancestors of the Slovenes of today. . . . In short, the very fact of survival bears witness to a status as an excremental remainder – as if a Slovene is living proof and/or the remainder of a compromise, of 'compromising one's desire', of choosing the wrong side in an ethical choice.

This 'wrong choice' is experienced as a humiliation of paternal authority – which is why, in Slovene mythology, the father is an impotent, frail drunkard, while the pillar of the family is always the mother, on whose silent sacrifice the entire social edifice is supposed to depend; one is tempted to propose the hypothesis that for Slovenes it is the Name-of-the-Mother, not the Name-of-the-Father, which guarantees the fundamental mechanism of socialization, of entry into the symbolic order. The proof that this myth structures social reality itself is the spread of alcoholism in Slovenia where, if one is to believe detailed clinical reports, the typical family constellation involves a humiliated alcoholic father cornered by the mother (his wife) into a double-bind: the mother implores him to cure himself, yet simultaneously her between-the-lines message to him is that he is too weak to do it, so that she effectively propels him in the direction of more drinking. . . .

33. In so far as the subject emerges from such an asymmetrical exchange (I not only get nothing in exchange for what I give, I even lose the very Thing on behalf of which I gave everything away), and in so far as the very kernel of Christianity, of the Christian 'supplement' to the Jewish Law, resides in a homologous traumatic disturbance of the balanced exchange (in exchange for what I lose, I even have to offer what I still possess – 'Whoever shall smite thee on thy right cheek, turn to him the other also', instead of 'An eye for an eye', etc.), it is no mere accident that the process of Christianization forms the background of Prešeren's poem: the modern subject is conceivable only within the Christian symbolic economy.

34. The truth of Modernity, of course, is that the renunciation of the particular (ethnic, etc.) Thing for the sake of the universal order (of Reason, etc.) undercuts the roots which keep this very universal order alive.

35. Against this background, one can also elucidate the strategy of a ruthless and perspicacious interrogator's effort to break down the resistance of his victim and wrest from him a confession that compromises his principles. He begins by inducing his victim to give way on some particular point which seems in no way to jeopardize his principles; then, after extracting from the victim a sufficient number of these 'inessential' concessions, the interrogator has only to remind him that the game is already up and

that it's time to drop the false pretences – the victim's high principles were compromised long ago, so why not call things by their proper name? . . . The trap in which the victim got caught consisted in his illusory belief that the universal Essence, the Thing he really cares about, can persist outside the network of 'inessential' concrete circumstances.

36. On a somewhat different level, the same goes for every attempt to 'accommodate' psychoanalysis to particular circumstances. Suffice it to recall Jung's infamous advice to Freud, on the ocean liner approaching New York, to avoid excessive emphasizing of sexuality in order to render psychoanalysis more palpable to puritan Americans, and Freud's bitter reply that if they leave out even more of its content, psychoanalysis will become all the more acceptable. . . . The fate of psychoanalysis in America – where, of course, it survived as the lifeless shell of its true content – fully justified Freud's rejection of such 'tactical concessions'.

37. In his reading of Claudel's Coufontaine trilogy, Lacan proposes three formulations of this gesture of *Versagung* (or, in Lacanese, symbolic castration):

- ' . . . castration is ultimately structured like this – we take away from somebody his desire, and in exchange for it we hand him over to somebody else – in this case, to the social order.'(Jacques Lacan, *Le Séminaire, livre VIII: Le transfert*, p. 380)

- ' . . . we deprive the subject of his desire, and in exchange for it we send him to the market where he becomes the object of general auction.' (ibid.)

- 'The effects on a human being of the fact that he becomes a subject of law are, in short, that he is deprived of what matters to him most, and in exchange for it, he is himself delivered to the texture which is woven between generations.' (ibid., pp. 380–81)

The very enchainment of these three formulations displays the structure of a Hegelian triad. What changes from the first formulation to the second is the nature of the order to which the subject is delivered: from the 'social order' in general, which suggests the complex edifice of the relations of domination and interdependence, we pass to the *market*, to this universal equalizer (in the act of exchange, all differences of social status are magically obliterated). On the other hand, the nature of what the subject is deprived of remains the same: his *desire*. In the third formulation, we return to the first as to the nature of the order to which the subject is delivered ('the texture of generations', i.e. the complex network of interdependences), whereas what the subject is deprived of is no longer his desire but 'what matters to him most': the object-cause of his desire, the hidden treasure that accounts for his value, *objet petit a*. The gap that separates this third formulation from the first two is crucial: in the last case the desire is no longer that of which the subject is deprived in the course of exchange but, rather, what the subject *gains* in the course of exchange – I become a desiring subject only in so far as I am deprived of 'what matters to me most'.

38. I am relying here on the excellent analysis of this scene by Elizabeth Cowie from her '*Film noir* and Women', in Joan Copjec, ed., *Shades of Noir*, London: Verso 1993, pp. 155–9. It would be of great theoretical interest to deploy all the different cinematic versions of this strange process of *aphanisis* in the course of which a subject from diegetic reality is killed or otherwise 'passes out' and then miraculously survives his/her own death: what we encounter here is the same structure of 'transubstantiation', i.e. the subject who survives his/her death is not substantially 'the same' as before. Suffice it to recall Hitchcock's *The 39 Steps*, in which Hannay is shot by the treacherous paternal figure (master of the spy ring) and saved by the Bible in his breast-pocket, which miraculously intercepts the bullet: it is deeply significant that *aphanisis* follows Hannay's confrontation with the 'anal father' who obscenely shows off his lack (the cut-off left third finger, his sign of recognition).

39. For an unsurpassed formulation of this key moment of the Hegelian dialectical process, see Gérard Lebrün, *La patience du concept*, Paris: Gallimard 1973.

40. According to the standard critique of the so-called 'representationalist notion of politics', one should renounce the notion of the political subject, since this notion refers

to the subject as an entity which pre-exists the (political) act and/or event and 'expresses' itself in it. It should now, however, be clear where this critique goes wrong: political subjectivity constitutes itself *in actu*, through its act; consequently, it is misleading to speak of 'its' act, since the subject is performatively posited by 'its' act – behind a true political act there is no pre-existing 'subject' whose 'interests' are 'represented' in it (as in the vulgar Marxist notion of political struggle, in which different positions 'represent' or 'translate' pre-existing economic class interests). In short, the problem with the critique of the 'representationalist notion of politics' is that it conceives the (political) subject as a substantial entity and not in the sense of German Idealism: in German Idealism, 'substance' designates the substratum which precedes the act/event and 'expresses' itself, its content, in it, whereas 'subject' coincides with 'its' act. The most pregnant formulation of this purely performative status of the subject is provided by Fichte's notion of *Tathandlung*, pointing towards the subject as the performative result of its own self-positing.

41. See Georges Bataille, *La part maudite*, Paris: Éditions de Minuit 1966.

42. I owe this line of thought to a conversation with Mark de Kessel.

43. One way of accounting for the paradox of the Hegelian *Aufhebung* is simply to conceive its two main recent French critiques, that of Deleuze and that of Derrida, as 'complementary'. Deleuze opposes *Aufhebung* as the limited-restrained negation, the negation which does not wholly annihilate its object but maintains and elevates its essential content to a higher, 'mediated' level, to the Nietzschean radical negation-destruction which 'clears the field' entirely, and thus opens up the space for the creation of the New; whereas Derrida, in clear contrast, plays upon the fact that *Aufhebung* never comes out without a remainder which resists being sublated–mediated. If, then, for Deleuze, Hegel is 'not radical enough', and does not go right to the end in the movement of negation, but gets entangled in the cobweb of deferrals–mediations, he is for Derrida 'all too radical', i.e. he underplays the extent to which the detour of deferral–mediation affects and displaces the very self-identity of the movement of negation–mediation, so precipitating its irretrievable 'dissemination'.

The solution resides in the 'dialectical synthesis' of these two opposites – not, of course, in the sense that Hegel offers the 'proper measure' of negation by way of avoiding the two extremes: Deleuze's excess of total annihilation, as well as Derrida's eternal deferral of it. The imagined Hegelian answer would, rather, consist in focusing on the level on which these two opposed critiques of *Aufhebung* coincide: the ultimate resort of *Aufhebung* is this very coincidence of the two modes of its own failure. Hegel's 'infinite judgement' *Der Geist ist ein Knochen* [The spirit is a bone], for example, designates the coincidence of pure, absolute, unconstrained negativity with an inert, non-dialectizable leftover. Or take the Monarch in Hegel's *Philosophy of Right*, who stands for the absolute negativity exempted from social mediation (he does not have to 'form' himself through the *work* of the negative, through its movement of deferral; he incarnates the threat of war which can engulf the complex social edifice at any moment . . .) precisely in so far as he is the remainder of biological 'immediacy', the last piece of raw, non-sublated, non-mediated nature (one is a King by birth, not by merit . . .).

Incidentally, in his otherwise exemplary formulation of the criticism that Hegel remains within the 'restrained economy' of sacrificing-negating only the 'inessential' (see Michael Hardt, *Gilles Deleuze*, Minneapolis: Minnesota University Press 1994), Hardt himself gets entangled in an 'essential' and unavoidable inconsistency. First, he quotes atomic disaster as an example of a radical destruction-negation in which nothing of the negated content is 'sublated', i.e. saved and elevated; then, all of a sudden, he claims that there is no need for the actual physical annihilation to take place – a radical rejection of the past and its tradition is sufficient. (Hardt's own example from the workers' movement: in contrast to the 'Hegelian' reformist demand that work, not capital, should rule – to such an inherent negation, 'sublation', of capitalism – one has to reject the very notion of work as already impregnated by the logic of capital. . . . From the Hegelian standpoint, one is tempted to retort that this radical rejection of the very notion of work, not merely of 'alienated' work, provides a nice example of the 'negation of negation', i.e. of the negation which negates the very presupposition shared by the 'position' – in this case, the rule of Capital – and its 'immediate' negation, the demand that work should rule). The moment we introduce this shift into the notion of 'radical negation', we leave behind pure, unrestrained negation and enter the domain of what Lacan calls the 'between-two-deaths': real death (physical destruction, atomic catastrophe) and the symbolic 'second death'. This difference, however, immediately involves us in Hegelian dialectical paradoxes, since it implies the difference between fully actualized power (which leads to the effective destruction of the other) and power which does not fully actualize itself but remains suspended, a potential threat (such a notion of power, which produces actual effects in its very potentiality, is indistinguishable from the symbolic 'second death'). In short, Hardt is forced silently to reformulate 'radical destruction' in such a way that this notion accommodates suspended power, power hindered in its act – something which, from a strictly Nietzschean perspective, cannot but appear as a sign of the nihilistic self-impediment of the life-force....

As for the relationship between Derrida and Deleuze, it is interesting to note how the difference in 'content' between these two critiques of Hegel overlaps with the difference in the very form of their respective writing. Derrida is a hyper-reflective philosopher who seems never to make a direct positive claim, but focuses on a search for inconsistencies in other philosophers' texts – or, rather, for inconsistencies in what philosopher B claims about philosopher A; consequently, his style is full of quotes, of reflective retreats which re-mark and reframe what has just been said. Deleuze, however, seems to effectuate a kind of return to the great 'pre-critical' innocence of directly deploying great ontological propositions on the nature of the Absolute, etc.; even when he interprets another philosopher (Nietzsche, Spinoza, etc.), he practises a version of the *discours indirect libre*, so that his rendition of the interpreted philosopher's line of reasoning becomes indistinguishable from his own thought.

44. Jacques Derrida, *Of Grammatology*, Baltimore, MD: Johns Hopkins University Press 1976, pp. 68–9.

45. Rodolphe Gasché falls most blatantly into this trap: according to his reading of Hegel, in the absolute identity of the Spirit 'all external conditions that may have seemed necessary to conceive it show themselves not only to be instances in which the Absolute is present, in that they sublate *themselves by themselves*, but also to be the Other in which the Absolute *relates to itself*. The Absolute, in relating to Other, consequently, relates to itself' (Rodolphe Gasché, *Inventions of Difference*, Cambridge, MA: Harvard University Press 1994, p. 205). What we have here is the standard story of Absolute Spirit as the full transparency and presence of self-mediation, internalizing every relation to Otherness into a self-relation.... What gets lost in this story is, as we have just seen, the price to be paid for this self-transparency: the loss of self-identity of the 'Self' itself – the Self which 'returns to itself' is not substantially the same as the one which previously got lost .... What remains the same in this process of loss and return is the void itself as its 'operator', i.e. the subject bereft of any substantial content ($). The Lacanian subject, of course, is not merely a 'pure void', but is sustained by a minimum of inert materiality which serves as its support (this paradoxical conjunction is designated by Lacan's matheme of fantasy: $\$ \lozenge a$). This support, however, is an object which is a direct counterpoint to the subject and, as such, gives body to a lack – that is to say, it is the 'originally missing object'.

46. '... after the mapping of the subject in relation to the *a*, the experience of the fundamental fantasy becomes the drive. What, then, does he who has passed through the experience of this opaque relation to the origin, to the drive, become? How can a subject who has traversed the radical fantasy experience the drive? This is the beyond of analysis, and has never been approached' (Jacques Lacan, *The Four Fundamental Concepts of Psycho-Analysis*, Harmondsworth: Penguin 1979, p. 273).

47. This is not to deny that these allusions are as a rule very pertinent. In *Le transfert*, for example, Lacan draws attention to the thoughtless superfluity of the Nietzschean syntagm 'beyond Good and Evil' ('not, as one is used to say in a kind of refrain, beyond Good and Evil, which is a nice formula to obfuscate what is in question, but simply beyond the Good' – Jacques Lacan, *Le Séminaire, livre VIII: Le transfert*, pp. 322–3): the moment one traverses the horizon of the Good, one also leaves behind the Evil.

48. At this level of the pure positivity of drive, 'do not compromise your desire [*ne pas céder sur son désir*]' is no longer operative, since, from the standpoint of drive, *desire as such is already a compromise*, a defence-formation against *jouissance*: 'For desire is a defence against going beyond a certain limit in *jouissance*.' (Jacques Lacan, *Écrits: A Selection*, p. 322). The ethics of desire and the ethics of drive are thus almost symmetrically opposed. Desire is always desire to desire, its primary aim is to maintain itself as desire, i.e. to keep open the gap of its unsatisfaction – apropos of an object, the experience of desire is always 'this is not *that*'; from this standpoint, of course, drive cannot but appear as the imbecilic self-enclosure which obfuscates the void of desire. Drive, on the contrary, is a circular motion which finds satisfaction in the very repetition of its failure; from this standpoint, desire appears as the endless postponing of the encounter with the Real Thing, as the escape from the satisfaction of *jouissance*, from the fact that we always-already *have* what we are after. Jean-Claude Milner is therefore fully justified in his claim that '*ne pas céder sur son désir*' is not part of the real core of Lacan's teaching, i.e. is not a proposition which returns again and again with ever new meaning (as is the case with 'desire is the desire of the other', 'the unconscious is structured like a language', the triad of Imaginary–Symbolic–Real, etc.), but a proposition limited to a certain phase of his teaching, which later disappears wihout trace. (See Jean-Claude Milner, *L'œuvre claire*, Paris: Seuil 1994.)

49. And does not this alternative – the eternal return of drives versus the endless metonymy of lack – bring us back to Schelling? Is not the eternal return of drives another name for Schelling's rotary motion, and is not the metonymy of lack another name for the infinite progress opened up by the emergence of the Word?

50. Another solution proposed by some Lacanians involves the attempt to articulate two distinct modes of the big Other: analysts form a *collective of knowledge* kept together by the shared reference to their Cause, *objet a*, in contrast to the usual *community of belief* (supposed knowledge) kept together by the shared reference to some Master-Signifier (S_1).

51. See Jacques Lacan, 'Logical time and the Assertion of Anticipated Certainty', in *Newsletter of the Freudian Field*, vol. 2, no. 2 (1988), and Chapter 2 of Slavoj Žižek, *Tarrying with the Negative*, Durham, NC: Duke University Press 1993.

52. Jacques Derrida, *The Gift of Death*, Chicago: University of Chicago Press 1995, p. 108.

53. See his excellent *La communauté virtuelle*, Combas: Éditions de l'éclat 1994.

54. As a rule, populist-corporatist leaders excel in the artifice of enabling every subgroup within the nation to recognize its own special content in the common Cause; as Ernesto Laclau has pointed out, Juan Perón presented himself to the trade unions as the representative of workers' interests against the corrupt capitalist plutocracy, to the Catholic Church as a devoted Christian fighting liberal decadence, to the Army as a zealous advocate of the patriotic values of defence of the country, and so on.

55. A careful reader, of course, has not missed the strict homology between this interdependence and the fundamental premiss of philosophical idealism: it is the subject's free act of positing which transforms the chaotic multitude of impressions into a consistent 'objective reality'.

56. The relationship between A and *a* is therefore *not* to be confused with the logic of the Universal and its constitutive exception: *objet petit a* is not the exception which guarantees the consistency of the big Other but, on the contrary, the very 'bone stuck in the throat' which prevents the big Other from establishing itself as a consistent field.

57. One often encounters, in different domains, similar strange cases of spectral objects lacking any inherent consistency, since they are generated solely by the inconsistency of a field – such an object dissolves into thin air the moment relations in this field are clarified. In pre-modern physics, for example, mysterious elements like 'aether' or 'phlogiston' merely give body to the inherent limitation of the conceptual apparatus to account for observable phenomena.

58. At a somewhat different level, therein resides the central problem of Hegel's *Philosophy of Right*: how are we to conceive a social order whose very positivity gives body, as it were, to radical negativity? This radical ambiguity is condensed in the figure

of the Monarch who, precisely as the place-holder of the negativity at the root of the entire social edifice, serves as the ultimate guarantee of the stability of the existing order.

59. See Dieter Hombach, *Vom Quark zum Urknall*, Munich: Boer 1994, pp. 70–80.

60. I am relying here on two books by Michel Poizat, *L'Opéra ou le cri de l'ange*, (Paris: Éditions A.M. Metailie 1986); and *La Voix du diable: La jouissance lyrique sacrée* (Paris: Éditions A.M. Metailie 1991).

61. There are, however, different versions of this voice. In Offenbach's *Hoffmann's Tales*, the three women stand not only for the three modes of the impossibility of the sexual relationship but also for the three types of a song: Olympia's is the song of a mechanical doll, of an automaton; Giulietta's is the seductive voice of a flirtatious woman; Antonia's is the deadly voice which follows the inner ethical 'demon' – it bears witness to the fact that the subject gave preference to *objet a* over the male sexual partner. And does not this triad obey the logic of Lacan's I–S–R: Giulietta's *imaginary* lure; Olympia's *symbolic* mechanism; Antonia's *Real* of drive? Antonia is therefore a properly ethical figure, like the Polish Veronika in Kieslowski's *The Double Life of Véronique*: in the choice between '*le père ou le pire* [father or the worst]', i.e. between a sexual relationship (guaranteed by the paternal metaphor) and the Voice, she opts for the Voice, although she knows that the price to be paid is death.

62. See Theodor Reik, 'Le schofar', in *Rituel: Psychanalyse des rites religieux*, Paris: Denoël 1975.

63. See Oswald Ducrot, *Le dire et le dit*, Paris: Éditions de Minuit 1984.

64. Hegel, *Jenaer Realphilosophie*, Hamburg: Meiner 1967, p. 161.

65. One can also say that this voice of a dying animal attests to a pure intention-to-signify prior to articulated meaning – no longer a mere meaningless reverberation, but not yet meaning. (See Giorgio Agamben's observations in his *Language and Death: The Place of Negativity*, Minneapolis: University of Minnesota Press 1991, pp. 33 ff.) This difference between meaning and intention-to-signify was first introduced in St Augustine's *De Trinitate*, apropos of our experience of a 'dead' foreign language (when I hear a foreign word, I know that it means – or at least, that it meant – something, but I do not know what). It was also St Augustine who pointed out how this experience gives rise to the *desire* to learn the true meaning of the word – in short, this 'empty' signifier is the signifier of *transference*. A fatal misunderstanding to be avoided here is to conceive of this experience as simply secondary, i.e. to follow the commonsensical intuition whereby the word in question 'originally' had to have its proper meaning: the intention-to-signify precedes meaning also with the speaker himself, it is an inherent constituent of the dialectics of meaning.

66. In a more detailed analysis, one should draw a parallel with the negativity of *labour*: in Hegel, labour, like articulated speech, also involves the experience of negativity, i.e. is a way of 'tarrying with the negative' – labour and speech are the two modalities of *deferring* the abyss of enjoyment-death.

67. Pointing out the true addressee of the interpreted text is perhaps the fundamental gesture of psychoanalytic interpretation: the 'repression' to be undone by the interpretative act does not primarily conceal the true meaning; rather, it furnishes a false addressee (of the patient's complaint, for example) in order to obfuscate the true one. A nice example of such an interpretation is found in one of Erle Stanley Gardner's Perry Mason novels in which the main witness to a murder, in the presence of his fiancée, describes in great detail to the police detective and Mason what took place at the time of the murder; Mason solves the mystery when he guesses the true addressee of this unexpectedly detailed account – the fiancée. The witness (who actually committed the crime) was unable to meet his fiancée in private prior to his conversation with the police detective and Mason; the true aim of his narrative is therefore to impart to her his concocted version of events, so that, while being separately questioned, they will both stick to the same false story.... The deception thus concerns the discursive, intersubjective status of the speech: what pretends to be an objective account of events effectively serves to inform the partner of the fabrication she is to stick with.

68. See Jacques Lacan, Seminar on *Anxiety* (unpublished), lecture of 22 May 1963. In this precise sense, one could say that the shofar is a defence against the psychotic figure

of a father who is not dead, who does not act as an agency of symbolic authority, and who thereby hinders the normal functioning of the symbolic order. That is to say: this order can normally function only if the primordial kernel of *jouissance* (the Freudian *Ding*) is evacuated, 'primordially repressed': articulated speech always surrounds the inaccessible void of the Thing.

For a psychotic, on the contrary, his speech directly equals the Thing, i.e. the Symbolic falls into the Real; the consequences of this short circuit are best exemplified by the case of Louis Wolfson, the Jewish-American schizophrenic writer who could not bring himself to hear or read his mother tongue, but was under an unconditional compulsion to translate its words into the words of some other, 'alien', tongue. In short, he maintained an incestuous relationship towards his mother tongue, this tongue remained for him an impossible–real, incestuous Thing – and since the Thing was not evacuated from the mother tongue, since this tongue did not involve any fundamental prohibition but simply remained his Thing, *the prohibition had to bear on the mother tongue itself,* thus leading to the compulsion to translate. We are thus dealing here with an exemplary case of psychotic displacement of the prohibition: the tongue that ignores the paternal prohibition becomes itself the object of a prohibition. (See Louis Wolfson, *Le Schizo et les langues,* Paris: Gallimard 1970.)

69. On this constitutive 'foreclosure' of the origins of Law, see Chapter 5 of Slavoj Žižek, *For They Know Not What They Do,* London: Verso 1991.

70. On these 'formulas of sexuation', see Jacques Lacan, *Le Séminaire, livre XX: Encore,* Paris: Éditions du Seuil 1975.

71. In the domain of politics, populist rhetoric offers an exemplary case of the exception which grounds universality: whenever the opinion prevails that *politics as such* is corrupt, not to be trusted, etc., one can be sure that there is always *one* politician who promulgates this universal distrust and thereby offers *himself* as the one to be trusted, as the neutral/apolitical representative of the people's true interests. . . .

72. Incidentally, one can see why one is fully justified in claiming that the transsexual subject, by installing Woman at the place of the Name-of-the-Father, disavows castration. If one adopts the usual feminist-deconstructionist commonplace according to which the psychoanalytic notion of castration implies that woman, not man, is castrated, one would expect that, on the contrary, when Woman occupies the place of symbolic authority, this place will be branded by castration; if, however, we take into account that both Woman and the primordial father are 'incastrable', the mystery immediately disappears.

73. A fact which – since it is a *negative* fact, something that Lacan *doesn't* do – usually escapes our attention can be adduced here as a further proof of our reading of the formulas of sexuation: Lacan does *not* link sexual difference to the opposition between language and *lalangue,* so that language (i.e. the formal-differential structure of the symbolic big Other) would be 'masculine' and the excess of homonyms, wordplays, etc., which constitutes *lalangue* 'feminine'. Therein resides the difference between Lacan's opposition language/*lalangue* and Kristeva's opposition Symbolic/Semiotic, notwithstanding certain similarities between these two couples: if Lacan were to conceive the feminine 'non-all' as the surplus, the excess which eludes the symbolic Law, then *lalangue* would effectively be 'feminine'; as it is, *lalangue* is strictly *not* sexualized.

74. See Chapter 3 of Slavoj Žižek, *The Metastases of Enjoyment,* London: Verso 1994.

75. Since, in our patriarchal society, male predominance is inscribed into the symbolic order itself, does not the assertion that women are integrated into the symbolic order without exception – i.e. in a sense more fully than men – run counter to their subordinate position within this order? Is it not more logical to ascribe the subordinate position to those who are *not* fully integrated into the symbolic order? What one must challenge here, however, is the underlying premiss according to which Power belongs to those who are more fully within the symbolic order. The exercise of Power, on the contrary, always involves a residue of the non-symbolized Real (in the guise of the unfathomable *je ne sais quoi* which is supposed to account for the Master's charisma, for example). It is by no means accidental that both our examples of the constitutive Exception, of the element not integrated into the symbolic order (primordial father, Lady in courtly love), involve the figure of an extremely cruel Master not bound by any Law.

76. This paradox points towards the delusion which is the proper object of psychoanalysis, a delusion more refined than a simple mistaking of a false appearance for the thing itself. When, for example, I daydream about sexual prowess and conquests, I am, of course, aware all the time of the illusory character of my fantasizing – I know very well that in reality I shall never effectively 'do it', that I am 'not really like that'. The delusion resides elsewhere: this daydreaming is a screen which provides a misleading image of myself – not only of my capacities, but also of my true desires. If, in reality, I were to find myself in a position to realize my daydreams, I would surely retreat from it in panic. At an even more complex level (in the case of indulging in sadistic fantasies, for example), the very soothing awareness of how I am 'merely daydreaming', of how 'I am not really like that', can well conceal the extent to which my desire *is* determined by these fantasies. . . .

77. One can also put it this way: in so far as the Symbolic constitutes itself by positing some element as the traumatic non-symbolizable Thing, as its constitutive Exception, then the symbolic gesture *par excellence* is the very drawing of a line of separation between Symbolic and Real; the 'Real', on the contrary, is not external to the Symbolic as some kind of Substance resisting symbolization – the Real is the Symbolic itself *qua* 'non-all', i.e. in so far as it lacks the constitutive Exception.

78. At a more general level, it would be productive to elaborate the link between the totalitarian Leader and the art of the comic absurd in which figures of the capricious Master *à la* Jarry's *Ubu roi* abound, i.e. to read Lewis Carroll with Samuel Goldwyn, the Marx Brothers with Stalin, etc.

79. This point is elaborated in detail in Elisabeth Bronfen, *Over Her Dead Body*, Manchester: Manchester University Press 1992.

80. See Carol Gilligan, *In a Different Voice: Psychological Theory and Women's Development*, Cambridge, MA: Harvard University Press 1982. Such a feminine 'substantialism' (this word is probably more appropriate than the usual 'essentialism') often serves as the hidden presupposition of feminist argumentation. Suffice it to recall the standard claim that a woman who actively participates in patriarchal repression (by following male ideals of feminine beauty, focusing her life on raising the children, etc.) is *eo ipso* a victim of male manipulation, and plays a role imposed on her. We are dealing here with the logic which is strictly analogous to the old orthodox Marxist claim that the working class is, as to its 'objective' social position, 'progressive', so that when workers engage in anti-Semitic right-wing populism, they are being manipulated by the ruling class and its ideology: in both cases, one has to assert that there is no substantial guarantee of the 'progressive' nature of women or the working class – the situation is irreducibly antagonistic and 'open', the terrain of an undecidable ideological and political struggle.

81. This ambiguity pertains already to the commonplace notion of femininity which, in line with Gilligan, associates women with intimacy, identification, spontaneity, as opposed to male distance, reflectivity, calculation; but, at the same time, also with masquerade, affected feigning, as opposed to male authentic inwardness – woman is simultaneously more spontaneous and more artificial than man.

82. See G.W.F. Hegel, *Phenomenology of Spirit*, Oxford: Oxford University Press 1977, pp. 79–103.

83. See F.W.J. Schelling, *On the History of Modern Philosophy*, Cambridge: Cambridge University Press 1994, pp. 115–16; for a more detailed account, see Chapter 1 above.

84. We can now see how the notion of femininity *qua* masquerade is strictly co-dependent with the position of woman as 'non-all': the very notion of mask implies that the mask is 'not all' (the mask is supposed to conceal something beneath); since, however, as we have just seen, there is nothing, no hidden truth, beneath the mask, there is also no positive, substantial element which is exempt from the masquerade, which is not a mask – the name for this void which is nothing in itself, but none the less makes the domain of masks 'non-all', of course, is the subject *qua* void ($).

85. 'It is for that which she is not that she wishes to be desired as well as loved' (Jacques Lacan, *Écrits: A Selection,* p. 290). Is not Edith Wharton's small masterpiece 'The Muse's Tragedy' the perfect exemplification of Lacan's thesis? It tells the story of a woman who was the alleged Muse – the great love and source of inspiration – of a dead famous poet.

When her young lover discovers that she wasn't really the poet's true love, he still clings to her, since he loves her for what she really is, not because of the aura bestowed on her by the fact that she was the great poet's love-object; she, however, rejects him – she wants to be loved for what she is not, i.e. as the poet's Muse, not for what she really is. . . . See Renata Salecl, 'I Can't Love You Unless I Give You Up', in *Gaze and Voice as Love Objects*, Durham, NC: Duke University Press 1996.

86. I owe this formulation of the Althusserian counter-argument to Robert Pfaller (personal communication, 21 March 1995).

87. Jacques Lacan, *Écrits: A Selection*, p. 5.

88. Ibid., p. 58.

89. Ibid., p. 312.

90. Ibid., p. 264.

91. Ibid., p. 312.

92. ' . . . if one has to do things for the good, in practice one is always faced with the question: for the good of whom? From that point on, things are no longer obvious' (*The Ethics of Psychoanalysis: The Seminar of Jacques Lacan. Edited by Jacques-Alain Miller, Book VII*, London: Tavistock/Routledge 1992, p. 319).

93. There is none the less a profound affinity between the Kantian moral universe and the universe of Sadeian perversion; perhaps the most convincing case for it can be made by focusing on the inherent inconsistency of Kant's postulate of the immortality of the soul in his *Critique of Practical Reason*. According to Kant, moral activity 'makes sense' only if its goal, the perfection of the moral subject, can effectively be achieved; however, since it is not possible to achieve perfection in our finite, mortal, bodily existence, we have to postulate the immortality of the soul – if he is to pursue the struggle for moral perfection, the subject has to survive his/her terrestrial life. . . .

It is easy to discern the fallacy of Kant's reasoning: as Kant himself emphasizes, moral activity 'makes sense' only with finite beings, i.e. with beings which, although rational, are also caught in the phenomenal universe and have a spatio–temporal bodily existence. The postulate of the endless asymptotic approach to the ideal of ethical perfection does not, therefore, call for the immortality of the soul but, on the contrary, for the *immortality of the body* – and it is precisely the fantasy of such an immortal-indestructible body that we find in de Sade, in whose literary universe the victim can be abused and tortured *ad infinitum*, but none the less remains alive and even miraculously retains her beauty, as if, beneath her ordinary, terrestrial body, caught in 'the way of all flesh', in the process of corruption and generation, she possesses another, sublime, ethereal, indestructible body. . . . See Alenka Zupančič, 'The Two Faces of Achilles: Don Juan and "Kant with Sade" ', in *On Radical Evil* (*S* Series, vol. 2), ed. Joan Copjec, London: Verso 1995.

94. Two outstanding examples in film are Hitchcock's *Murder* and Cronenberg's *M. Butterfly*.

95. It is against this background that one should approach the complex problem of the relationship between Kant and Kierkegaard. Kierkegaard's 'religious' is uncannily close to Kant's 'ethical': Kierkegaard's 'religious stage' and Kantian 'moral Law' both aim at the same traumatic kernel, though each misses it in its own specific way. In both cases, the subject encounters an impossible demand that a priori cannot be complied with (Kant emphasizes how one can never self-complacently exclude the possibility that some hidden pathological motivation was at work in what presents itself as the ethical act accomplished for the sake of duty; in a strictly homologous way, Kierkegaard was eternally gnawed by doubt concerning his belief – I can never be quite sure that I truly believe; all I can say is that I believe I believe; so that towards the end of his life Kierkegaard himself was compelled to admit that he was not a believer . . .). The obverse of this proximity is that Kierkegaard's 'ethical' ultimately coincides with what Kant dismissed as the 'pathological', ordinary notion of religion whose fundamental assumption is that I accomplish good deeds because I know that God will reward me in the afterlife, i.e. as part of an exchange with God.

The difference between Kant and Kierkegaard which immediately catches the eye, of course, is that the call of duty in Kant is universal, it concerns every rational being; whereas in Kierkegaard, the call of God is addressed only to the few who have been chosen by what to us, common mortals, cannot but appear as an unfathomable, contingent decision; however, does not Kant's assertion of moral Law as an unexplicable *fact* of pure reason also point towards a homologous contingency in the very foundation of ethics? Kant's radical refusal to ground ethics in the reference to whatever kind of substantial Good reappears in Kierkegaard in the guise of the difference between belief and virtue: *the opposite of sin is belief, not virtue.* Virtue is a pre-Christian notion; it belongs to the pagan era when, since Revelation had not yet taken place, sin as such was *stricto sensu* an unknown entity; in strict analogy to Kierkegaard's dismissal of virtue, Kant depreciates any form of compassionate striving for the Good of our neighbours as ethically irrelevant. For Kierkegaard, 'sin' is emphatically *not* a matter of the immediate content of our acts, it does *not* directly refer to the horrible deeds of a sinner – it concerns solely the denial of belief; along the same lines, for Kant, 'unethical activity' is defined not by its immediate content ('such and such acts are unethical') but in a purely formal way, as an activity which, although beneficent to our fellow-men, is not motivated solely by respect for the moral Law.

96. Lacan's assertion (from his unpublished Seminar on *Anxiety*, lecture of 5 December 1962) that (symbolic) castration coincides with the subject's interpretation of castration involves an analogous 'Hegelian' reflective inversion. To *cognoscenti* of Lacan, this paradoxical, seemingly nonsensical coincidence immediately recalls the far better known thesis on the relationship between desire and interpretation: desire *is* its own interpretation. When the subject is confronted with the enigma of desire, he strives desperately to fix the co-ordinates – the sets, props and costumes – of what is the true cause of his desiring, he produces ever new interpretations of what he actually wants – and this very unending search, this questioning attitude of never being quite certain what we desire, *is* desire *tout court*. The same goes for castration: 'castration' ultimately designates the very gap that forever separates the raw fact of castration (of a pure, 'non-economic' lack or loss) from the subject's attempts to integrate this raw fact into his or her symbolic economy.

PART II

Related Matters

3

Quantum Physics with Lacan

The 'wired' desire

The impasse that lurks in the background of late-capitalist liberal-democratic permissiveness, to which different fundamentalisms provide desperate answers, is: How we are to re-stimulate the desire to copulate today, in an age when, owing to its direct accessibility – to the lack of obstacles that would heighten its value – the sexual object is more and more depreciated – or, to quote Freud's classic formulation:

> the psychical value of erotic needs is reduced as soon as their satisfaction becomes easy. An obstacle is required in order to heighten libido; and where natural resistances to satisfaction have not been sufficient men have at all times erected conventional ones so as to be able to enjoy love.[1]

Within this perspective, courtly love appears as simply the most radical strategy for elevating the value of the object by putting up conventional obstacles to its attainability. When, in his seminar *Encore*, Lacan provides the most succinct formulation of the paradox of courtly love, he says something apparently similar, yet fundamentally different: 'A very refined manner of supplanting the absence of the sexual relationship by feigning that it is us who put the obstacle in its way.'[2] The point is therefore not simply that we set up additional conventional hindrances in order to heighten the value of the object: *external hindrances that thwart our access to the object are there precisely to create the illusion that without them, the object would be directly accessible* – what such hindrances thereby conceal is the inherent impossibility of attaining the object.

In order to make this deadlock palpable, let us turn for a moment to an example from another domain, that of the so-called 'computer highway'. If, in the near future, all data, movies, and so on, were to become instantly available, if the delay were to become minimal so that the very notion of 'searching for' (a book, a film . . .) were to lose its meaning, would not this instant availability suffocate desire? That is to say: what sets human desire in motion is a short circuit between the primordially lost Thing and an empirical, positive object, that is, the elevation of this object to the dignity of the Thing – this object thus fills out the 'transcendental' void of the Thing, it becomes prohibited, and thereby starts to function as the cause of desire. When, however, every empirical object becomes available, this absence of the prohibition necessarily give rise to anxiety: what becomes visible via this saturation is that the ultimate point of prohibition was simply to mask the inherent impossibility of the Thing, that is, the structural deadlock of desire.[3] One thing, therefore, is certain: the advent of cyberspace will shatter, and transform beyond recognition, the very basic structure of our capacity to desire, since it will lay bare the paradox of desire by cutting the ground from under the feet of the creative sublimation that enables us to escape this paradox (the fact that desire is sustained by lack and therefore shuns its satisfaction, that is, the very thing for which it 'officially' strives): we elevate an empirical, ordinary object to the 'dignity of the Thing' – we posit it as unattainable/prohibited, and this inaccessibility keeps the flame of our desire alive.

On account of its logic of instant gratification, the universe of 'virtual reality' signals the very opposite of what its name announces: the *end* of the virtual space of symbolization, or, as Winnicott put it, of the space of transitive objects – everything is instantly here, but bereft of its substance and thus instantly devalued.[4] 'Virtual reality' is therefore a kind of Orwellian misnomer: it stands for the very opposite of virtuality, for the saturation of the virtual space of symbolic fiction. Or – to put it in yet another way – in contrast to the standard situation in which the very inaccessibility of the object, the fact that the object is 'hard to get', *guarantees its reality*, the availability of the object is paid for by its *de-realization*, by the frustrating experience that 'this (what we get) is not that'. So the big enigma is: how, through what kind of limitation of access, will capitalism succeed in reintroducing lack and scarcity into this saturation?

This predicament allows us to throw some new, perhaps unexpected, light not only on the contemporary resurgence of different 'fundamentalisms', but also on so-called 'political correctness'. One of the aspects of the PC attitude is to reintroduce Prohibition in the domain of sexuality, and to make us discern everywhere the hidden traces of 'incorrect' (patriarchal, racist, etc.) enjoyments. One is therefore tempted to conceive PC as a Foucauldian 'strategy without subject' aimed at arousing our interest in what its official, public discourse pretends to prohibit. From this perspective, PC appears as a kind of 'cunning of reason' by means of which history counteracts the alarming fact that in the aftermath of the 'sexual revolution' of the 1960s, people are less and less prone to copulate (according to the latest polls in Western Europe, 70 per cent of young women prefer dinner in an expensive restaurant to a passionate night of love . . .). What we are witnessing is an ironic reversal of the 1960s, when (sexual) desire was experienced as a 'progressive', liberating agency enabling us to get rid of rigid traditional values – (sexual) desire in its effectively disturbing dimension, from obscene talk to self-humiliation, is now on the side of 'reaction'. The irony lies in the fact that, from the PC point of view, 'straight', 'normal' sexuality is almost prohibited, while the more one's sexuality approaches the so-called 'perverted' forms, the more it is approved of – one has almost to apologize if one is to indulge in old-fashioned penetrative heterosexual activity. . . . The 'False Memory Syndrome' (in which, on the psychiatrist's suggestion, the patient projects his disavowed phantasmic content into external reality and 'recalls' how, in his youth, he was seduced and/or sexually abused by his parents), is for that reason the *symptom* of PC, an exemplary case of how 'what was foreclosed from the Symbolic returns in the Real'. The primordial 'politically incorrect' sexual harasser is, of course, none other than the Father-Enjoyment, the phantasmic figure of the obscene pre-symbolic father.[5]

The very rehabilitation of the theory of seduction is to be conceived of as an index of the changed status of subjectivity in our postmodern late-capitalist society – that is to say, of the shift towards a 'pathological Narcissus' to whom the Other (desiring subject) as such appears as a violent intruder: whatever he or she does (if he or she smokes, laughs too loudly or not loudly enough, casts a covetous glance at me . . .), amounts to a disturbance of my precarious imaginary balance. Threatened by every encounter with the Other's desire, this 'pathological Narcissus' endeavours to dwell in *virtual* space (in the precise sense this term acquires in the computer universe): in the space of virtual communities in which one is free to change one's identity, in which no link is effectively binding, since I can withdraw from any 'relationship' at any moment; the form of sexuality which fits this universe is *bisexuality*, with its fluid, shifting identities.[6]

Therein resides the fatal flaw of the PC strategy of fighting 'hate speech' by replacing 'aggressive' with neutral terms (a weak-sighted person is 'visually challenged', an undeveloped country is 'developing', etc.). The problem with this strategy is that the power discourse can easily turn it to its advantage by using it to render aseptic the raw brutality of exploitation: why should not brutal rape become 'non-consensual sexual satisfaction', and so on? In short, PC-newspeak simply imitates today's bureaucratese, in which the murder of a political opponent becomes the aseptic 'annihilation of the target', and so forth – what is at stake in both cases is the endeavour to suspend the 'stinging' dimension of speech, the level at which the other's word impinges on the very kernel of my being. And is not this protection against the encounter *qua* real the true underlying impetus of 'debasement in the sphere of love' today?

Our point is therefore that the PC attitude effectively contributes to 'debasement in the sphere of love' via its effort to suspend all traces of the encounter of the Real, of the Other *qua* desiring subject. With what does it strive to replace it? Here, the underlying fantasy of Robert Heinlein's *Puppetmasters* can provide an answer. Today, the theme of parasitic aliens which invade our planet, stick to our back, penetrate our spinal cord with their prolonged stings, and thus dominate us 'from within' tastes like stale soup; the film, shot in 1994, strikes us visually as a rather mismatched combination of *Alien* and *Invasion of the Body Snatchers*. Its phantasmic background is none the less more interesting than it may seem: it resides in the opposition between the human universe of sexual reproduction and the aliens' universe of cloning. In our universe, reproduction occurs by means of copulation, under the auspices of the symbolic agency of the Name-of-the-Father; whereas the alien invaders reproduce themselves asexually, via direct self-copying duplication, and therefore possess no 'individuality'; they present a case of radical 'immixing of subjects', that is, they can communicate directly, bypassing the medium of language, since they all form one large organism: One. Why, then, do these aliens pose such a threat?

The immediate answer, of course, is that they bring about the loss of human individuality – under their domination, we become 'puppets', the Other (or, rather, the One) directly speaks through us. However, there is a deeper theme at work here: we can experience ourselves as autonomous and free individuals only in so far as we are marked by an irreducible, constitutive loss, division, splitting; only in so far as our very being involves a certain 'out-of-joint'; only in so far as the other (human being) ultimately remains for us an unfathomable, impenetrable enigma. The 'aliens', on the other hand, function precisely as the complement that restores the lost plenitude of a human subject: they are what Lacan, in his *Seminar XI*, calls 'lamella', the indestructible *asexual* organ without body, the mythical part that was lost when human beings became sexualized. In contrast to a 'normal' sexual relationship, which is always mediated by a lack and, as such, 'impossible', doomed to fail, the relationship with 'aliens' is therefore fully satisfying: when a human subject merges with an alien, it is as if the round plenitude of a complete being, prior to sexual divisions, about which Plato speaks in his *Symposium* is reconstituted – a man no longer needs a woman (or vice versa), since he is already complete in himself. We can see now why, in Heinlein's novel, once a human being gets rid of the grip of the parasitic alien, he is completely bewildered and acts as if he has lost his footing, like a drug addict deprived of his fix. At the end, the 'normal' sexual couple is reconstituted by means of a (literal) parricide: the threat to sexuality is dealt with.

Our point, however, is that what this novel stages in the guise of a paranoiac fantasy is something that is slowly becoming part of our everyday life. Is not the personal computer increasingly evolving into a parasitic complement to our being? Perhaps the choice between sexuality and compulsive playing with a computer (the proverbial adolescent who is so immersed in a computer that he forgets about his date) is more than a media invention: perhaps it is an index of how, via new technology, a complementary relationship to an 'inhuman partner' is slowly emerging which is, in an uncanny way, more fulfilling than the relationship to a sexual partner – perhaps Foucault was right (although not for the right reasons); perhaps the end of sexuality is looming on the horizon, and perhaps the PC is in the service of this end.[7] Any relationship to the intersubjective Other is therefore preceded by the relationship to an object on to which the subject is 'hooked' and which serves as a direct complement, a stand-in for the asexual primordially lost object. In pop-psychoanalytic terms, one could say that the subject who, via computer *qua* object-supplement, participates in a virtual community, 'regresses' to the polymorphous perversity of 'primordial Narcissism' – what should not escape our notice, however, is the radically 'prothetic' nature of this (and every) Narcissism: it relies on a mechanical foreign body that forever decentres the subject.

The Cartesian cyberpunk

The outstanding feature of computerized 'interactive media' is the way they are giving birth to a renewed 'drive-to-community' as a substitute for the progressive disintegration of our 'actual' community life: what fascinates people far more than the unprecedented access to information, the new ways of learning, shopping, and so on, is the possibility of constituting 'virtual communities' in which I am free to assume an arbitrary sexual, ethnic, religious, and so on, identity. Or, as some journalist put it: 'Forget race, gender. In cyberspace, you are what you care about.' A gay man, for example, can enter a closed sexual community and, via on exchange of messages, participate in a fictionalized group sexual activity as a heterosexual woman. . . . These virtual communities, far from signalling the 'end of Cartesian subjectivity', represent the closest attempt hitherto to actualize the notion of the Cartesian subject in the social space itself: when all my features, including the most intimate, become contingent and interchangeable, only then is the void that 'I myself am' beyond all my assumed features the *cogito*, the empty Cartesian subject ($). One must be careful, however, to avoid various traps that lurk here. The first among them is the notion that, prior to the computer-generated virtualization of reality, we were dealing with direct, 'real' reality: the experience of virtual reality should, rather, make us sensitive to how the 'reality' with which we were dealing *always-already was* virtualized. The most elementary procedure of symbolic identification, identification with an Ego Ideal, involves – as Lacan had already put it in the 1950s, apropos of his famous schema of the 'inverted vase' – an identification with a 'virtual image [*l'image virtuelle*]': the place in the big Other from which I see myself in the form in which I find myself likeable (the definition of Ego Ideal) is by definition virtual. Is not virtuality, therefore, the trademark of every, even the most elementary, ideological identification? When I see myself as a 'democrat', a 'Communist', an 'American', a 'Christian', and so on, what I see is not directly 'me': I identify with a virtual place in the discourse. And in so far as such an identification is constitutive of a community, every community is also *stricto sensu* always-already virtual.[8]

This logic of virtuality can be further exemplified by Oswald Ducrot's analysis in *Le dire et le dit* of the different discursive positions a speaker can assume within the same speech act: assertive, ironic, sympathetic, and so on – when I speak, I always constitute a virtual place of enunciation from which I speak, yet this is never directly 'me'. Today, it is often pointed out how the universe of virtual community, with its arbitrarily exchangeable identities, opens up new ethical dilemmas: suppose that I, a gay man, assume in a virtual community the identity of a heterosexual woman – what if, within the virtual sexual play constituted by the interchange of descriptions on the screen, somebody brutally rapes me? Is this a case of 'true' harassment or not? (Things will get even more complex with the prospect of more people encountering each other and interacting in the same virtual reality: what, precisely, will be the status of violence when somebody attacks me in virtual reality?) Our point, however, is that these dilemmas are not really so different from those we encounter in 'ordinary' reality, in which my gender identity is also not an immediate fact but 'virtual', symbolically constructed, so that a gap separates it for ever from the Real: here, also, every harassment is primarily an attack on my 'virtual', symbolic identity. That is the true horror of virtual sex: not the experience of the loss of 'real', flesh-and-blood sex, but the awareness that *this 'real' sex never existed in the first place*, that sex always-already was virtual. The same goes for virtual reality as such: what gives rise to anxiety is not the loss of 'real reality' but the awareness that (what we experience as) reality always-already *was* virtual, sustained by a symbolic fiction.

This, however, in no way implies that nothing really important is taking place with today's technological virtualization of reality: what takes place is, in Hegelese, the very formal inversion from In-itself to For-itself, that is, the virtualization which was previously 'in-itself', a mechanism which operated implicitly, as the hidden foundation of our lives, now becomes explicit, is posited as such, with crucial consequences for 'reality' itself. What we have here is an exemplary case of Hegel's Minerva's owl which 'flies in the evening': a spiritual principle effectively reigns as long as it is not acknowledged as such; the moment people become directly aware of it, its time is up and the 'silent weaving of the spirit' is already laying the groundwork for a new principle. In short, the properly dialectical paradox resides in the fact that *the very 'empirical', explicit realization of a principle undermines its reign.* Or – to put it in a different way – what takes place in this passage from In-itself to For-itself is a kind of conflation of the two dimensions which remain apart in the 'normal' or 'standard' functioning of the symbolic order, that of *symbolic fiction* and that of *fantasy*.

On the one hand, virtual space is the space of symbolic fictions *par excellence*: the Other Scene of purely virtual entities which, although they are not to be found anywhere in 'reality', are none the less effective and regulate our lives. In 'reality', there are only individuals and the screens at which they stare; none the less – to quote the now classic words of William Gibson – the individuals hooked on the screen 'develop a belief that there's some kind of *actual space* behind the screen, some place that you can't see but you know is there'. On the other hand, however, the screen of a PC is the window of fantasy in its essence: an empty frame on to which phantasmic scenarios are projected. Cyberspace is thus at the same time both a space for the transmitting of messages, for communication, *and* the imagery of virtual reality. The result of this conflation is a kind of psychotic short circuit in which the symbol, in so far as it overlaps with (or, rather, falls into) phantasmic reality, loses its performative power, that is, no longer effectively 'engages' the subject.

The inherent obverse of this disengagement – of the fact that the subject maintains towards the computerized virtual universe the distance which suspends the dimension of performativity, of symbolic engagement, of being obliged by one's word – is, of course, a kind of short circuit between the signifier and the real: in virtual reality proper we will have a simulated, virtual (and in this sense still symbolic) universe which we will experience directly as 'reality itself'. The other side of distance is thus a kind of *direct immersion into the 'virtual' universe on the screen*: 'virtual reality' gives rise to the dream of a language which no longer acts upon the subject merely through the intermediate sphere of meaning, but has *direct effects in the real* (like Hitchcock's fantasy about the machine by means of which a future film director will be able to manipulate the emotions of his public directly, bypassing the visual medium). The key point to grasp is the interdependence of these two opposing features. In so far as the 'wired universe' is effectively 'post-Oedipal', a universe no longer relying on the paternal symbolic authority, one should recall Lacan's classic definition of psychosis (the 'foreclosure of the Name-of-the-Father') – and psychosis is characterized precisely by the paradoxical coincidence of overproximity and externality. That is to say, psychosis involves the external distance the subject maintains towards the symbolic order (in psychosis, the subject is confronted with an 'inert' signifying chain, one that does not seize him performatively and does not affect his subjective position of enunciation: towards this chain, the subject maintains a 'relation of exteriority')[9] *and* the collapsing of the Symbolic into the Real (a psychotic treats 'words as things'; in his universe, words fall into things and/or things themselves start to speak). If, in 'normal' symbolic communication, we are dealing with the distance (between 'things' and 'words') which opens up the space for the domain of Sense and, within it, for symbolic engagement, in the case of virtual reality, on the contrary, the very overproximity (of the sign and the designated content) *disengages* us, closes up the space for symbolic engagement.

The problem of communication in virtual communities is thus not simply that I can lie (that an ugly old man can present himself as a beautiful young woman, etc.) but, more fundamentally, that I am never truly engaged, since at any moment I can pull back, unhook myself. In virtual community sex games I can be ruthless, I can pour out all my dirty dreams, precisely because *my word no longer obliges me*, is not 'subjectivized'. Perhaps the crucial question the 'computerization' of our symbolic exchanges compels us to confront is that of the *performative*: how will the progressive 'computerization' of our intersubjective contacts affect the fundamental dimension of the symbolic universe, that of the pact, of the obligation, of engagement, of 'trust', of 'relying upon another's word'? The point, of course, is not simply to bemoan the loss of the old universe of the symbolic bond – the appropriate starting point would be, rather, the fact that communication in virtual communities is uncannily close to the exchange between analyst and analysand in the psychoanalytic cure: here also the performative force of words is somehow suspended; this is why I can say anything to my analyst, reveal all my obscene fantasies about him, knowing that he will not be offended, will not 'take it personally'.

This parallel with psychoanalysis is especially pertinent with regard to the initial gesture of the subject's 'entry' into a new symbolic dimension. The very cancellation of 'normal' performativity in the psychoanalytic cure involves a kind of 'transcendental' performative gesture by means of which both analysand and analyst accept that what will take place from now on is no longer 'normal' intersubjective speech but mere 'free associations' whose performative dimension is suspended (no matter how violently the analysand verbally attacks the analyst, for example, they are both aware that this is not to be taken 'personally', as a 'real threat'). And things are strictly homologous in the 'wired universe': here also, a primordial 'Yes!' is needed, an 'act of faith' by means of which the subject agrees to participate, to 'play the game', to act as if, over and above him (the user) and the machine (computer), there is the virtual universe of fictions on the screen, this Popperian Third World which – although purely virtual and, as such, lacking both psychical and physical reality – none the less determines the user's very 'real' activity. In this precise sense, the very cancellation of the 'normal' performativity of intersubjective speech in the 'wired universe' continues to rely on a symbolic pact, on the same 'Yes!' by means of which the speaker accepts the fictitious existence of the 'big Other', of the universe of symbolic fictions.

The second trap, the opposite of the first, lies in too hastily proclaiming every reality a virtual fiction: one should always bear in mind that the 'proper' body remains the unsurpassable anchor limiting the freedom of virtualization. The notion that in some not too distant future human subjects will be able to weigh the anchor that attaches them to their bodies and change into ghost-like entities floating freely from one virtual body to another is the phantasm of full virtualization, of the subject finally delivered from the 'pathological' stain of *a*. Let us recall the restaurant scene from Terry Gilliam's *Brazil* which perfectly exemplifies this ultimate limit of virtualization: in a high-class restaurant, the waiter recommends to his customers the best suggestions from the daily menu ('Today, our tournedos is really special!', etc.), yet what the customers get when they have made their choice is a dazzling colour photo of the meal on a stand above the plate, and on the plate itself a loathsome excremental paste-like lump. That is the central antinomy of our 'postmodern' experience of reality: the virtualization of reality always produces an excremental remainder of the real which resists virtualization.[10]

Which of these two traps is worse? Since they are co-dependent, heads and tails of the same coin, one can only repeat Stalin's immortal answer to the question 'Which of the two deviations is worse, the left-wing or the right-wing?': 'They are both worse!' The more urgent question is, rather: What are we effectively running away from when we take refuge in the virtual community? *Not* directly from authentic symbolic engagement – there is something between symbolic engagement proper and the virtual community. Let us recall the distinction between the traditional marriage arranged by parents and the modern, post-traditional marriage based on love. The replacement of the traditional marriage by marriage based on love is usually celebrated as the sign of liberating progress; however, things are far more ambiguous, and can always take an unpleasant dive into murky superego waters. The traditional marriage asks of the spouses only fidelity and respect (or, rather, the semblance of respect) – love follows the wedding, it is an accident which emerges (or fails to emerge) out of marital familiarity, so I am not *obliged* to love my spouse. In a marriage based on love, on the contrary, I soon find myself in the paradox of obligatory love: since I am married, and since marriage should be based on love, *I must love my spouse* – a superego command which terrorizes me from within. The worm of doubt is thus soon at work, setting in motion the incessant questioning ('Am I really still in love with my spouse?') which, sooner or later, gives rise to a guilt feeling. . . . *This* unbearable superego injunction is what the subject runs away from into the 'cold' universe of virtual relations in which the other is no longer a true intersubjective other – his or her death, for example, has, rather, the status of the death of my imaginary opponent in a video game.

Cynicism as reflected ideology

Another trap to be avoided apropos of the 'wired universe' is that of technological determinism: the old Marxist lesson still holds – that is to say, the way computerization affects our lives does not depend directly on technology, it results from the way the impact of new technology is refracted by the social relations which, in their turn, co-determine the very direction of technological development. So which are these social relations?

In one of his letters, Freud refers to the well-known joke about the new husband who, asked by his friend how his wife looks, how beautiful she is, answers: 'I personally don't like her, but that's a matter of taste.' The paradox of this answer does not point towards an attitude of selfish calculation ('True, I don't like her, but I married her for other reasons

– her wealth, her parents' social influence . . . '). Its crucial feature is that the subject, in providing this answer, pretends to assume the standpoint of universality from which 'to be likeable' appears as an idiosyncrasy, as a contingent 'pathological' feature which, as such, is not to be taken into consideration. The joke therefore relies on the impossible/untenable position of enunciation of the new husband: from this position, marriage appears as an act which belongs to the domain of universal symbolic determinations and should, as such, be independent of personal idiosyncrasies – as if the very notion of marriage did not involve precisely the 'pathological' fact of liking a particular person for no particular rational reason. (Incidentally, such an undermining of a statement by means of reference to its subjective position of enunciation is what characterizes Hegelian dialectics.)[11]

One encounters the same 'impossible' position of enunciation in contemporary 'postmodern' racism. We all remember one of the highlights of Bernstein's *West Side Story*, 'Officer Krupke', the song in which the delinquents provide the amazed policeman with the socio-psychological explanation of their attitude: they are victims of disadvantageous social circumstances and unfavourable family relations. . . . Asked why they are violent towards foreigners, neo-Nazi skinheads in Germany tend to give the same answers: they suddenly start to talk like social workers, sociologists and social psychologists, quoting diminished social mobility, rising insecurity, the disintegration of paternal authority, and so on. The same goes even for Zhirinovsky: in interviews for the 'enlightened' Western press, he also speaks the language of pop-sociologists and psychologists. That is to say, there are two main pop-scientific clichés about the rise of populist demagogues: they feed on the frustrations of ordinary people caused by the economic crisis, and social insecurity; the populist totalitarian leader is a distorted personality who, by means of his aggression, abreacts a traumatic personal past, a lack of genuine parental love and support in his childhood – the very two reasons quoted by Zhirinovsky when he is asked to explain his success: 'If there were a healthy economy and security for the people, I would lose all the votes I have'; 'It seems to have been my fate that I never experienced real love or friendship.'[12]

This is what Lacan had in mind when he claimed that 'there is no metalanguage': what Zhirinovsky or the skinheads assert is a lie even if – or rather, precisely in so far as – it is factually true: their assertions are belied by their very position of enunciation, by the neutral, disengaged position from which the victim is able to tell the objective truth about himself. And it is easy to imagine a more theoretically updated version of such a false attitude – a racist, for example, who claims that he is not the true author of his violent verbal outbursts against African-Americans or Jews or Arabs: the charges against him presuppose traditional metaphysical notions which have to be deconstructed; in his performative utterance, which by itself perpetrated an act of violence, he was merely referring to, quoting, drawing from, the historically available stock of insults, so that the entire historical tradition, not himself, must be put on trial; the very notion that there exists a self-identical responsible subject who can be held accountable for racist outbursts is an illusion already denounced by Nietzsche who proved that the deed – or rather, the doing – is original, while the 'doer' behind the doing is a symbolic fiction, a metaphysical hypostasis, and so forth.[13]

This impossible position of enunciation characterizes the contemporary cynical attitude: in it, ideology can lay its cards on the table, reveal the secret of its functioning, *and still continue to function*. Exemplary here is Robert Zemeckis's *Forrest Gump*, a film which offers as the point of identification, as the ideal ego, a simpleton, and thus directly asserts stupidity as a key category of ideology. The principal ideological axis of *Forrest Gump* is the opposition of the hero and his lifelong love. Gump is a blessedly-innocent simpleton with a 'heart of gold' who executes the orders of his superiors undisturbed by any ideological qualms or fanatical devotions. Renouncing even a minimum of 'cognitive mapping' (Jameson), he is caught in a tautological symbolic machine towards which he lacks any ironic distance – a passive witness of and/or participant in great historico-political battles whose significance he does not even try to understand (he never asks himself why he has to fight in Vietnam, why he is suddenly sent to China to play ping-pong, etc.). The object of his love is a girl fully engaged in the ideological struggles of recent decades (anti-Vietnam demonstrations, etc.) – in a word, she *participates in history* and endeavours to understand what is actually going on.

The first thing to note about the film is that *Gump is ideology at its purest*: the opposition of Gump and his girlfriend does not stand for the opposition between the extra-ideological zero-degree of social life and ideological struggles which divide the social body; rather, it exemplifies the tension between Ideology in its zero-degree (the meaningless ideological machine) and the antagonisms Ideology endeavours to master and/or render invisible. Gump, this slow-witted, automatic executor of orders, who does not even try to understand anything, gives body to the impossible *pure subject of Ideology*, to the ideal of a subject in whom Ideology would function flawlessly. The ideological mystification of the film resides in the fact that it presents Ideology at its purest as non-ideology, as extra-ideological good-natured participation in social life. That is to say, the ultimate lesson of the film is: don't even try to understand; obey, and you shall succeed! (Gump ends up as a famous millionaire.) His girlfriend, who endeavours to acquire a kind of 'cognitive mapping' of the social situation, is symbolically punished for her thirst for knowledge: at the end of the film, she dies of AIDS.

Forrest Gump reveals the secret of ideology (the fact that its successful functioning involves the stupidity of its subjects) in such an open way that in different historical circumstances it would undoubtedly have subversive effects; today, however, in the era of cynicism, ideology can afford to reveal the secret of its functioning (its constitutive idiocy, which traditional, pre-cynical ideology had to keep secret) *without in the least affecting its efficiency.*[14]

This cynical attitude also provides a key to today's resurgent ethnic and religious 'fundamentalisms'. Lacan had already emphasized how a cynic does not believe in words (in their 'symbolic efficiency'), but only in the real of *jouissance* – and is not the Nation-Thing today's supreme embodiment of political *jouissance?* This accounts for the paradox that today cynically 'enlightened' intellectuals who are no longer able to believe in any social Cause are the first to fall prey to 'fanatical' ethnic fundamentalism. The link between cynicism and (ethnic or religious) fundamentalism does not concern primarily the fact that in today's 'society of spectacle' fundamentalism itself is just another mediatic show and, as such, feigned, a cynical mask of power interests, but, rather, its opposite: the cynical distance itself relies on the unacknowledged attachment to an ethnic (or religious) Thing – the more this attachment is disavowed, the more violent its sudden eruption. . . . We should always bear in mind that within our ideological space the reference to one's Nation is the supreme form of ideology in the guise of anti- or non-ideology (in short, of ideology *tout court*): 'Let's put our petty political and ideological struggles aside, it's the fate of our nation which is at stake now'.

We encounter an analogous falsity in the attitude of those traditional psychoanalysts who prefer their patients to be 'naive' and ignorant of psychoanalytic theory – this ignorance allegedly enables them to produce 'purer' symptoms, symptoms in which their unconscious is not too distorted by their rational knowledge. For example, the incestuous dream of a patient who already knows all about the Oedipus complex will be far more distorted, resorting to more complex strategies to conceal its desire, than the dream of a 'naive' patient. We all have a longing for the good old heroic times of psychoanalysis, in which a patient told his analyst: 'Last night, I had a dream about killing a dragon and then advancing through a thick forest to a castle . . . ', whereupon the analyst triumphantly answered: 'Elementary, my dear patient! The dragon is your father, and the dream expresses your desire to kill him in order to return to the safe haven of the maternal castle . . .'. Lacan's premiss here is exactly the opposite: the subject of psychoanalysis is the modern subject of science, which means – among other things – that his symptoms are, by definition, never 'innocent', they are always addressed to the analyst *qua* subject supposed to know (their meaning) and thus, as it were, imply, point towards, their own interpretation. For that reason one is quite justified in saying that we have symptoms which are Jungian, Kleinian, Lacanian, and so on – that is to say, whose reality involves implicit reference to some psychoanalytic theory. Today, the 'free associations' of a typical educated analysand consist for the most part of attempts to provide a psychoanalytic explanation of his or her disturbances. . . .

This is also what Lacan's thesis on 'Joyce-the-symptom' aims at: Joyce's famous statement that he wrote *Finnegans Wake* in order to keep literary historians busy for the next four hundred years has to be read against the background of Lacan's assertion that within a psychoanalytic cure a symptom is always addressed to the analyst and, as such, points forward towards its interpretation. The 'modernism' of Joyce resides in the fact that his works – at least *Ulysses* and *Finnegans Wake* – are not simply external to their interpretation but, as it were, take into account in advance their possible interpretations, and enter into dialogue with them. In so far as an interpretation or a theoretical explanation of a work of art endeavours to 'frame' its object, one can say that this modernist dialectics provides another example of how the frame is always included in, is a part of, the framed content: in modernism, a theory about the work is comprised in the work, the work is a kind of pre-emptive strike at possible theories about itself.

On that account, it is inappropriate to criticize Joyce for no longer writing for a naive reader capable of an immediate consumption of his works but for a reflected reader who is able to read only with an eye on possible theoretical interpretations of what he is reading – in short, for a literary scientist: such a 'reflected' approach in no way diminishes our enjoyment of the work – on the contrary, it supplements our reading with a surplus-enjoyment which is one of the trademarks of true modernism.[15] And what the so-called 'postmodernist' turn adds to it is, perhaps, just the experience of a certain '*ça n'empêche pas d'exister*'. That is to say: modernism still clings to the illusion that reflection somehow radically affects its object (once a symptom is properly interpreted, it should dissolve; once one explains to a racist the true causes of his hatred of foreigners, this hatred should disappear . . .), whereas a postmodernist takes into account the fact that even if my racism is 'reflected', *it still remains racism pure and simple*, and – even worse – that a first-level racism can become operative only when it is accompanied by a second-level reflection that contains and disavows its true scope. . . .[16]

So, on the political level, the problem today is how to counteract this 'reflected' racism: is there a specific kind of *knowledge* which renders the act impossible, a knowledge which can no longer be co-opted by cynical distance ('I know what I'm doing, but I'm doing it nevertheless')? Or must we leave the domain of knowledge behind and have recourse to a direct, extra-symbolic, bodily intervention, or to an intuitive 'Enlightenment', a change of subjective attitude, beyond knowledge? The fundamental premiss of psychoanalysis is that there exists such a knowledge which produces effects in the Real, that we *can* 'undo things (symptoms) with words' – the whole point of the psychoanalytic cure is that it operates exclusively at the level of 'knowledge' (words), yet has effects in the Real of bodily symptoms.

Cynicism versus irony

How, then, are we to specify this 'knowledge' which, even in our era of cynicism, brings about effects in the Real? Perhaps the best approach to it is via the opposition between violent coercion and 'genuine' subordination. This opposition, of course, is never to be accepted at face value: subordination (of women to men in a patriarchal society, of a 'lower' race to a 'higher', of a colonized to colonizer, etc.), precisely when it is experienced as 'genuine' and 'sincere' by the subordinated subjects themselves, presents a case of ideological delusion beneath which critical analysis should be able to discern the traces of (internalized, 'naturalized') external brute coercion. However, what about the far more sinister *inverse* operation which makes us (mis)perceive as mere coercion, to which we submit ourselves in a wholly external way, something which effectively has a hold on us 'from within'? On a first approach – that is to say, at an immediate-abstract level – our yielding to this brute coercion is, of course, to be contrasted to a relationship towards some 'genuine' authority in which I experience my subordination to it as the fulfilment of my personality, not as something that thwarts my self-realization – by subordinating myself to a genuine authority, I realize my own essence (in a traditional patriarchal society, for example, a woman is supposed to fulfil her inner vocation by subordinating herself to her husband).

The 'spirit' of such an immediate opposition between external coercion and genuine subordination is, however, profoundly anti-Hegelian: Hegel's aim is precisely to demonstrate how the two opposites pass over into each other (see his exemplary analyses of 'noble' and 'low' consciousness in the *Phenomenology of Spirit*). On the one hand, a close dialectical analysis renders visible how our external subordination to brute coercion is never simply external – how this very experience of the force to which we yield as simply external is an illusion of abstract consciousness. Suffice it to recall the traditional liberal attitude towards the State as a 'mechanical' instrument of external coercion which limits my freedom: what this liberal individualist attitude fails to notice is how this limitation of my freedom involved in the notion of citizen is not external but the self-limitation which actually increases my true freedom, that is, elevates me to the level of a free rational being: that part of me which resists State order, experiences this order as a threat, is the unfree aspect of my personality. Here, I am effectively enslaved to the contingent 'pathological' features of my non-rational nature, to the insignificant whims of my particular nature – this part of my personality *has* to be sacrificed if I am to become a truly free individual. Perhaps an even better example is an adolescent who resists his father's authority and experiences it as external 'repression', misrecognizing thereby the extent to which this authority holds him in sway 'from within' and guarantees the integrity of his self-experience – witness the disorientation, the sense of loss, which takes place when paternal authority effectively disintegrates. . . .

As a true Hegelian, Lacan was fully justified in inverting the commonplace about the liberating potential of unconscious impulses which resist the 'repression' of the Authority to which we consciously submit: the Master is unconscious, he exerts his hold upon us in the unconscious. On the other hand, in so far as 'human being' implies the infinite freedom of subjectivity, an element of falsehood adheres to every allegedly 'genuine' subordination: beneath it, there always lurks a hypocritical calculation or a fear of raw violence. The dialectic of liberation resides precisely in breaking the spell of 'genuine' authority, denouncing it as a mask of brute coercion; exemplary here (again) is the case of the feminist critique that discerns the traces of brute coercion in what, within the patriarchal space, appears as woman's 'natural' vocation. At a more general level, one can assert that 'progress' does not consist only in reducing the amount of violent coercion but also in recognizing violent coercion in what was previously perceived as the 'natural' state of things. The logic of this recognition involves the properly Hegelian dialectical tension between the In-itself and the For-itself: it is wrong simply to claim that the patriarchal subordination of women was always founded on violent coercion, and that liberating reflection simply brings to light an already existing state of things; yet it is no less wrong to claim that, prior to feminist critical reflection, things simply took their course without any antagonistic tension, and that violence becomes violence only when it is experienced as such. The paradox of reflection is that it retroactively makes the past state of things what it always-already 'truly was': by means of the feminist retroactive gaze, the past is retroactively posited in its 'truth'.

On that account, one should be very careful not to reify the psychical impact of a certain sexual practice into its immediate property. For some feminists, for example, fellatio stands for the worst humiliation and debasement of woman – what if, on the contrary, we imagine an intersubjective relationship in which fellatio bears witness to *man's* humiliation, to his abasement to a passive bearer of his phallus, a plaything in woman's hands? Our point here is not merely that the relationship of domination in a sexual contact is always tainted with ambiguity, but that it is the very ambiguity, 'undecidability', of a Master/Servant relationship that 'sexualizes' it. In the minimal mechanism of sexual intercourse, one stares blindly, intoxicated with enjoyment, while the other 'works' – who is the Master here, and who the Servant? Who effectively serves whom as the means of his or her enjoyment? Is not the apparent Master the Slave of his Slave, is not the true Master he who demands of his Slave that he play the role of Master? In the standard (hetero)sexual act, man 'takes', 'makes use of', a woman – but with a slight shift in perspective, it is possible to assert that he effectively reduces himself to an instrument of her enjoyment, subordinating himself to the insatiable superego injunction 'Encore!' (the title of Lacan's *Seminar XX*).

What we must avoid here, apropos of such dialectical passages of an opposite into its other, is the lure of symmetry: Hegel's point is not that the two reversals (of 'genuine' authority into external coercion and vice versa) are somehow exchangeable, that they follow the same logic. Their asymmetry is best epitomized by reference to the couple *cynicism* and *irony*. The fundamental gesture of cynicism is to denounce 'genuine authority' as a pose, whose sole effective content is raw coercion or submission for the sake of some material gain, while an ironist doubts if a cold calculating utilitarian is really what he pretends to be – he suspects that this semblance of calculating distance can conceal a much deeper commitment. The cynic is quick to denounce the ridiculous pretence of solemn authority; the ironist is able to discern true attachment in dismissive disdain or feigned indifference. In matters of love, for example, the cynic excels in denigrating exalted declarations of deep spiritual affinity as a stratagem to exploit the partner sexually or otherwise, whereas the ironist is prone to ascertain, in a melancholic mood, how brutally making sport of our partner, even humiliation, often simply expresses our unreadiness to admit to ourselves the full depth of our attachment. . . . Perhaps the artist of irony *par excellence* was none other than Mozart – suffice it to recall his masterpiece *Così fan tutte*. The trio 'Soave il vento', of course, can be read in a cynical way, as the faked imitation of a sad farewell which barely conceals a glee at the coming erotic intrigue; the ironic point of it is that the subjects who sing it, *including Don Alfonso, the manipulator who staged the event,* are none the less authentically touched by the sadness of the situation – this unexpected authenticity is what eludes the grasp of the cynic.

On a first approach, cynicism may appear to involve a much more radical distance than irony: is not irony benevolent ridicule 'from above', from within the confines of the symbolic order – that is to say, the distance of a subject who views the world from the elevated position of the big Other towards those who are enticed by vulgar earthly pleasures, an awareness of their ultimate vanity – while cynicism relies on the 'earthly' point of view which undermines our belief in the binding power of the Word, of the symbolic pact, 'from below', and advances the substance of enjoyment as the only thing that really matters: Socrates versus Diogenes the Cynic? The true relationship, however, is the reverse: from the correct premiss that 'the big Other doesn't exist' – that the symbolic order is a fiction – the cynic draws the mistaken conclusion that the big Other doesn't 'function', that its role can simply be discounted: owing to his failure to notice how the symbolic fiction none the less regulates his relationship to the real of enjoyment, he remains all the more enslaved to the symbolic context that defines his access to the Thing-Enjoyment, caught in the symbolic ritual he publicly mocks.[17]

This is precisely what Lacan has in mind with his '*les non-dupes errent*': those who are not duped by the symbolic fiction are most deeply in error. The ironist's apparently 'softer' approach, on the other hand, far more effectively unbinds the nodal points that hold the symbolic universe together – that is to say, it is the ironist who effectively assumes the nonexistence of the Other. One is therefore tempted to use this couple of cynicism and irony in order to define one aspect of the 'spiritual' gap that continues to separate the East (ex-Communist Eastern Europe) from the West. What persists in the East is a kind of cynical mistrust of the Word, of the symbolic pact, of its binding authority;[18] whereas the West entertains the suspicion that the allegedly 'free' utilitarian-calculating cynical subject is himself caught in a web of unacknowledged inner impediments and symbolic debts.

A common notion of psychoanalysis, of course, makes it almost an epitome of cynicism as an interpretative attitude: does not psycho-analytic interpretation involve, in its very essence, the act of discerning 'lower' motivations (sexual lust, unacknowledged aggression) behind the apparently 'noble' gestures of spiritual elevation of the beloved, heroic self-sacrifice, and so on? Perhaps, however, this notion is somewhat too glib; perhaps the original enigma that psychoanalysis endeavours to explain is exactly the opposite: how can the actual behaviour of a person who professes his or her freedom from 'prejudices' and 'moralistic constraint' bear witness to inumerable inner impediments, unavowed prohibitions, and so on? Why does a person who is free to 'enjoy life' engage in a systematic 'pursuit of unhappiness', methodically organizing his or her failures? What's in it for him or her, what perverse libidinal profit?

The proof that cynicism, far from effectively undermining the symbolic bond, thoroughly relies on it – that this reliance is the inherent correlative and foundation of cynical distance – is provided by a feature which apparently contradicts the attitude of cynical distrust characteristic of East European Socialism: its almost paranoiac *belief in the power of the Word*. The State and the ruling Party reacted with utter panic to the slightest public criticism, as if some vague critical hints in an obscure poem published in a small circulation literary journal, or an essay in an academic philosophical journal, possessed the potential capacity to trigger an explosion of the entire socialist system. Incidentally, this feature renders 'real Socialism' almost sympathetic to our retrospective nostalgic view, since it bears witness to the legacy of the Enlightenment (the belief in the social efficiency of rational argumentation) that survived in it. This, perhaps, was why it was possible to undermine 'real Socialism' by peaceful civil society movements that operated at the level of the Word – belief in the power of the Word was the system's Achilles heel.

What we encounter here is yet another example of how, in ideology, opposites coincide: the 'ideological' is not only the false, mystifying presentation of raw coercion as 'genuine' domination and authentic respect for the Master, but also – perhaps even more so – the illusory misrecognition of the inner 'hold' a figure of authority exerts upon us, that is, the notion that we are merely yielding to external coercion when effectively, at the level of the unconscious libidinal economy, we need the Master in order to avoid the deadlock of our desire. Perhaps this couple of cynicism and irony is more than just one in a series of complementary ideological procedures; perhaps it provides us with the key to the fundamental deadlock that generates the radical ambiguity of the notion of ideology, on account of which the opposite of an ideological procedure sooner or later proves itself no less ideological. The cynic reduces ideological chimeras to raw reality, he is in search of the real ground of elevated ideological fictions; whereas the ironist entertains a suspicion that perhaps reality itself is not real but always-already structured as a fiction, dominated, regulated by an unconscious fantasy. Each of the two attitudes involves its own trap: the cynic's, a naive belief in ultimate reality outside the cobweb of symbolic fictions; the ironist's, the opposite: the reduction of reality itself to a fiction – so how are we to break this vicious cycle, how are we to avoid the mutual depreciation of the two positions that necessarily entraps us in a paradox similar to Escher's famous drawing of two hands holding a pencil and drawing each other? Lacan shows the way by introducing the distinction between reality (structured as a fiction) and the Real as, precisely, that which resists symbolization.

Quantum physics' 'thesis eleven'

Perhaps the key feature of quantum physics is that for the first time, it has included this reflectivity into science itself, by positing it as an explicit moment of the scientific process.[19] Because of this self-reflective character of its propositions, quantum physics joins ranks with Marxism and psychoanalysis as one of the three types of knowledge which conceives itself not as a neutral adequate description of its object but as a direct intervention in it. 'There are theories which do not aim at congruence with their object, but want to change it' – significantly, this almost literal paraphrase of Marx's 'thesis eleven' is a quote from a recent book on quantum physics.[20] In quantum physics, as well as in Marxism and psychoanalysis, the 'true' knowledge affects its object: in Marxism, the theory describes society from the standpoint of its revolutionary change, and thereby transforms its object (the working class) into a revolutionary subject – the neutral description of society is formally 'false', it involves the acceptance of the existing order; in psychoanalysis, the act of interpretation itself intervenes in its object (dissolves the symptom); in quantum physics, the act of measurement itself brings about the 'collapse of the wave function'. In all three cases, the self-relativization of the theory, far from undermining its cognitive claim, serves as the ultimate proof of its validity.

The true scope of the revolutionary impact of quantum physics has been the object of passionate debate for more than half a century. A cursory examination of the responses of philosophy (or, more precisely, of what passes itself off as philosophy) to quantum physics suffices to validate fully Althusser's thesis on the co-dependence of positivism and obscurantism: the 'spontaneous philosophy' of quantum physics consists of a bricolage of positivist confinement to what is measurable/observable, and spiritualist obscurantism ('there is no reality outside the observer', 'reality exists only in our mind' ...).

Stephen Hawking undoubtedly had in mind such obscurantist talk of 'consciousness which begets reality', such associations of quantum physics with ESP phenomena, with curving a spoon from a distance by means of the sole 'power of the mind', and so on, when he risked a provocative paraphrase of Joseph Goebbels: 'When I hear of Schroedinger's cat, I reach for my gun.'

The first antidote against such obscurantism is to situate quantum physics in relation to the split between the pre-modern universe of meaning and the universe of modern science, which is inherently 'meaningless', 'incomprehensible', since it runs against the most elementary spontaneous preconceptions which determine our sense of 'reality'. How does psychoanalysis relate to the universe of (modern) science? Is it a science, a pre-scientific interpretative-mantic procedure, or something entirely different (a self-reflective procedure in the lineage of the dialectic of German Idealism, for example)?

Lacan displaced the very terrain of this standard question by asserting that the *subject* of psychoanalysis (the analysand) is the Cartesian subject of science. Therein resides the difference (one of many differences) between Freud (as read by Lacan) and Jung: Jung advocates a return to the pre-modern universe of Wisdom and its sexo-cosmology, the universe of a harmonious correspondence between the human microcosm and the macrocosm – that is to say, for him the subject of psychoanalysis is the pre-modern subject living in a universe in which 'everything has a meaning'; for Lacan, on the contrary, the analysand is the 'empty' Cartesian subject living in a 'disenchanted' world, a subject deprived of his roots in the universe of Meaning, confronted with an inherently 'incomprehensible' universe in which the power of everyday hermeneutic evidence is suspended. This difference accounts for the divergence in their respective approaches to a symptom; in the case of agoraphobia, for example, a Jungian would have direct recourse to some archetype, grounding the fear of open spaces in the experience of birth, being thrown into the open space outside the maternal body, and so on; whereas a Freudian would follow the lead of modern science and apply himself to a concrete analysis, in order to unearth some contingent link to a particular experience with no inherent connection to open space (recently, the patient witnessed a violent fight in an open space which stirred up a long-forgotten childhood trauma, for example).[21]

How, then, does quantum physics stand with respect to this split? Of all sciences, it has most thoroughly broken with our everyday comprehension of 'reality' opened up by modern Galilean physics: Galileo broke with the Aristotelian ontology that gave systematic expression to our everyday pre-comprehension (bodies are naturally 'falling-down', and tend towards a state of rest, etc.). By carrying this break to extremes, however, quantum physics also confronts its inherent deadlock most radically: in order to enter the circuit of scientific communication, it has to rely on the terms of our everyday language, which unavoidably call to mind objects and events of 'ordinary' tangible reality (the *spin* of a particle, the *nucleus* of an atom, etc.) and thereby introduce an element of irreducible disturbance – the moment we take a term too 'literally', we are led astray.

The only adequate formulation of quantum physics would be to replace all terms which, in any way whatsoever, relate to the universe of our everyday experience with a kind of jabberwocky, so that we would be left with pure syntax, with a set of mathematically formulated relations. Consequently, scientists are quite justified in emphasizing that one cannot 'understand' quantum physics (to 'understand' a phenomenon means precisely to locate it within the horizon of our meaningful comprehension of reality): quantum physics simply 'works', it 'functions', yet the moment one tries to 'understand' how it works, one is swallowed up into the Black Hole of un-reason. On the other hand, difficulties arise with the so-called collapse of the wave function: one can pass from potentiality to actuality only by means of an observer who functions at the level of everyday experience, so that the very line that separates the quantum universe from our everyday reality runs *within* quantum physics. John Wheeler provided perhaps the only adequate answer to one of the great enigmas of quantum physics – when, at what precise point, does the collapse of the wave function occur – by identifying it with the emergence of intersubjectively recognized *meaning*: we are dealing here neither with automatic registration in a machine (a photo, for example) nor with consciousness, but simply with language meaning.[22]

'Complementarity'

This radical break of quantum physics with our everyday comprehension of 'reality' belies all attempts to combine quantum physics with Eastern thought, which remains thoroughly rooted in pre-modern sexualized ontology (the cosmic polarity of male and female principles, Yin and Yang, etc.). Attempts to bring quantum physics and Eastern wisdom together usually evoke the notion of 'complementarity' – does not this notion point back to the 'complementarity' of principles in pre-modern cosmology (no Yin without Yang, etc.)? A closer examination, however, immediately compels us to call this analogy into question.

Let us begin with Heisenberg's infamous 'uncertainty principle': even some popular introductions to quantum physics fall prey to the epistemological fallacy of interpreting the uncertainty principle as something which hinges on the inherent limitation of the observer and/or his or her measuring instruments – as if, on account of this limitation (i.e. because our observation intervenes in and affects the observed process), we could not simultaneously measure a particle's mass *and* momentum (or any other couple of complementary features). The uncertainty principle is actually much 'stronger': far from concerning merely the limitation of the observer, its point is, rather, that complementarity is *inscribed into the 'thing itself'* – a particle itself, in its 'reality', cannot have a fully specified mass and momentum, it can have only one *or* the other. The principle is thus profoundly 'Hegelian': what first appeared to be an epistemological obstacle turns out to be a property of the thing itself; that is to say, the choice between mass and momentum defines the very 'ontological' status of the particle. This inversion of an epistemological obstacle into an ontological 'impediment' which prevents the object from actualizing the totality of its potential qualities (mass and momentum) is 'Hegelian'.

And this is what 'complementarity' is about: two complementary properties do *not* complement each other, they are mutually exclusive. The relationship between mass and momentum resembles that between a figure and its background: we see either two human faces in profile or a vase, no 'synthesis' is possible here; we can never have two figures. The two terms of a choice do not form a Whole, since each choice already constitutes its own Whole (of a figure and its background) which excludes its opposite. The 'complementarity' of quantum physics is thus much closer to the peculiar logic of a *forced choice* articulated in Lacan's psychoanalysis than to the pre-modern balance of cosmic principles: its counterpart in our human condition is a situation in which the subject is forced to choose and to accept a certain fundamental loss or impossibility. This impossibility is what the Enlightenment ideal of a self-awareness that enables us to act, of an empowering knowledge exemplified by the expressions like 'know-how' or '*savoir-faire*', endeavours to elude: once I know too much, I am no longer in a position to accomplish the act – that is to say, a 'man who knows too much' is a man who can no longer act. 'Complementarity', as the fundamental mystery of the human act in its relationship to knowledge-awareness, thus points towards the real of an impossibility; Jon Elster formulated this impossibility as the paradox of 'states that are necessary by-products' – *it is impossible* for a subject to strive consciously for the property X and effectively to produce it (where X stands for properties which are crucial for our self-esteem: love of others, dignity, etc.). In short, a true act can be accomplished only in unawareness of its conditions: *it is impossible* to comprise in the act an awareness of its 'objective' dimension, of its consequences, and so on.[23]

The same paradox is at work in the so-called 'hermeneutic circle': meaning emerges only if there is a gap in the causal chain.[24] The 'determinist' solution (the more I become aware of the actual causal chain which determines my activity, the more I lose the illusion of freedom) falls short here: the point it misses is that my reflective awareness of all the circumstances which condition my act can never lead me to act: it cannot explain the fact of the act itself. By endlessly weighing the reasons for and against, I never manage to act – at a certain point, I must decide to 'strike out blindly', saying to myself: 'I really don't care about all the consequences, let's simply do it, whatever the cost'; once this decision is taken, the conditions and circumstances themselves retroactively appear in a new light. (This is analogous to religious belief: the decision to believe never results from a careful weighing of *pro* and *contra*, that is, one can never say: 'I believe in Christ because, after careful consideration, I came to the conclusion that reasons for prevail' – it is only the act, the decision to believe, that renders the reasons to believe truly comprehensible.) One should therefore fully endorse the (Nietzschean) paradox of 'active forgetfulness', of a forgetting which alone enables us to act. Similarly, in the domain of law, a legal order is in force only in so far as its subjects 'repress' its contingent, 'illegal' origins and accept its claim to validity at face value. On a somewhat different level, this is what Heidegger is aiming at when he insists again and again that true philosophical deliberation is not only 'of no practical use' but can even hurt our 'practical efficiency': a scientist, for example, if he is to be efficient in his particular domain, *must not* 'think', that is, reflect upon the ontological horizon of pre-comprehension which discloses this domain – therein resides one of the dimensions, an often misrecognized one, of 'ontological difference'.

Yet another version of the impossibility – that is, of the kernel of the Real – contained in the notion of 'complementarity' is provided by the paradox of freedom: on its most radical level, freedom is experienced in the guise of my awareness of the inexorable, often self-destructive, necessity to act in a certain way: 'I cannot do otherwise, since to act in this way is part of my very nature'. As Schelling puts it, it is as if, in a timeless, eternally past, primordially unconscious act, I have chosen myself, my 'eternal nature': radical freedom and consciousness are incompatible, the truly free founding decision was unconscious, and must remain such if it is to stay in force – the moment it is raised to consciousness, it is already called into question and, for all practical purposes, retracted. The most pathetic example, of course, is that of love: the decision to love somebody is free (compulsory love is no love), yet this decision can never be a present and conscious one (I can never say to myself: 'Now I will decide to fall in love with this person . . . ') – all I can do in the present is to ascertain that *the decision has already been taken* and that I am caught in the inexorable necessity to love.[25]

This notion of complementarity also enables us to discern what is perhaps the weak point in the otherwise path-breaking politico-philosophical essays of Chantal Mouffe. One of the principal targets of Mouffe's critique is contemporary liberal-democratic attempts to provide a meta-political foundation of politics in some neutral frame of reference which would account for the set of universally binding ethical rules (Rawls's 'original position', Habermas's discursive rationality, etc.): she denounces these attempts at foundation as naturalizing gestures which obfuscate the Political [le *politique*], the field of antagonisms in which different positions are grounded only in themselves, in the performative act of opposing themselves to the political adversary. According to Mouffe, an ethical foundation of politics is not only theoretically wrong but also politically dangerous, since it harbours totalitarian potential by rendering invisible the violent gesture of its own imposition: there is always an extreme violence involved in imposing a set of normative rules as a neutral-universal ground of judgement. . . .

Although this critique is fully justified, it continues to shirk the paradox of complementarity in so far as it contains the illusion of a politics delivered from naturalizing mystification, dispensing with any reference to some extra-political foundation: as if it were possible to play the pure game of antagonism; as if naturalization – that is, a reference to some non-antagonistic neutral (ethical) foundation – illusory as it is, were not an irreducible, necessary condition of a politically efficient *prise de position*. In this precise sense, ethics is a *supplement* of the Political: there is no political 'taking sides' without minimal reference to some ethical normativity which transcends the sphere of the purely Political – in other words: without the minimal 'naturalization' involved in legitimating our position via a reference to some extra-political (natural, ethical, theological . . .) agency. And – to dot the i's – the 'Yes!' of the Hegelian 'reconciliation' is, in the last analysis, precisely a 'Yes!' to complementarity: a 'Yes!' of fully accepting that one cannot simultaneously 'know it' and 'do it'; a 'Yes!' of bidding farewell to the Enlightenment illusion of a self-transparent activity, an activity wholly aware of its implications.

Against historicism

The trap to be avoided here is the reduction of this theme of complementarity to the now-fashionable critique of universalism and the related assertion of the plurality of particular narratives: complementarity – conceived as the impossibility of the complete description of a particular phenomenon – is, on the contrary, *the very place of the inscription of universality into the Particular*. A particular social phenomenon can never be completely 'contextualized', reduced to a set of sociohistorical circumstances – such a particularization would presuppose the crudest universalism: namely, the presumption that we, its agents, can speak from a neutral-universal place of pure meta-language exempt from any specific context.

Within the social-symbolic field, each particular totality, in its very self-enclosure, (mis)perceives itself as universal, that is to say, it comprises itself and its own perspective on its Outside, on all other particular totalities (epochs, societies, etc.) – why? Precisely because it is in itself *incomplete*, 'open', not wholly determined by its context. The point is thus not that we, the observing subjects embedded in our particular situation, can never wholly comprehend the set of particular circumstances which determine the Other, the object of our scrutiny; the deficiency is 'ontological', not merely 'epistemological' – this Other is already in itself not wholly determined by circumstances. It is this very overlapping of the two deficiencies (or, in Lacanese: the intersection of the two lacks) that opens up the dimension of universality.

Marx, in a famous passage from his Introduction to *Grundrisse*, clearly perceived this enigma of universality: how is it that Homer's poetry, although conditioned by its time, has retained its quasi-universal appeal up to our day? The problem is not to explain how something akin to the *Iliad* was possible only in the early Greek society; the problem, rather, is to explain why this product of early Greek society still speaks to us and arouses our enthusiasm. Marx's answer, unfortunately, does not live up to his question: by a naive recourse to the parallel between the epochs of European history and stages in the development of a human individual, a parallel deeply indebted to the tradition of German Romanticism, he interprets the irresistible charm of Ancient Greek society as the eternal charm of the 'childhood of humanity'. Even this erroneous answer, however, involves a correct principle of explanation: it relies on the premiss that what accounts for the universal appeal of Homer's poetry is *its very attachment to specific historic conditions*. The problem is not why Homer's poetry, *in spite of* its roots in a specific historical constellation, retains its universal appeal, but the exact opposite: why does a product of *these* (and not some other) historical conditions retain a universal appeal?

This deadlock of the historicist critique of universalism is clearly illustrated apropos of the problematic of *human rights*: are they embedded in their specific Western context, or are they universal? It is easy to historicize the notion of universal human rights by demonstrating their emergence in the modern Western context of the bourgeois struggle for emancipation; the true problem, however, is to explain *their universal appeal*, on account of which the critique which dismisses them as imposed Western values falls short'.[26] This universal appeal is founded upon the gap, implied by the notion of human rights, between their universality and their always-imperfect realization. That is to say: the crucial difference between the democratic universe of human rights and other political orders is that the structuring principle in all these orders is immediately identified with their particular, determinate content, whereas the very functioning of the democratic order relies on the difference between the 'ordering' and the 'order' – between the structuring principle of the system, the system 'in its becoming' (as Kierkegaard would have put it), and any determinate, positive form of this order. In other words, human rights can never be simply enumerated, presented as a closed set – the very modern notion of human rights implies that they are never 'all', that there is always something to be added to the list. They are 'universal' not simply in the sense that they are supposed to include all human beings, but also in the sense that they cannot be reduced to any particular, determinate form of their positive articulation – the second sense is a *sine qua non* of the first. On that basis, all kinds of so-called minorities (ethnic, sexual, religious . . .) can always, in their very critique of a particular (sexist, Western, etc.) bias of the predominant formulation of human rights, again refer to their universality, claiming that their own rights are not properly taken into consideration in this predominant formulation. Universality becomes 'for itself', is 'posited as such', when some particular content is hindered in its self-fulfilment.[27]

We can now see where, precisely, the Hegelian approach to universality differs from the standard one: the standard approach is concerned with the historicist problem of the effective scope of a universal notion (is a notion truly universal, or is its validity actually constrained to a specific historical epoch, social class, etc.?), whereas Hegel asks exactly the opposite question: how, in what precise historical conditions, can a 'neutral' universal notion emerge at all? Under what conditions do people become aware of the universal notion of 'labour' irrespective of particular professions? When does the neutral notion of a 'style' become operative in art theory? When, for example, did painters begin to assume that they were free to choose from a multitude of styles (Expressionist, Impressionist, Cubist, Surrealist . . .)? In what type of society does one experience one's own cultural background as something contingent, as one exemplification of the neutral-universal notion of 'culture', so that one can then play the game called 'multiculturalism'?

I can be a feminist, socialist, conservative, free-market . . . ecologist – in each case, my particular (socialist, conservative, feminist . . .) orientation is constitutive of my identity as an ecologist: the capitalist profit-orientated economy (or the excess of modernity, or patriarchal domination) is for me the very root of the ecological catastrophe. The properly Hegelian problem is not to ascertain that my particular (socialist, conservative, feminist . . .) brand of ecological orientation is just one species of the universal genus of ecological movements; the true problem is how, under what conditions, *my own particular sociopolitical experience leads me to abandon the immediate identification of 'being an ecologist' with my particular brand of it*, so that I apprehend the link that connects ecology in general with my particular orientation as contingent. The answer, of course, is provided by the notion of *lack*: only in so far as I experience my own particular position as fundamentally *deficient* does the universal dimension involved in (and obfuscated by) it appear as such – or, in Hegel's terms, is it 'posited', becomes 'for itself'.

Or – to put it in a slightly different way – the historicist reduction of Marx or Freud to an expression of their age is false and itself ideological, although quite accurate at the factual level. Marx's analysis of capitalism is, of course, 'a child of its time', embedded in a concrete and unique historical constellation; the true enigma, however, is how it was possible for Marx, at that precise moment of history, to provide the key that enables us to unravel the secret of the whole of history hitherto. Freudian psychoanalysis is, of course, a product of the late nineteenth century; what one has to explain, however, is how it was possible for Freud to gain an insight into the universal logic of human sexuality. . . . In a proper dialectical analysis, universality and historicization are thus strictly correlative.

Therein resides also the falsity of a certain kind of multiculturalism: the fact that cultures are different, that each culture possesses its own irreducible specificity, is a *factum brutum*, a banality that lacks the dignity of an object of thought; the problem, on the contrary, is to explain how, in spite of their differences, cultures none the less interact; how a certain (poetic, ideological, etc.) theme can have universal repercussions and cross the barriers that separate different cultures. Incidentally, the first thing to do here is to reject the cliché according to which Western cultural imperialism suppresses differences between cultures – quite the contrary, imperialism actually *accentuates* these differences, since it literally lives by them. Even in the 1920s, Aldous Huxley remarked in *Jesting Pilate* how the English colonists in India were deeply respectful of Indian traditional life, of the wisdom of old Hindu or Buddhist religion. An educated Englishman was always ready to admit Indian wisdom's superiority to modern Western civilization – what he feared more than a vampire fears a string of garlic was an Indian who had become Westernized and successfully integrated Western science and politics, without renouncing his Indian identity. In short, what the English feared was those Indians who endeavoured to transform India into a modern nation like England itself.

Along the same lines, one can also clarify the allegedly 'unhistorical' character of the Lacanian 'formulas of sexuation'. Every epoch, every society, every ethnic community, of course, furnishes its own ideological connotation of the difference between the sexes (in Europe, for example, 'man' is posited as the neutral universality of the human species, whereas 'woman' stands for the specific difference, i.e. for 'sexualization' as such; in Ancient China, on the contrary, 'woman' designated continuity and 'man' discontinuity, breach, separation). What the Lacanian 'formulas of sexuation' endeavour to formulate, however, is not yet another positive formulation of the sexual difference but the underlying impasse that generates the multitude of positive formulations as so many (failed) attempts to symbolize the traumatic real of the sexual difference. What all epochs have in common is not some universal positive feature, some transhistorical constant; what they all share, rather, is the same deadlock, the same antinomy – in Schelling's terms, one is tempted to say that this same impasse persists and repeats itself in different powers/potentials in different cultures. The notion of the Real *qua* traumatic antagonism which returns as the same in all successive failed attempts at its symbolization thus leads us to invert the standard formula of the relationship between Universal and Particular (the Universal as the genus which divides itself into particular species): here, it is as if Universal and Particular change places – we have a series of Universals, of universal interpretative matrices, which are all answers to the 'absolute particularity' of the traumatic Real, of the imbalance of an antagonism which throws out of joint, and thereby 'particularizes', the neutral-universal frame, so that the schema of the relationship between Universal and Particular is now the following:

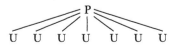

217

The criticism that Lacan 'reifies' the Real into a non-historical kernel excluded from historical change therefore thoroughly misses the point: not only is there no conceptual incompatibility between the Real *qua* non-historical kernel and historicity, but it is the very trauma of the Real which again and again sets in motion the movement of history, propelling it to ever new historizations/symbolizations.

How does one make a rat human?

In what – beyond the New Age 'holistic' speculations on the spiritual nature of the universe, and so on – resides, then, the properly philosophical interest of quantum physics? Philosophers usually refer to quantum physics to enlist its help in their eternal battle against everyday common-sense naive realist ontology, or – when they are in a more spiritual New Age mood – as a proof that within contemporary science itself, the so-called 'Cartesian mechanical paradigm' is losing ground against a new 'holistic' approach. Perhaps, however, the true breakthrough of quantum physics lies elsewhere: it compels us to call into question the ultimate and most resilient philosophical myth (as Derrida called it), that of the absolute gap that separates nature from man – from the universe of language in which human beings 'dwell', as Heidegger put it.

It was Sartre, perhaps, who provided the most astute formulation of this gap in his opposition between the In-itself of the inert presence of things and the For-itself of human consciousness as the vortex of self-negation. It is interesting to note how even Lacan, Sartre's great opponent in the heyday of the 'structuralist' debate in the 1960s, remained at that time thoroughly within these co-ordinates: the standard Lacanian theme in the 1950s and 1960s was the unsurmountable opposition between the animal universe of imaginary captivity, of the balanced mirror-relationship between *Innenwelt* and *Aussenwelt*, and the human universe of symbolic negativity, imbalance. Lacan thereby fully participates in the line of thought that begins with Hegel, according to which man is 'nature sick unto death', a being forever marked by traumatic misplacement, thrown 'out of joint', lacking its proper place, in contrast to an animal which always fits into its environment, that is to say, is immediately 'grown into' it. Symptomatic here is Lacan's 'mechanistic' metaphorics: an almost celebratory characterizing of the symbolic order as an automaton that follows its path, totally impervious to human emotions and needs – language is a parasitic entity that battens on the human animal, throwing his or her life rhythm off balance, derailing it, subordinating it to its own brutally imposed circuit.

What accounts for the specific Lacanian flavour of this renewed assertion of the gap that separates 'culture' (the symbolic order) from the fullness of the immediate life-experience is the reversal of the usual Cartesian idealist contrast between the life of the spirit and the mechanics of nature: with Lacan, it is the machine in its very 'blind', senseless, automatic repetitive movement that elevates the human universe above the immediate animal life-experience. The political connotation of this theme of man being constitutively 'out of joint' is radically ambiguous – it functions as a 'floating signifier' that can be appropriated by the Left option (the celebration of man's negativity as the power of the permanent transcending and revolutionizing of every routine, inert situation) as well as by the Right one (Arnold Gehlen's anthropology, for example, whose main thesis is that, owing to the lack of an innate instinctual pattern, man needs a Master, i.e. the authority of a strong Institution that can keep his excesses in check and guarantee a stable point of reference).[28]

Jacques-Alain Miller's comments on an uncanny laboratory experiment with rats (from one of Lacan's unpublished Seminars) provide a thrilling and somewhat uneasy exemplification of this philosophical *topos*. In a labyrinthine set-up, a desired object (a tasty morsel of food or a sexual partner) is first made easily accessible to a rat. Then the set-up is changed in such a way that the rat sees and thereby knows where the desired object is, but cannot gain access to it; in exchange for it, as a kind of consolation prize, a series of similar objects of inferior value is made easily accessible – how does the rat react? For some time, it tries to find its way to the 'true' object; then, upon ascertaining that this object is definitely out of reach, the rat will renounce it and put up with some of the inferior substitute objects – in short, it will act as a 'rational' subject of utilitarianism. It is only now, however, that the true experiment begins: the scientists perform a surgical operation on the rat, messing about with its brain, doing things to it with laser beams about which – as Miller delicately put it – it is better to know nothing.

So what happened when the operated rat was again let loose in the labyrinth, the one in which the 'true' object was inaccessible? *The rat persisted*: it never became fully reconciled to the loss of the 'true' object, resigning itself to one of the inferior substitutes, but repeatedly returned to it, attempted to reach it.[29] In short the rat, in a sense, was *humanized*: it assumed the tragic 'human' attitude towards the unattainable absolute object which, because of its very inaccessibility, forever captivates our desire.[30] Miller's point, of course, is that this quasi-humanization of the rat resulted from its biological *mutilation*: the unfortunate rat started to act like a human being in relation to its object of desire when its brain was butchered and crippled by an 'unnatural' surgical intervention. . . . (A detailed reading of Lacan's last texts demonstrates that in the last years of his teaching he left this traditional philosophical *topos* behind – when he evokes examples from animal behaviour, he no longer uses them as mere 'analogies': that is to say, these examples are to be taken *literally*; that, however, is another story. . . .)

How, then, are we to break with this tradition without falling prey to naive naturalism and/or its complementary double, evolutionary teleology? How are we to avoid the standard procedure of filling in the gap that separates man from animal via man's 'naturalization', that is, via the endeavour to explain all specifically 'human' characteristics in terms of natural evolution? Is the only alternative really that of 'spiritualizing' nature itself? Quantum physics opens up a totally different path: what it calls into question is not the specificity of man, his exceptional position with regard to nature, but, rather, the very notion of nature implied by the standard philosophical formulation of the gap between nature and man, as well as by the New Age assertion of a deeper harmony between nature and man: the notion of nature as a 'closed', balanced universe, regulated by some underlying Law or Rule. True 'anthropomorphism' resides in the notion of nature tacitly assumed by those who oppose man to nature: nature as a circular 'return of the same', as the determinist kingdom of inexorable 'natural laws', or (more in accordance with 'New Age' sensitivity) nature as a harmonious, balanced Whole of cosmic forces derailed by man's *hubris*, his pathological arrogance. What is to be 'deconstructed' is this very notion of nature: the features we refer to in order to emphasize man's unique status – the constitutive imbalance, the 'out-of-joint', on account of which man is an 'unnatural' creature, 'nature sick unto death' – must somehow already be at work in nature itself, although – as Schelling would have put it – in another, lower power (in the mathematical sense of the term).[31]

Five lessons of the 'double-slit'

So how does quantum physics enable us to break the standard deadlock of the 'naturalization' of man and/or the 'spiritualization' of nature? Let us take as our starting point the (deservedly) famous 'double-slit experiment' – it was Richard Feynman who claimed that this experiment reveals the central mystery of the quantum world.

To simplify the procedure, let us imagine a wall with two small holes – slits – in it. On one side there is a source of a beam of electrons, on the other another wall incorporating an array of electron detectors. Electrons emitted by the source pass through (one of) the two holes and hit the other wall, where the array of detectors allows us to observe the pattern of the way they hit this wall. The enigma, of course, concerns the particle–wave duality: when is the observed pattern that of particles and when is it that of the interference of two waves? When both slits are open, the pattern observed is that of the interference of two waves. When one slit *or* the other is opened in turn, there is no interference. When, with both slits open, we slow down the beam so that only one electron goes through the whole set-up at a time, *we still get the pattern for interference by waves.* If, however, we observe the two slits to see which slit each electron goes through, we get no interference pattern. That is the mystery: it is as if a single electron (a particle which, as such, must go through one of the two slits) 'knows' whether the other slit is open, and behaves accordingly: if the other slit is open, it behaves as a wave; if not, it behaves as an 'ordinary' particle. Even more: a single electron seems to 'know' if it is being observed or not, since it behaves accordingly. . . . So what are the implications of this experiment?

- Its first lesson is that the potentiality of the wave function is not a 'mere possibility' in the ordinary sense of the term: the point is not simply that the trajectory of a particle is not determined in advance – that what is determined in advance is just the probability that a particle will pass through one slit or the other; the point is, rather, that the 'actual' result (the fact that when only one electron goes through the whole set-up at a time, we still get the pattern for interference by waves) can be accounted for only by accepting the 'incomprehensible' hypothesis according to which a particle 'effectively' did not follow only one path but, in an unheard-of sense, *all the paths which are possible within the constraint of its wave function.*

What is thereby called into question is a feature which, according to philosophical *doxa* from Kierkegaard to Heidegger, distinguishes man from nature: nature does not know possibility as such, it is only in the human universe – that is, with the advent of language – that possibility as such becomes effective, determines our actual performance. Suffice it to mention the obvious example of guilt feelings: I am devoured by the awareness that I *could have* acted differently, in accordance with my duty – in the human universe, failure to do something is a positive fact that can brand my entire life. For Lacan, this short circuit between possibility and actuality is a fundamental feature of the symbolic order: power, for example, is *actually* exerted only in the guise of a *potential* threat: only in so far as it does not strike fully but 'keeps itself in reserve'. Take the logic of paternal authority: the moment a father loses control and displays his full power (starts to shout, or to beat his child), we necessarily perceive this display as impotent rage, that is, as an index of its very opposite.[32] The supreme example in psychoanalysis, of course, is provided by symbolic castration: the mere *threat* of castration brings about psychical consequences which amount to a 'castrating' effect – it brands the subject's *actual* behaviour with an indelible mark of restraint and renunciation.[33] And do we not encounter an analogous short circuit between possibility and actuality in the quantum universe in which the actual behaviour (trajectory) of a particle can be explained only by taking into account the fluctuation of virtual particles?

• The second lesson of the double-slit experiment concerns the enigma of what Lacan, in his Seminar *Encore*, calls 'knowledge in the real': nature seems to 'know' which laws to follow; leaves on a tree 'know' the rule that enables them to ramify according to a complex pattern, and so on. One of the basic themes of the philosophy of self-consciousness is that our (the subject's) awareness of a thing affects and transforms this thing itself: one cannot simply assert that a thing, inclusive of its properties, exists 'out there' irrespective of our awareness of it. Take the ambiguous status of patriarchal violence against women: one could claim that this violence becomes actual violence *only when it is experienced* – 'registered' – *as such by a woman*. In a society in which the traditional patriarchal ideology exerts unquestionable hegemony – one which lacks even a minimal of 'feminist awareness' – a certain kind of 'possessive' attitude of a man towards a woman is not only not perceived by a woman as 'violent', but even received with open arms as a sign of authentic passionate devotion. The point here, of course, is not to 'soften' this violence by reducing it to something 'merely imagined': violence is 'real', yet its raw, indeterminate reality becomes the reality of 'unacceptable violence' only via its 'registration' in the symbolic order.

Another example is provided by Edith Wharton's *Age of Innocence* – what we have in mind is the reversal that takes place in the last pages of the novel, when the hero learns that his allegedly ignorant and innocent wife knew all the time that his true love was the fatal Countess Olenska. This is the 'innocence' alluded to in the novel's title: far from being an ingénue blessedly unaware of the emotional turmoils of her beloved, she knew everything, yet she persisted in her role as ingénue, thereby safeguarding the happiness of their marriage. The hero, of course, mistook her for precisely such an ingénue: *had he known that she knew*, not only would their happiness have been impossible, but his passionate affair with Countess Olenska would also have been ruined – such an affair can blossom only in so far as it is unrecognized by the big Other (epitomized here by the allegedly ignorant wife). That is the most unpleasant and humiliating surprise for someone who is involved in a clandestine love affair: suddenly I become aware that my spouse knew all the time, and merely feigned ignorance. . . .

The lesson of the double-slit experiment is that a similar 'knowledge in the real', a knowledge that affects the 'actual' behaviour of a particle, is already operative at the level of microphysics: if we observe the electron's trajectory in order to discover through which of the two slits it will pass, the electron will behave as a particle; if, on the other hand, we do not observe it, it will display the properties of a wave – as if the electron somehow *knows* whether it is being observed or not. . . . Therein resides the enigma of 'knowledge in the real': how can a particle that passes through slit A *know* the state of slit B (is it open or not?) *and act accordingly*?

• It was no accident that in our second paragraph we resorted to the term 'registration' which, taken literally, designates the inscription of an event or object into a symbolic network. According to quantum physics, the 'hard' external reality of 'actual' material objects in space and time is constituted by means of the 'collapse' of the wave function, which occurs when the quantum process affects the level defined by the second law of thermodynamics (irreversible temporality, etc.). And it is deeply symptomatic that in an effort to specify this 'collapse', quantum physicists resort again and again to the metaphorics of *language*: the 'collapse' of the wave function occurs when a quantum event 'leaves some kind of *trace*' in the observation apparatus, that is, when it is '*registered* in some way'. What is crucial here is the relationship to externality: an event becomes fully 'itself', realizes itself, only when its external surroundings 'take note' of it. Does not this constitutive relationship to externality not prefigure the logic of 'symbolic realization', in which an event x 'counts', becomes 'effective', via its inscription in the symbolic network that is external to the 'thing itself'? As I have already pointed out, when John Wheeler, one of those who have consistently tried to work out the philosophical consequences of quantum physics, was cornered by an interviewer who asked him about the exact moment of the collapse of the wave function, he offered as a last refuge the inter-subjective community of scientists: one can be absolutely sure of a collapse only when the result of a measurement is integrated into the intersubjectively acknowledged scientific discourse. . . . The parallel that imposes itself here is that between quantum mechanics and the symbolic process of decision, of the intervention of a 'quilting point [*point de capiton*]' which stabilizes meaning.[34]

Let us recall Agamemnon's decision to sacrifice his daughter; at first,

223

he hesitates; the arguments for both sides seem conclusive, the situation is undecidable: 'Oh but doom will crush me / once I rend my child, / the glory of my house – / a father's hands are stained, / blood of a young girl streaks the altar. / Pain both ways and what is worse?'[35] At Aulis, however, Agamemnon takes a strange turn:

> Without transition or pause, he changes tone. From one verse to the next, the conflict of obligations is carried off – as if by favorable winds, effective even before they blow. 'It is right and holy that I should desire with exceedingly impassioned passion the sacrifice staying the winds, the maiden's blood'.[36] The either–or, which just an instant ago was so cruel in its two opposing laws, is now *decided*. What is more, the law embraced by Agamemnon is no longer evil, it is right, just, sacred.[37]

Do we not encounter here, in this operation of *capitonnage* which 'quilts' the freely floating multitude of arguments, something strictly analogous to the 'collapse' of the wave of potentialities into an unambiguously determined position? And are we not also dealing with the same logic in the Schellingian passage from the universe of potentialities which are present in the guise of Ideas in God's mind (the spectral, shadowy proto-existence of a thing previous to its actual existence) to our actual spatio–temporal world? Schelling himself speaks of the difference between the passive multitude in the subject and the subject which effectively posits itself as One.

In any case, the exact interpretation of the collapse of a wave function contains the fundamental aporia of quantum physics: it concerns the enigma of the relationship between *potentia* and actuality, that is, of the passage from the quantum universe of potentialities into our 'effective' reality. Ultimately, only two interpretations seem to be viable: either so-called 'Copenhagen orthodoxy', in which this collapse is linked to the function of the observer, and eventually to consciousness; or the 'Many Worlds Interpretation', which simply dispenses with the collapse by claiming that all possibilities are realized in a plural, infinitely ramified universe. Some interpreters (Alistair Rae, among others[38]) look for a way out of this uncanny and crippling dilemma in which – as Stalin would have put it – both choices are worse via an 'objective' redefinition of the observer's function: the collapse occurs when a quantum event is inscribed into, registered by, a process which is no longer potential-reversible, since in it the second law of thermodynamics (prescribing the irreversibility of a temporal succession) is already in force. Rae relies here on Ilya Prigogine's claim that the fundamental reality of our universe is not that of 'being', of the reversible micro-reality of particles, but that of 'becoming', of the irreversible process of reality regulated by the second law of thermodynamics.

The passage from quantum reality to measured observable reality, however, is not a passage from being to becoming but, rather, the opposite: is not quantum reality the domain of pure becoming, of an undetermined potentiality which, by means of measurement, 'collapses' into the determined being of a real object? And, on the other hand, is not the tension between particles and processes (Prigogine's fundamental conceptual frame of reference) characteristic of the classical, pre-quantum physics which moves between a mechanicist Newtonian reduction of complex processes to their elementary constituents (particles) regulated by strict laws, so that the laws directly describing global processes are merely statistical approximations, and its inherent inversion, which posits global processes as the only true reality? In this case, we have *three* levels, not just two: the quantum level with its 'undecidable' wave–particle duality; the 'mechanicist' level of bodies, particles, or some other elementary constituents; and, finally, the 'thermodynamic' level of global processual functions.

Here, perhaps, a reference to Schelling renders possible, if not a solution, at least a productive reformulation of the problem. The quantum universe is a universe of potentialities in which there is as yet no actuality proper (no linear deployment of time, since temporal processes are reversible, etc.); in this universe, wave–particle duality remains 'indifferent', a non-exclusive, non-contradictory coexistence of two features which, the moment we pass to actuality proper, become incompatible (i.e. in actuality proper, an entity cannot be a wave and a particle at the same time). The 'collapse' of the quantum universe then stands for the Schellingian *Ent-Scheidung*, the act of decision/discrimination by means of which wave–particle duality is posited as an actual difference: it is only now that we can speak about the actual difference between bodies (formerly: particles) and processes (formerly: waves). In short, is not the opposition between level 2 and level 3 – between elements/bodies and global processes – a kind of 'explicatio' of the opposition wave–particle, which remains 'implicit'?

• One is tempted here to take a step further: according to the Lacanian reading of the Freudian notion of *Nachträglichkeit* ('deferred action'), the symbolic inscription, 'registration', of an event always occurs 'after the fact', with a minimum of delay – reality always 'will have been': that is, by means of its symbolic inscription it 'becomes what it always-already was'. Now, John Wheeler has proposed a change in the double-slit experiment, the so-called 'delayed double-slit', which brings about the same paradox of the 'retroactive writing of history'. In short, the experiment can be set up in such a way that our decision to observe the trajectory of a particle or not is taken *after the particle has already passed through the slits*: in that brief period of time when the particle is already beyond the two slits but has not yet hit the measuring apparatus. Our decision therefore decides what went on *retroactively*: it determines whether we have been dealing with an (observed) 'particle' or an (unobserved) 'wave'.

This minimal delay of the inscription with regard to the 'event' itself also opens up the space for a kind of ontological 'cheating' with virtual particles: an electron can create a proton, and thereby violate the principle of constant energy, only if it reabsorbs it quickly enough – that is, before its environs 'take note' of the discrepancy. 'Quantum indeterminacy' lives off this minimum of 'free space' between an event and its inscription: what we encounter here is, again, the basic paradox of the process of symbolization (reality 'becomes what it was' via its inscription in the external symbolic medium) in its 'lower power'.

It is here, once we come upon virtual particles, that things become really interesting. So-called 'vacuum fluctuation', a process in the course of which a particle springs up 'out of nowhere' and then returns to Nothingness, this 'virtual' existence of a particle which annihilates itself before reaching full actuality, is generally formulated in terms of 'knowledge' and 'registration': 'A pion is created, crosses to another proton and disappears all in the twinkling of uncertainty allowed while the universe "isn't looking".'[39] All this must take place in the minimum of time, before the surroundings take note of the discrepancy. In his popular book *In Search of Schroedinger's Cat*, Gribbon goes one step further and projects this assuming of knowledge into the particle itself:

> First it [an electron] appears, popping out of the vacuum like a rabbit out of a magician's hat, then it travels forward in time a short distance before realizing its mistake, acknowledging its own unreality, and turning around to go back from whence it came[40]

– that is, into the abyss of Nothingness. And it is perhaps in the insistence on this gap, on this minimal delay between the event itself and its registration, that we find the most far-reaching epistemological revolution of quantum physics: in classical physics, 'knowledge in the real' asserts its hold directly, without any delay – that is to say, things simply know what laws they are to obey – whereas quantum physics allows for a minimum of 'ontological cheating'. A whole new domain is thus opened up, the domain of the shadowy pseudo-being of pure potentialities, of uncanny events which go on 'in the twinkling of uncertainty . . . while the universe "isn't looking" ' . . . .

Is not this virtual state of an electron which, upon admitting its mistake and acknowledging its unreality, returns to non-existence, equivalent to what Lacan describes as the state 'between the two deaths'? An entity exists only so long as it does not 'register', 'take note of', its nonexistence – like the proverbial cartoon cat which, although it has no ground under its feet, is unaware of this, and so calmly continues to walk in the air. . . . What is thereby attested is the discord between knowledge and being: knowledge always involves some loss of being and, vice versa, every being is always grounded upon some ignorance. The supreme example of this discord in psychoanalysis, of course, is the notion of symptom: a symptom, in its very painful reality, disappears as the result of a successful interpretation. In quantum physics, this same discord is in force not only at the level of micro-particles but also at the macro level: the hypothesis of quantum cosmology is that the universe as such resulted from a gigantic vacuum fluctuation – the universe in its entirety, its positive existence, bears witness to some global 'pathological' disturbed balance, to a broken symmetry, and is therefore doomed to return to a primordial Void.

The difference between quantum cosmology and the *New Age* mythology of cosmic balance is insurmountable here: the 'New Age' attitude engages us in an endeavour to 'set our derailed world right' by re-establishing the lost balance of cosmic principles (Yin and Yang, etc.), whereas the ontological implication of quantum cosmology and its notion of 'vacuum fluctuation' is that 'something exists' at all only in so far as the universe is 'out of joint'. In other words, the very existence of the universe bears witness to some fundamental disturbance or lost balance: 'something' can emerge out of 'nothing' (the vacuum) only via a broken symmetry. Quantum physics and cosmology are thus within the tradition of what Althusser called 'aleatoric materialism', the tradition that begins with Epicurus, according to whom the cosmos was born out of the declination [*klinamen*] of falling atoms. The lesson of Lacan (and of Hegel, *pace* the usual platitudes about the complementary relationship of opposites in dialectics) ultimately amounts to the same: *hubris* is constitutive; the bias of our experience accounts for its fragile consistency, 'balance' is another name for death.

Quantum physics therefore cuts off the very possibility of a retreat into the New Age mythology of natural balance: nature, the universe in its entirety, results from a 'pathological' tilt; as such, it also 'is only in so far as it does not take note of its nonexistence'. . . . That is to say: here, at this crucial point, we must draw all the consequences from the fundamental impasse of quantum cosmology: the wave function collapses – that is to say, reality as we know it is constituted – when the quantum event is 'registered' in its surroundings, when an observer 'takes note of it'; so how does this collapse take place when the 'event' in question is the universe in its entirety? Who, in this case, is the observer? Here, of course, there is a strong temptation to introduce God in the role of this universal Observer: the universe actually exists because its existence is 'registered' by Him. . . . The only consistent way to resist this temptation while remaining within the co-ordinates of the quantum universe is fully to embrace the paradox that the universe in its entirety is 'feminine': like 'Woman' in Lacan, the universe in its entirety *does not exist*, it is a mere 'quantum fluctuation' without any external boundary that would enable us to conceive it as 'actual'.

• The fifth lesson of the double-slit experiment concerns the dialectical relationship between an object and the process of searching for it. To illustrate the strange logic of the collapse of a wave function by means of which the quantum potentiality 'coagulates' into one reality, Wheeler mentions a somewhat nasty variation on the well-known society game of guessing the name of an object: what if, unbeknown to the questioner, the participants agree not to pick out an object in advance, so that when a participant has to answer 'Yes' or 'No' to a question ('Is it alive?', 'Does it have four legs?', 'Does it fly?', etc.), he should pay attention only to the consistency of his answer – the object he has in mind must be such that his answer is consistent with all the previous answers of the other participants. Thus, the questioner unknowingly participates in the determination of the object: the direction of his questioning narrows the choice down.

This situation is not unlike the joke about the conscript who tries to evade military service by pretending to be mad: he compulsively checks all the pieces of paper he can lay hands on, constantly repeating: 'That's not it!' The psychiatrist, finally convinced of his insanity, gives him a written certificate releasing him from military service; the conscript casts a look at it and says cheerfully: 'That *is* it!' What we have here is a paradigmatic case of the symbolic process which creates its cause, the object that sets it in motion. Wheeler's point, of course, is that things are analogous in quantum physics: the modality and direction of our search participate in the creation of the object for which we are searching: if we decide to measure the position of a particle, it will 'collapse' from potentiality into one actual set of spatial co-ordinates, while the same particle's mass will remain potential-undecided, and vice versa.[41]

Creatio ex nihilo

Let us, however, risk one more step, and go to extremes – which, in philosophy, usually means: to the fundamental Hegelian theme of 'determinate negation', of a Nothingness which none the less possesses a series of properties (in accordance with the differential logic of the signifier in which the very absence of a feature can function as a positive feature, as in the well-known Sherlock Holmes story in which the 'curious incident' with the dog consists in the fact that the dog *did not* bark). Hegel's 'determinate negation', of course, is the speculative reformulation of the old theological notion of *creatio ex nihilo*. In his Seminar on the *Ethics of Psychoanalysis*, Lacan insists that a *creatio ex nihilo* can occur only in a symbolic order: *creatio ex nihilo* points towards the miraculous emergence of a new symbol against the background of the void of the Thing; in the Real, on the contrary, nothing comes out of nothing. . . . Does not 'vacuum fluctuation', however, provide a perfect case of *creatio ex nihilo?* In quantum physics, 'vacuum' is conceived as Nothingness, as a void, but a void which is none the less 'determinate', that is to say, contains a whole set of potential entities. Vacuum 'fluctuation' refers to the very process by means of which something (a particle) emerges out of the void and then again evaporates, disappears in it – here quantum physics suddenly speaks the language of Hegelian dialectics. . . .

One could go on and supplement our list with numerous further parallels between quantum physics and cosmology, and Lacanian psychoanalysis: the astounding homology between the duality of 'imaginary' and 'real' time in Hawking and the duality of feminine and masculine 'formulas of sexuation' in Lacan;[42] the parallel between the Black Hole and the traumatic Thing [*Ding*] in Freud and Lacan;[43] up to the purely 'differential' definition of the particle which directly recalls the classic Saussurean definition of the signifier (a particle is nothing but the bundle of its interactions with other particles). . . . The conclusion imposed by quantum physics, therefore, is the following: what we experience as the 'hard reality' of objects in time and space is not the 'ultimate reality'; 'beneath' it there is another universe of potentialities with no irreversible temporal line, a universe in which something can emerge out of nothing, and so on. In short, the quantum universe displays in a 'wild' state, at a more 'primitive' level, a series of features which, according to our philosophical tradition, constitute the *differentia specifica* of the human universe of language – as if the old Schelling was right, as if in human freedom and language something that already underlies 'external reality' itself is raised to a higher power.

Quantum physics thus enables us to avoid not only the twin strategies of the vulgar-materialist naturalization of man and the obscurantist spiritualization of nature, but also the more 'modern', 'deconstructionist' version according to which 'nature' is a discursive construct.[44] Its ultimate lesson is not that nature is already in itself 'spiritual', but something incomparably more *unheimliches*: in the strange phenomena of the quantum universe, the human Spirit as it were encounters itself outside itself, in the guise of its uncanny double. Quantum processes are closer to the human universe of language than anything one finds in 'nature' (in the standard meaning of the term), yet this very close-ness (i.e. the fact that they seem to 'imitate' those very features which, according to the common understanding of the gap that separates nature from man, define the *differentia specifica* of the human universe) makes them incomparably stranger than anything one encounters in 'nature'. Therein resides the uncanniness of quantum physics with regard to the Kantian transcendental dimension: on the one hand it seems as if, in quantum physics, Kant's fundamental insight according to which (what we experience as) reality is not simply 'out there' but is constituted by the observing subject is finally verified and fully confirmed by science itself; on the other hand, this very 'empirical' realization of the transcendental model appears somehow excessive and unsettling, like the proverbial bore who spoils the game by observing its rules too literally.

Is not all we have developed hitherto, however, just a set of metaphors and superficial analogies which are simply not binding? To this criticism, which imposes itself with a self-evident persuasiveness, one can provide a precise answer: the irresistible urge to denounce the homologies between the quantum universe and the symbolic order as external analogies with no firm foundation – or, at least, as mere metaphors – is itself an expression and/or effect of the traditional philosophical attitude which compels us to maintain an insurmountable distance between 'nature' and the symbolic universe, prohibiting any 'incestuous' contact between the two domains. . . .

The emergence of human freedom can be accounted for only by the fact that nature itself is not a homogeneous 'hard' reality – that is to say, by the presence, beneath 'hard' reality, of another dimension of potentialities and their fluctuations: it is as if, with human freedom, this uncanny universe of potentialities re-emerges, comes to light. . . . Consequently, one is tempted to claim that Schelling's freedom *qua* pure 'possibility of being [*Seinkönnen*]' which of itself, by its own power, actualizes itself and acquires existence (this highest enigma which Schelling failed to explain again and again) is prefigured and/or concretized (here also, linear temporal succession is suspended) in quantum physics' notion of the emergence of 'something' (a particle) out of the 'nothingness' of a vacuum fluctuation. Is not this vacuum fluctuation Schelling's freedom which does not yet exist? Such a reading is further confirmed by the repetition of this micro-process at the macro level of cosmology: as we have already seen, according to the most daring hypothesis of quantum cosmology, our universe as such, in its entirety, is a kind of gigantic vacuum fluctuation; it popped up out of nothing as a result of a disturbed balance, and is destined to return to nothing. In other words, does not the Big Bang stand for the primordial expansion which follows the primordial contraction of the void of Freedom into the absolutely condensed singular point of matter? Prior to the primordial contraction there was only the void of pure *Seinkönnen*, the Freedom of a will which wills nothing; against this background one can fully appreciate Schelling's definition of the emergence of man: in man, possibility is no longer automatically realized but persists *qua* possibility – precisely as such, man stands for the point at which, in a kind of direct short circuit, the created universe regains the abyss of primordial Freedom.

Notes

1. Sigmund Freud, 'On the Universal Tendency to Debasement in the Sphere of Love' (1912), in James Strachey, ed., *The Standard Edition of the Complete Psychological Works of Sigmund Freud*, vol. XI, London: Hogarth 1986, p. 187.

2. Jacques Lacan, *Le Séminaire, livre XX: Encore*, Paris: Éditions du Seuil 1975, p. 65.

3. Therein resides one of the antinomies of late capitalism: on the one hand this saturation, this instant gratification that suffocates desire; on the other, the growing number of the 'excluded', of those who lack the basic necessities of life (proper food, shelter, medical care, etc.) – here excess and lack, suffocation and deprivation, are structurally co-dependent, so that it is no longer possible to measure 'progress' by an undisputed standard. That is to say: it is inappropriate to claim that since some people live in abundance while others live in deprivation, we must strive for universal abundance: the 'universalization' of the form of abundance which characterizes late capitalism is impossible for structural reasons, since, as Hegel pointed out in his *Philosophy of Right*, in capitalism, abundance itself produces deprivation.

4. As an indicator of this approaching crisis, suffice it to recall the 'negation of negation' which marks the use of computer technology in the domain of publishing: first, one puts computers to use in order to produce printed newspapers or journals (desktop editing, etc.) more efficiently; sooner or later, however, the fatal question is raised: why should we continue to print newspapers at all? Why shouldn't we consider the 'virtual' text on the screen as the finished product, and distribute it directly via internet? In other words, new technology is first adopted as a means of realizing old needs more efficiently; then, all of a sudden (when it is already too late), one becomes aware that these old needs are no longer functional, that they are rendered obsolete by new technology. And is it not the same with *sexuality*? At first, computers were used to organize the old business of dating, of finding an appropriate sexual partner more efficiently, it soon became clear, however, that the exchange of information about what I would like to do with a virtual partner *is sufficient in itself* – it no longer serves as a prelude to 'real' sex, since *talking about sex is already experienced as the 'thing itself'*.

5. See Leonardo S. Rodriguez, 'Le False Memory Syndrome', *L'Âne: Le magazine Freudien*, no. 57–8, Paris 1994, pp. 53–4.

6. Here, however, one should avoid the ideological trap of the standard notion of 'narcissistic personality' (a hedonistic individual who aims at instant gratification and disregards all symbolic prohibitions). As an antidote to this notion, one should recall Lacan's reversal of Dostoevsky's famous proposition from *The Brothers Karamazov* (see p. 118 above).

7. Incidentally, the newly fashionable notion of 'interactive media' is also an Orwellian misnomer which conceals its exact opposite: the tendency to promote the subject as an isolated individual who no longer *interacts* properly with others: the 'interactive' computer network enables the subject to do his buying (instead of going out to the shops), to order food by home delivery (instead of going to a restaurant), to pay bills (instead of going to a bank), to work (on a computer connected via a modem with his company, instead of going out to the office), to engage in political activities (by participating in 'interactive' TV debates), etc., up to his or her sex life (masturbating in front of the screen, or 'virtual sex', instead of an encounter with a 'real' person). What is slowly emerging here is the true 'post-Oedipal' subject, no longer attached to the paternal metaphor.

8. An exemplary case of this virtual 'mediation' of our self-experience is the way the citizens of Sarajevo perceive themselves in these difficult times for the city under siege. Their suffering is, of course, very material, but it is impossible not to notice the narcissistic satisfaction contained in their narrativization of their predicament: they are well aware that their city has become a symbol, that they are in a sense the 'centre of the world', that the eyes of the media are turned on them. Consequently, in their very direct self-experience of their painful everyday life, they are already playing a role for the gaze of the virtual Other – what they fear (at an unconscious level, at least) is the loss of this privileged 'sacred' role of the exemplary victim, i.e. the moment when Sarajevo will become a city like any other. . . .

9. *The Seminar of Jacques Lacan. Book III: The Psychoses (1955–1956)*, New York: Norton 1993, p. 251.

10. To avoid a fatal misunderstanding: this remainder does not point towards the irreducible self-presence of 'our own' body, accessible to us in an immediate self-experience – our bodily self-experience is, on the contrary, always-already 'virtual', i.e. sustained by a series of imaginary and symbolic identifications. To this 'ordinary' body of everyday reality, one should oppose the sublime-undead body of what Lacan calls 'lamella' (the body of the 'alien' from Ridley Scott's film, the body of the Sadeian victim which retains its beauty even when it is tortured to infinity . . .).

11. Strangely enough, this central feature of Hegelian dialectics is sometimes denied to Hegel, as, for example, in the following passage of an otherwise admirable book on Deleuze:

The central question for Platonic inquiry, Deleuze claims, is 'Qu'est-ce que?': 'What is beauty, what is justice, etc.?' Nietzsche, though, wants to change the central question to 'Qui?': 'Who is beautiful?', or rather, 'Which one is beautiful?' . . . In effect, the two questions point to different worlds for their answers. Deleuze will later call the materialist question 'the method of dramatization' and insist that it is the primary form of inquiry throughout the history of philosophy (except perhaps in the work of Hegel). The method of dramatization, then, is an elaboration of perspectivism as part of a critique of interest and value: 'It is not enough to pose the abstract question "what is the true?"; rather we must ask "who wants the true, when and where, how and how much?" ' (Michael Hardt, *Gilles Deleuze*, Minneapolis: University of Minnesota Press 1994, p. 30.)

What remains somewhat enigmatic in this counterposition of the traditional philosophical question and its 'Leninist' materialist reversal (the first suspends the subject of enunciation of a thesis under discussion and constrains itself to its enunciated content, to its validity, etc.; whereas the second, by means of the 'dramatization', involves the position of enunciation of the subject who stands behind the thesis, like Lenin, whose question apropos of a pathetic assertion of freedom, for example, was never 'What is freedom?' but, rather, 'Freedom for whom? To do what?') is the notion that Hegel occupies the exceptional position of the only pure idealist in the history of philosophy. Enigmatic, if we consider the fact that Hegel's entire *Phenomenology of Spirit* is a repeated 'dramatization' of each 'shape of consciousness': each particular 'shape' is subverted, belied – not by means of a comparison with some 'objective' measure of truth but by means of 'reflective' reference to the position of enunciation of the subject who defends it. Hegel refutes asceticism, for example, by 'dramatizing' the ascetic attitude and posing the 'materialist' Leninist question 'Who advocates ascesis? From what position does he do it? In whose interest?'. For a more detailed account of this Hegelian 'dramatization', see Chapter 4 of Slavoj Žižek, *For They Know Not What They Do*, London: Verso 1991.

12. Quoted from *Time* magazine, 11 July 1994, pp.27–8.

13. To avoid misunderstanding, one should point out here that Derrida is fully aware of the pitfalls of such historicist reductionism: one of his recurrent themes is that every theoretical position, 'neutral' as it may appear, always relies on some (usually unacknowledged) *ethico-political choice*.

14. Incidentally, the Jim Carrey figure in *Dumb and Dumber* is far less ideological than Forrest Gump: he is – potentially, at least – more subversive precisely in so far as he offers *less* than Forrest Gump. In *Dumb and Dumber*, stupidity plain and simple is bereft of the aura of 'heart-of-gold' natural goodness which provides its ideological sugar-coating.

15. Two additional remarks are necessary here. First, what modernism retroactively makes clear, of course, is that even the most traditional work of art implies a certain subconscious 'theory about itself' embodied in the hermeneutic horizon of expectations which determines our approach to it. Secondly, at a more detailed level, Lacan's thesis on 'Joyce-the-symptom' involves the claim that Joyce was a psychotic who used his work of art as the substitute-formation destined to supplement the failed paternal metaphor, thereby enabling him to avoid the loss of reality. What Lacan has in mind here is Freud's crucial thesis from his reading of Schreber's memoirs: that paranoid delirium is not an illness but, rather, an attempt at healing, a formation by means of which the psychotic subject pulls himself out of the true illness, complete autistic breakdown (the 'end of the world'): delirium enables the psychotic subject to participate again in social life (albeit in a distorted way, identifying his fellow-men as persecutors, etc.) – and Joyce's work possesses precisely the status of such a psychotic delirium. . . .

16. The triad realism–modernism–postmodernism therefore, *grosso modo*, corresponds to the three logics of the relationship between reality and its reflection: in traditional realist logic, reality is 'out there', unaffected by reflection (whether the subject is aware of it or not, reality takes its course . . .); modernism believes in the redemptive/liberating power of reflection (the fundamental premiss of the critique of ideology, this modernist procedure *par excellence*, is that our awareness of the true causes of ideological distortion will make it disappear); postmodernism not only does not return to premodern naivety but, rather, adds a supplementary turn of the screw to modernist reflectivity – the very immediate state of things can sustain itself only via a reflective distance (I can be wholly submitted to Power, wholly integrated in it, only if I maintain a cynical distance towards it; I can be a racist only if I do not take my racism 'seriously' but water it down with self-irony; etc.). On a first, superficial approach, postmodernism may seem to undermine the Hegelian logic of mediating, thereby reflectively dissolving the immediate starting point; a deeper approach, however, soon shows how the paradoxical dependency of pre-reflective immediacy on reflective distance is the true secret of Hegel's notion of 'In- and For-itself': the In-itself of presupposed immediacy is sustained by the very force of reflection that apparently corrodes it.

17. Another way to define the trap in which cynicism gets caught is via the difference between public Law and its obscene underside, unwritten superego rules: cynicism mocks public Law from the position of its obscene underside which, consequently, it leaves intact.

18. To illustrate this point with an unpleasant everyday experience, let us imagine a plane exposed to strong turbulence: when the pilot reassures us on the loudspeaker that there is nothing really dangerous going on, a Westerner's mind is immediately set at rest,

whereas an Easterner automatically suspects that he is actually listening to a pre-recorded message, and that the crew has already parachuted. . . .

19. It was Lyotard who, in *La condition postmoderne*, emphasized as the most striking feature of postmodern scientific knowledge its self-reflectivity, its disposition to question the validity of its statements incessantly: the traditional distinction between science and philosophy is thereby suspended, since science itself includes epistemological reflections which previously fell into the domain of philosophy.

20. Dieter Hombach, *Vom Quark zum Urknall*, Munich: Boer 1994, p. 7.

21. The thesis according to which the subject of psychoanalysis is the subject of modern science has far-reaching consequences for psychoanalytic practice: far from being a disturbing factor, the analysand's knowledge of (psychoanalytic) theory is an inherent constituent not only of the psychoanalytic cure but of the very formation of symptoms. A symptom is always addressed to some 'subject supposed to know'; it is formed with an eye to its interpretation; and the problem is precisely *what kind* of interpretation is implied by it, the 'correct' one or the 'wrong' one. Crazy as it may sound, the 'reflectivity' of desire means, among other things, that we have *theoretically wrong* and *theoretically correct* symptoms.

22. See P.C.W. Davies and J.R. Brown, eds, *The Ghost in the Atom*, Cambridge: Cambridge University Press 1993, p. 62.

23. On this relationship of 'complementarity' (in the sense of quantum mechanics) between the awareness of concrete historical conditions and our ability to act, see Stanley Fish's perspicacious observations, especially 'Critical Self-Consciousness, Or Can We Know What We're Doing?', in *Doing What Comes Naturally*, Durham, NC and London: Duke University Press 1989; and 'The Law Wishes to Have a Formal Existence', in *There's No Such Thing as Free Speech*, New York and Oxford: Oxford University Press 1994.

24. See Chapter 5 of Slavoj Žižek, *For They Know Not What They Do*.

25. Another exemplary case of this logic of complementarity is provided by the relationship between so-called 'dynamic' and 'static' hierarchies of authority in political theory. Why does a state employee have to carry out the orders of his superiors? On the one hand, orders are to be executed if and in so far as they are in compliance with the existing legal norms regulating the exercise of power; on the other hand, I am formally obliged to obey the orders of those who, according to the legal hierarchy of authority, are my superiors. Problems arise, of course, when these two levels collide: do I have to obey the superior authority irrespective of the (possibly illegal) content of its orders, or do I have the right (the duty, even) to counteract orders which, in my view, violate existing legal norms? Here also we encounter a kind of 'quantum constant', a minimal grey zone in which, due to a structural necessity, clear demarcations are blurred.

26. We are also dealing here with the problem of remembrance and forgetting: the forgetting of the origins of human rights in the early-capitalist historical context is not *only* ideological, it does not serve *only* the expansion of Western cultural-political imperialism; it *also* enables a specific ideological complex to cut loose from the contingency of its origins and start to float freely, as it were, so that wholly different classes, social groups and discursive formations *can* make use of it. The very problematic of human rights offers an exemplary case of such a liberating 'active forgetfulness' (Nietzsche): although it is undoubtedly a 'child of its (white – male – early-bourgeois . . .) time', it can (and did) lose its anchoring in this historical moment and be used by non-whites, women, workers, etc., to legitimate their claims. Marx himself interprets the institution of a government responsible to Parliament (and not to the Monarch) as the case of a similar productive misreading: although it took shape in the political confusion around the English Glorious Revolution, as an improvised solution to a particular problem (what to do with an imported monarch who did not even speak English, etc.), it evolved into the norm of liberal-democratic political life.

In this precise sense, synchrony has the advantage over diachrony: what matters is not the contingency of the origins of a certain phenomenon, but its function here and now – even if today's function of the phenomenon in question is clearly based upon a misunderstanding of its original role, there is more 'truth' in it than in the contingency of the original role. (The same goes, of course, for words: etymology can serve as the perfect form of a 'lie in the guise of truth', since evoking the original meaning of a word, for example, can well serve to obfuscate the racist, etc. connotation this word displays in today's context.)

27. The same goes for the notion of democracy: it has a potentially universal appeal, i.e. it cannot be simply reduced to one of the political 'language games', in so far as the gesture of self-questioning, of permanent problematization of its determinate, positive forms, is built into it – here again, one can see how lack and universality are strictly co-dependent.

28. Such a veneration of the (symbolic) Institution which provides a minimum of stability to the otherwise disorientated human herd was not foreign to Lacan himself – witness his long-standing fascination with the Catholic Church as an *institution* regulating the lives and desires of its believers, a fascination wholly in line with the typical French tradition of authoritarian right-wing 'atheist Catholicism' *à la* Maurras.

29. The most viable theory of man's difference is therefore that according to which man is distinguished not by some advantage over animals – some outstanding ability, etc. – but, rather, by some primordial deficiency, stupefaction, idiocy or tomfoolery: by the fact that, in contrast to animals, he falls prey to some lure. This is what Lacan's theory of the 'mirror stage' is about: man is a dupe who fixes his eyes upon his mirror-image, immobilizing it and extracting it from its temporal continuum. . . . The epigram 'To err is human' thereby acquires a precise meaning beyond the banal tolerance of human weaknesses: man is defined by his ability to get caught in an illusion, to 'take seriously' the symbolic fiction. Or – to put it another way – man is an animal who definitely *does not learn from history*, and is condemned to repeat the same mistakes all over again.

The author of these lines was (deservedly) the victim of such an argumentation during the examination of his doctoral thesis at the Department of Psychoanalysis in the University of Paris-VIII, when François Regnault drew attention to an inaccurate quote from Mallarmé's *Un coup de dés*: I simplified the correct 'rien *n'aura eu* lieu que le lieu' into 'rien *n'aura* lieu que le lieu' – Regnault's sarcastic remark was that this mistake is pardonable to French native speakers (since everybody in France commits it . . .) but totally inexcusable for a foreigner who is not at home in French. . . .

30. This shift is precisely the shift from (biological) *instinct* to *drive*. For that reason, an animal's (say, a dog's) unconditional attachment to its Master, its 'faithfulness unto death', is no longer properly animal: it already results from the poor animal's being trapped (entrapped, even) in the symbolic universe. The image of a faithful animal which 'persists to the end' in serving its Master (a horse which carries its Master till it drops dead, for example) stands for the drive at its purest.

31. Here we have another example of how, in ideology, opposites coincide: both the New Age 'holistic' notion of man as a part of the natural-spiritual global process, and the notion of man as derailed nature, as an entity 'out of joint', are ideological – what both notions 'repress' is the fact that *there is no (balanced, self-enclosed) Nature* to be thrown out of joint by man's *hubris* (or to whose harmonious Way man has to adapt).

32. For a more detailed analysis, see Chapter 4 of Slavoj Žižek, *Tarrying with the Negative*, Durham, NC: Duke University Press 1993.

33. Lacan elaborates this paradox of potentiality that possesses an actuality of its own apropos of the notion of (symbolic) power: in 'Subversion of the Subject and Dialectic of Desire', for example, he characterizes the Master-Signifier as 'this wholly potential power [*ce pouvoir tout en puissance*], this birth of possibility' (Jacques Lacan, *Écrits: A Selection*, New York: Norton 1977, p. 306).

34. For the notion of the 'quilting point', see Chapter 3 of Slavoj Žižek, *The Sublime Object of Ideology*, London: Verso 1989.

35. Aeschylus, 'Agamemnon' (lines 207–12), in *The Oresteia*, trans. Robert Fagles, Harmondsworth: Penguin 1979, p. 225.

36. Fagles's translation of these verses (lines 214–17) is: '. . . stop the winds with a virgin's blood, / feed their lust, their fury? – feed their fury! – / Law is law! – / Let all go well.'

37. See Reiner Schürmann, 'Ultimate Double Binds', *Graduate Faculty Philosophy Journal*, New York: New School for Social Research, vol. 14, no. 2 (Heidegger and the Political), pp. 216–18.

38. See Chapter 9 of Alastair Rae, *Quantum Physics: Illusion or Reality?*, Cambridge: Cambridge University Press 1994.

39. John Gribbon, *In Search of Schroedinger's Cat*, London: Corgi Books 1984, p. 198.

40. Ibid., p. 201.

41. This same procedure also seems to be at work in the search for the new Dalai Lama in Tibetan Buddhism: the boy who is celebrated as the new reincarnation of the Dalai Lama is not actually 'found'; the very search for him creates him, as in Wheeler's version of the social game where the very search for the unknown object produces its features – the monks themselves, by the direction of their inquiry, gradually narrow the circle of possible candidates until only one remains. . . .

42. See Slavoj Žižek, *Looking Awry*, Cambridge, MA: MIT Press 1991, pp. 46–7. Incidentally, the Lacanian 'formulas of sexuation' also seem to provide the matrix of the two main interpretations of quantum physics: is not the so-called 'Copenhagen orthodoxy' phallic, does it not involve an universality with the observer *qua* its constitutive exception? And is not the 'Many Worlds Interpretation', in so far as it involves the unfathomable infinity of universes, 'excessive' in a feminine way? Furthermore, does not David Bohm's 'quantum potential' theory provide an androgynous false exit?

43. This parallel was proposed by Jacqueline Rose in *Why War?*, Oxford: Blackwell 1993, pp. 171–76. Rose draws attention to Stephen Hawking's thesis that a black hole is not just an abyss swallowing everything that approaches it too closely: it also *emits* particles (at least outwardly, since these particles effectively rebound from its edge). The analogy with the Freudian–Lacanian *Ding* imposes itself here: *das Ding* is a kind of black screen on to which we project our fantasies and then, when they rebound from it, misperceive them as an irradiation of *das Ding* itself.

44. Here one should add a self-critical note: in *Looking Awry*, I conceived the parallel between Hawking's opposition of imaginary and real time and the feminine and masculine side in Lacan's formulas of sexuation as an index of how the fundamental deadlock of symbolization (over)determines even our approach to the most abstract problematic of physics. Now, however, my position is that of 'realism': in nature we effectively encounter the symbolic order, inclusive of its constitutive deadlock, in a lower power/potential.

Index

Printed in the United States
by Baker & Taylor Publisher Services